BOMBER SQUADRON

Men who flew with XV

Martyn R. Ford-Jones

WILLIAM KIMBER · LONDON

First published in 1987 by
WILLIAM KIMBER & CO. LIMITED
100 Jermyn Street, London SW1Y 6EE

ISBN 0-7183-0659-7

Photoset in North Wales by
Derek Doyle & Associates Mold, Clwyd
and printed in Great Britain by
Redwood Burn Limited, Trowbridge

In memory
of the men of XV Squadron
who did not survive

Contents

List of Illustrations

MAPS

Acknowledgements

The idea for this book was born one Saturday evening as I sat in the Galaxy Club at RAF Mildenhall listening to a group of men reminiscing about some of their wartime experiences. The occasion was a reunion of Nos XV and 622 Squadrons, to which Don Clarke, the Secretary of the Mildenhall Register (The Squadron Association), had invited me.

During that evening the thought occurred to me that unless recorded, the day would come when these stories would be told no more. A small but human sentence in the chapter of Bomber Command's history gone forever.

I am therefore indebted, in the first instance, to Don Clarke for the introduction to the members of the Mildenhall Register.

Compiling and writing a book of this nature involves many hours of interviews, research and collating specific data. This in turn involves a number of people, not least of all those whose stories have been recorded in this book. They have all given freely of their time and patience, their only concern being, 'Why do you want to write about me?' I have been made welcome in their homes, their hospitality has known no bounds and I have remained friends with the majority of them.

It is of course to these ex-flyers, and their wives, that my first thanks must go. In chronological order of the book they are: The late Air Vice-Marshal Stewart Menaul CB, CBE, DFC, AFC; Squadron Leader Peter Boggis, DFC; Group Captain T.H.B. Taylor; Frederick 'Steve' and Marion Stevens; Graham 'Mick' and Brenda Cullen; Doug and Margaret Fry; Gil and Amy Marsh; Oliver Brooks, DFC, and his wife Vera; Len Miller, DFC; Bernard and Margaret Dye; Arthur and Elizabeth Horton; Harry Bysouth, DFM and his wife Rene; Pat Russell; Frank and Brenda Watson; Frank Diamond; George Allom.

Others involved in piecing the stories together include George and Joyce Wright, Ken Pincott, Tony and Olive Godfrey, Alf Lorimer, Norman Bibbing, Ernie Fitch, Kay Godfrey, Grace 'Archie' Button, née Archer, and Percy Pluck and Ken Rogers who have both now sadly passed-on.

Amongst the others to whom I offer thanks are the author, and my good friend Norman Franks, who although busy with his own books has always found time to help a friend in need. His encouragement and inspiration must also be acknowledged.

Another author whom I met at one of the reunions, and found to be most helpful is Martin Middlebrook, whose books, *The Bomber Command War Diaries, The Battle of Hamburg* and *The Nuremberg Raid,* are all recommended reading matter, and have proved useful sources of reference to me.

To Mr L. Howard and the staff of the Air Historical Branch at Lacon House, and the staff of the Public Record Office at Kew. To Alan Cooper, who has often pointed me towards the right documents at the PRO. To my good friends Geoff Thomas, for his help with photographs, and John Reid, the Secretary of the Fenland Aircraft Preservation Society and to Steven Blanchard. Finally to my wife Valerie who has supported me throughout, as well as acting as unpaid secretary, personal assistant and purveyor of camera equipment. To my two daughters Alexandra, who made many cups of coffee, and Emma, who, when I wondered whether I should carry on, commented, 'Too many people have helped you for you to let them down now.'

Introduction

Many accounts have been written recording the courage and heroic deeds of some of the men who served with either Fighter Command or Bomber Command, Royal Air Force during World War Two.

The Battle of Britain drew the public's attention to the fighter pilots, who to some extent were the 'glamour boys' of the skies. Their stories were related both during and immediately after the war in great numbers. By comparison, those who served in Bomber Command did not share the same degree of public awareness. Only occasionally did the name of a member of Bomber Command become known to the public. This usually occurred after a morale boosting raid or the press announced the award of a decoration to a member of bomber aircrew by the King.

During those years of conflict, approximately 125,000 men flew with Bomber Command; some of them were regular officers but many others were volunteers. Of that number over 47,000 lost their lives flying on operations.

It appears that only in recent years have some of the survivors been persuaded to tell their stories, and there are still many more to be recorded.

One could argue that one bomber squadron was much like another; this is probably true, but the individuals who flew night after night taking the war to the enemy could all tell different tales of their air war.

Apart from being in Bomber Command the men whose stories are recorded in this book also have a common bond which still unites them; they all flew, at some period during the war, with one particular squadron – No XV Squadron RAF. All, that is, except one. Arthur Horton flew with No 622 Squadron, XV's sister unit. He is included for two reasons: because his story is an integral part of Bernard Dye's and because it is an excellent one in its own right.

The bond shared by members of XV Squadron still unites them to this day. They came from all walks of life, different backgrounds and different trades or professions. Some came almost directly from school. They all had one aim in life, to see freedom and democracy returned to Europe.

The struggle was fierce, the life expectancy of a rear gunner for example was estimated at only eleven hours, and many crews never completed a tour, but still these young men continued to come forward. The fighting and strain of trying to complete a tour of 'ops' was interspersed with incidents which now may seem silly to some, but at the time broke the strain of war and brought forth merriment and humour. The memories of such incidents still bring the sound of laughter when the stories are retold at reunions. These help to soothe the hurt of losing friends and colleagues almost nightly, while having themselves to carry on.

Set out in chronological order, the stories in this book give, I hope, an insight into how these young men of another generation lived, loved, played and fought over six years of war, each man telling his own story. It is not intended to present them as heroes; indeed they do not see themselves as such. There was a job to do and they did it to the best of their ability. Some of them were at first reluctant to impart the information regarding the service side of their lives, but in the knowledge of a genuine interest they relented. One fact these men are proud to acknowledge is that they flew with No XV Squadron, or, as they could be termed, a few of 'Fifteen's Flyers'.

Martyn R. Ford-Jones
Swindon
Wilts

PROLOGUE

No 15/XV Squadron RAF

No XV Squadron, unofficially known as 'Oxford's Own', is one of the oldest operational squadrons in the Royal Air Force. It was formed as part of the Royal Flying Corp at South Farnborough, Hampshire, on 1st March 1915. Personnel were drawn from No 1 Reserve Squadron and the Recruits Depot. Its first commanding officer was Captain P.B. Joubert de la Ferté, who later became Air Chief Marshal Sir Philip Joubert de la Ferté KCB, CMG, DSO, twice C-in-C Coastal Command.

Equipped initially with an assortment of aeroplanes, the squadron re-equipped with BE2c's for army co-operation duties during the late summer. The squadron moved to France during December that same year, where it carried out photographic, artillery sorties. The assistance XV Squadron rendered to the Fifth Army during the attacks on the Ancre Salient in January 1917 was recognised by Field Marshal Sir Douglas Haig, the Commander-in-Chief of the Expeditionary Force. At the end of May 1917, the squadron converted to RE8 aeroplanes, or as they were commonly known, 'Harry Tates'.

The squadron stayed in France after the war returning to England in February 1919. It was disbanded in December at Fowlmere, in Cambridgeshire.

On 20th March 1924, No XV reformed as a bomber squadron, at Martlesham Heath, near Ipswich, Suffolk. Its equipment consisted of de Havilland DH9A's, one Vickers Vimy and two Bristol F2b Fighters. The latter aircraft were to be used in the experimental role as part of the squadron's work with the Aeroplane and Armament Experimental Establishment at Martlesham. The DH9A's were to enable the squadron to revert to a bomber role in the event of a war. During its ten-year association with the A&AEE, XV Squadron carried out a whole range of experimental trials including bomb ballistics, bombing cameras, parachute flares and high altitude gunnery trials, to name but a few.

The squadron reverted back to its day bomber role on 1st June 1934, under the command of Squadron Leader T.W. Elmhirst AFC. It was equipped with twelve Hawker Hart Mk I's which were delivered to the squadron's new base at Abingdon, in Oxfordshire, between 2nd June and 8th August. It was at this time that the now famous XV Squadron roman numeral markings were first applied to the fuselage of the unit's aircraft.

March 1936 saw another change of equipment when the squadron converted to Hawker Hind aircraft. It was as a result of converting to this type of aircraft that the squadron decided to change the hart on the unit's badge to a hind. This was approved by King Edward VIII in the summer of 1936 when the first set of squadron badges were approved. By the end of September, the hind's head was proudly displayed on the tail fins of all squadron aircraft.

The Air Defence Command of Great Britain was reorganised during July 1936. This resulted in the formation of four new Commands: Training, Coastal, Fighter and Bomber. No XV Squadron, as part of No 1 (Bomber) Group, was absorbed into the latter Command and hence began its long association with RAF Bomber Command.

During June and July 1938, No XV gave up its Hind aircraft in exchange for Fairey Battle bombers, with which it was to go to war in 1939.

In an effort to foster good relations between the public and the RAF, the Air Ministry approved a scheme which affiliated some squadrons to certain cities and towns throughout Great Britain. The scheme commenced in April 1939 and No XV was linked to the city of Oxford. Although the name was not embodied in the official title No XV became known as 'Oxford's Own ' squadron.

When a state of emergency was declared at the end of August, the squadron changed the code letters EF, which it had worn on the fuselage of its aircraft since the spring of 1939, to LS which it was to retain until 1951.

When war was declared in September 1939, No XV was ready. History had repeated itself when the squadron moved to France the day before the declaration. It stayed there until December. During this period it carried out armed daylight reconnaissance flights over the Siegfried Line.

On 9th and 10th December, No XV returned to England, flying its out-dated Battle aircraft to Wyton, where it was to convert to Bristol Blenheims. RAF Wyton, a No 2 Group station, was to become No XV's home until August 1942. The squadron did however move to Alconbury for a month between April and May 1940.

The squadron re-equipped twice during its stay at Wyton, first in November 1940 with the twin-engined Vickers Wellington bomber and then in April 1941, when it became the second squadron to receive the Short Stirling four-engined bomber. Whilst at Wyton it also participated in many of the major raids against enemy targets, including the first 'Thousand Bomber Raid' on the night of 30th May and the second 'Thousand Bomber Raid' against Essen two nights later.

On Thursday 13th August 1942, No XV Squadron re-located to Bourn in Cambridgeshire, from where it continued the fight against Germany. The squadron's stay at Bourn was a relatively short one, for almost exactly nine months to the day No XV moved to Mildenhall in Suffolk. RAF Mildenhall had re-opened as an operational station in April 1943, after being closed during the winter months for the construction of concrete runways. This in fact proved to be the last move made by the squadron during the war years, although another change of equipment was made in December when the squadron converted to Avro Lancasters.

On Tuesday 10th August 1943, No 622 Squadron RAF was formed at Mildenhall from the personnel and equipment of 'C' Flight No XV Squadron. The two squadrons remained at Mildenhall and operated alongside each other for the duration of the war. Unfortunately, No 622 Squadron was disbanded two years later in August 1945. Although re-formed as a Royal Auxiliary Air Force transport squadron in 1950 with Valetta aircraft, No 622 was again disbanded in September 1953.

Although XV Squadron has been disbanded a number of time

since the war, it has always been re-formed with new equipment. In 1983, whilst flying Buccaneer aircraft, the squadron was disbanded, only to reform on 31st October as the first Tornado squadron assigned to RAF Germany.

During the war years, No XV Squadron acquitted itself in a creditable manner. It participated in numerous raids, dropping over 17,000 tons of bombs and laying more than 1,600 mines in enemy waters. The squadron also took part in the 'Manna' operations, near the wars end, dropping food supplies to the Dutch people, and later the 'Exodus' operations whereby released British prisoners of war were flown back to England following the German surrender.

Many of those who served with No XV Squadron later attained Air Rank including Lord Elworthy GCB, CBE, DSO, MVO, DFC, AFC, MA (1935) who became Marshal of the Royal Air Force. The squadron also fostered four air chief marshals, four air marshals, four air vice-marshals and eight air commodores.

Many members of aircrew who were later awarded decorations for courage or acts of bravery with other squadrons, passed through the ranks of No XV Squadron. These include four recipients of the Victoria Cross, Second Lieutenant William Barker who joined XV Squadron in July 1916 and flew BE2c's in France, Sergeant Thomas Gray who served as a leading aircraftman during the pre-war years 1933-36, Air Commodore Hughie Edwards who, in 1936, flew Hawker Hinds with the squadron at Abingdon and Group Captain Leonard 'Len' Trent who was with No XV the day war was declared, and served with the squadron during the Battle of France.

Decorations earned by members of No XV Squadron included one Croix de Guerre (to Flying Officer H.T. Rudall), one Order of the British Empire, three Distinguished Service Orders, one hundred and twenty-four Distinguished Flying Crosses, six Bars to the DFC, one Air Force Medal, one Conspicuous Gallantry Medal and seventy-seven Distinguished Flying Medals.

CHAPTER ONE

Three Times Fifteen

Air Vice-Marshal Stewart Menaul
CB, CBE, DFC, AFC

Flak bursts peppered the sky in a continuous barrage of anti-aircraft fire. As each salvo exploded the black smoke dissipated on the wind, as if to make room for the next barrage. The staccato rattle of machine gun fire audible over the straining roar of aircraft engines, as fighter and bomber twisted and turned in evasive manoeuvres around the sky. The whole action punctured by the whistle of cascading bombs which rained down to explode, with devastating impact, on or near the target.

*

The above could be descriptive of the majority of the operations undertaken by Air Vice-Marshal Stewart Menaul, during his long and distinguished career with Bomber Command.

Stewart Menaul's association with the Royal Air Force began in 1936 at the RAF College, Cranwell, where he received the peacetime training of a regular officer. On leaving Cranwell he was sent to No 19 (Fighter) Squadron, based at Duxford in Cambridgeshire. The posting was probably one of the shortest on record, and brought forth a home truth.

Stewart Menaul recalls:

> When I left Cranwell I was sent to No 19 Squadron at Duxford. I reported for duty, but before I had time to unpack my kit I received a telegram directing me to No XV Squadron based at Abingdon. I duly made my way to Abingdon, where I was

welcomed by Flying Officer 'Sam' Elworthy, the 'A' Flight Commander, who later became a group and personal assistant to the AOC-in-C.*

XV Squadron at that time was flying Hawker Hinds, which I flew two or three times during the first couple of weeks I was there. I had only been at Abingdon about a month, and was just getting to know the area, when another telegram arrived marked for my attention. It requested myself and another officer to report to No 21 Squadron at Lympne, in Kent.

With all this changing about I suddenly realised the truth in the old RAF cliché, 'Why bugger about by yourself, when you can join the Air Force and be buggered about by experts.'

No 21 Squadron, which also flew Hinds, had been disbanded after the First World War but reformed on 3rd December 1935, at Bircham Newton, Norfolk. After a spell at Abbotsinch, No 21 moved south to Lympne in November 1936. The training took a leisurely pace and the location of the airfield had, in those closing years of peace, a distinct advantage.

Stewart Menaul remembers with nostalgia:

Lympne was a marvellous place. The Cinque Ports Flying Club was based on the airfield, and myself and another chap would hire a De Havilland Puss Moth and fly, with two young ladies, to Le Touquet for the weekend. The whole damn thing cost ten shillings, including the fuel for the aeroplane.

In August 1938 No 21 moved to Eastchurch, on the Isle of Sheppey. Then in March 1939 the squadron was moved again, this time to a new base at Watton in Norfolk. It was still at Watton in September when the Prime Minister of the day, Neville Chamberlain, made his now famous speech to the nation, declaring that Britain was at war with Germany.

Initially, No 21 Squadron, who had converted to Blenheims in 1938, was employed in photographing enemy airfields, but its main

*'Sam' Elworthy eventually rose to the rank of Marshal of the Royal Air Force.

role was anti-shipping operations in the English Channel and North Sea. Some targets on the Continent were also attacked. Stewart Menaul comments on those raids:

> Those first attacks, when I was with No 21 at Watton during the early part of the war on places like Kiel, were absolutely suicidal. Some of the boys almost blew themselves up with their own bombs, going in at low level.
>
> Furthermore the Blenheims we flew were slow, underarmed and totally unsuitable. They were hacked down like butterflies by the Me109's.

The qualities of his leadership soon showed and Stewart Menaul was appointed to higher rank. By the time he departed from No 21 during the summer of 1940, he was a squadron leader. His association with No XV Squadron, which was now based at Wyton and had also converted to Blenheims, was resumed later in the year when he was posted there in September.

The first operation that he carried out with No XV occurred on the evening of 22nd September, when ten aircraft were detailed to attack Ostend. The attacking force was led away by Pilot Officer Megginson flying Blenheim L8800. One by one the other aircraft raced across the airfield until the last Blenheim, T2227 piloted by Squadron Leader Menaul, lifted gently into the air.

Having arrived over the target, Megginson carried out a very shallow diving attack on the new tidal harbour. He was unable to observe the results, unlike Stewart Menaul, whose bombs started a large fire between the docks, after a high level attack. On this raid both the flak and enemy fighters were quiet, and all attacking aircraft returned safely.

Two nights later the squadron despatched nine aircraft to attack the docks at Le Havre. Stewart Menaul was first away, again in Blenheim T2227.

Over the target the weather was clear with 2/10th cloud at 10,000 feet. Squadron Leader Menaul executed a high level attack on the docks, but was unable to observe the results due to the approach of two enemy aircraft. These aircraft, which appeared to be carrying headlights, approached the Blenheim from astern, but by swift evasive action Menaul managed to evade them before they had a chance to attack.

The flak defences put up a weak barrage to signify its presence but which did nothing to deter the attackers. By comparison the flak batteries defending the harbour at Boulogne threw up a heavy and accurate barrage of steel, when six aircraft from XV Squadron attacked on the night of 26th September. The pattern was similar to the previous raid with Menaul leading the mission and making a high level attack.

Searchlights assisted the flak batteries, by scanning the night sky. For one heart-stopping moment Menaul's aircraft was caught by a single beam, but using skilful evasive action he managed to evade it.

An identical raid, by the same number of aircraft, was carried out against the same target on 7th October. Again the flak barrage was heavy but the gunners' efforts continued to be in vain, for all aircraft returned safely.

An opportunity for Stewart Menaul to get even with the flak batteries arose on the night of 10th/11th October, when XV Squadron assisted the Royal Navy in a combined operation against Cherbourg. The squadron detailed eleven aircraft, nine of which were to bomb the town in an effort to create a diversion which would allow HMS *Revenge* to get within range. The bombs would hopefully start fires to give the ship's guns an aiming point.

The two remaining aircraft, flown by Squadron Leader Menaul and the squadron commander, Wing Commander Joe Cox, were to bomb any shore batteries which endeavoured to return the Navy's fire.

A large fire was started by the exploding bombs in the target area, which the Royal Navy did not hesitate to enlarge. The shore batteries opened fire in retaliation, which was the cue Stewart Menaul and Joe Cox had been waiting for. Wing Commander Cox swung into the attack and unleashed his bombs on some gun emplacements. Menaul following his commander's example hit the same positions with his first stick of bombs, adding to the fires already burning. The second stick exploded in the docks, but the results were not observed.

Stewart Menaul has cause to remember the raid:

Vickers Wellington Mk IC T2961, LS-S, flown by Squadron Leader Stewart Menaul, from Wyton in 1941.

Squadron Leader Stewart Menaul (*centre*) with the members of his crew, Flying Officer Cochane, Flying Officer Downs, Sergeant Cosser and Sergeant Warner.

> I well remember flying over Cherbourg whilst the Navy were bombarding it. It was quite a remarkable performance. Joe Cox and I were supposed to cruise around dropping flares and bombs on the gun emplacements below, whilst the Navy pumped shells into the town. I considered this a very unhealthy pastime. Keeping one eye on the instruments and the other on what was going on, Joe Cox and I circled separately over the target area. At one point we bloody nearly collided head on, but saw each other just in time.

Squadron Leader Menaul hauled back on the control column and kicked the rudder bar, jinxing the Blenheim out of its path to destruction. Wing Commander Cox obviously took the same action and the two aircraft skimmed past each other, a hair's breadth from disaster.

> It was a remarkable thing we didn't collide. Fortunately too we didn't both turn in the same direction; if we had the aircraft would most certainly have met!
>
> On the way home my wireless operator tuned his set into the BBC wavelength, and picked up a dance band playing one of the popular compositions of the day, a number called 'Fools rush in where angels fear to tread'. When I got back to Wyton I said to Joe Cox, 'You probably didn't hear it, but the title of the tune playing on the radio could not have been more appropriate.'

The operation was a great success and the Navy, by way of thanks, commented on the excellent co-operation it received from the RAF, thus enabling the raid to be carried out according to plan.

The last major attack in which XV Squadron was to participate flying Blenheims occurred on 29th October 1940. At approximately 06.15 hours seven aircraft took off to bomb a fuel plant near Hamburg. Although there was no cloud, visibility over the target area was reduced by severe ground haze. Flares were dropped to assist the bombing, but still little could be seen. To avoid wasting his bombload Stewart Menaul looked for a suitable alternative target, which he found in the shape of a searchlight battery in the Ruhr.

On 1st November, both XV Squadron and the airfield of Wyton, which had been part of No 2 Group Bomber Command, were transferred to No 3 Group. At the same time the squadron converted to Vickers Wellington MkIc bombers. The conversion period took up the whole of November and the first two weeks of December.

The new twin-engined aircraft had distinct advantages over its predecessor, including rotating front and rear Frazer-Nash turrets. The Wellington also necessitated the addition of two new members to each crew, a co-pilot and a rear gunner. The conversion period allowed these two to be integrated with their crew both on duty, as part of the team learning about the new aircraft, and off duty getting to know one another.

With the increase in numbers of aircrew there were many new faces to be seen at Wyton, at the end of 1940. On 14th December another new face arrived, when Wing Commander H.R. Dale was appointed to take over the squadron.

The weather during the third week of December precluded the squadron from participating in any operations. On the night of 16th December Squadron Leader Menaul and three other crews stood by to attack Boulogne, but the raid was cancelled due to the weather. The following night the same four crews stood by to bomb Le Havre, but again bad weather intervened. The pattern was repeated on the next two nights as well.

Eventually, on the night of 20th December, one aircraft got away. The other three bombers due to participate in the operation were grounded at the last minute by a Group signal. The lone Wellington was loaded with 10 × 250 lbs bombs and two small bomb containers (SBC), which it dropped on its target, a fuel depot at Antwerp.

Two days after Christmas, Squadron Leader Menaul, piloting Wellington R1280, M, took off at 16.45 hours with five other aircraft and headed for the docks at Le Havre. The weather was again bad with 10/10th cloud over the target area.

Although conditions were not good the searchlights scanned the clouds, whilst the gun batteries sent up the familiar barrage of flak. The Wellington crews not being able to locate the target area dropped their bombs on the searchlight and gun batteries.

With the new year came a change in the weather. The cloud which had been hanging around, during the day, on 1st January began to dissipate as the evening wore on. This change enabled 141 aircraft of Bomber Command, to carry out a highly successful raid on Bremen that night.

No XV Squadron detailed five aircraft to participate in the raid, their specific target being the docks. Menaul, flying Wellington R1280, took off at 16.45 hours closely followed in turn by Pilot Officer Gilmour, Pilot Officer Raymond, Flying Officer Manahan and Pilot Officer Giles.

Visibility over the target was excellent, although there had been light haze at the start of the raid. The target was sighted and successfully bombed by the crews, with the exception of Pilot Officer Raymond whose bombs blasted the railway junction at Lesum. Although the ground defences responded to the attack all the aircraft returned safely. However, of the total force, four aircraft crashed in England.

The squadron detailed crews to participate in a number of raids over the next couple of weeks, but Stewart Menaul did not fly again until 16th January when he attacked the port of Wilhelmshaven.

> As a flight commander my name was not on the battle order every night, unlike other crews. Due to certain commitments associated with the position, as a flight commander one's tour took, in consequence, longer to complete.

The raid on Wilhelmshaven was considered a success despite the active defences. One aircraft, T2847 flown by Pilot Officer Dove, abandoned the mission due to heavy icing and returned home. The six other crews detailed followed Menaul to the target area. The weather over the target was perfect with good visibility, enabling the crews to identify the aiming point; the main railway yards.

The searchlights threw their cold beams of light up into the night sky. Similarly, the flak batteries threw up a barrage of bursting shells, in an effort to bring down the night intruders. The aircraft continued their mission to drop their mixed load of 500 lb bombs and SBCs on the railway yards, regardless of the heavy curtain of steel exploding around them. Numerous explosions on the ground were reported, with large fires seen burning in the target area. The intense activity of the searchlights and flak batteries was all in vain. No losses were reported by Bomber Command, who left the target burning fiercely.

The continual strain of operational flying was occasionally broken by an evening of drinking, dancing or both, when time permitted as Stewart Menaul recalls:

> When the squadron was stood down we would jump into a car or van and tear off in search of some amusement. Cambridge was, of course, a favourite place, especially at weekends, because there was an officers' club there. The only thing that spoilt our enjoyment was one ghastly chap, who insisted on making us wear our gas masks in the action position. One Sunday afternoon he came into the club, while we were dancing, and started 'cutting up rough'! Imagine trying to dance with a girl with this bloody thing between you, especially if she was big-bosomed. We were thoroughly brassed off with this character and decided to get our own back. The following weekend he was found in the local drain culvert. He wasn't hurt but he was certainly wet. That fortunately was the end of his jaunts to the officers' club. He really was an objectionable sod. We all felt he could be more usefully employed, especially after we had been on 'ops' the night before and wanted some relaxation.

Returning to operations on the night of 7th February, Stewart Menaul participated in a raid on the Channel ports. Eight crews led by Wing Commander Dale were charged with bombing Boulogne harbour. Although the searchlights were fewer in number than usual, the flak was intense. A stiff barrage of both heavy and light flak burst around the aircraft.

Squadron Leader Menaul's bombs rained down, and he watched as they burst across the gates of dock number four, causing three large explosions. The incendiaries fell close by, adding to the fires. Having completed his task, instead of turning for home, he pushed forward the control column of R1280 and dived towards two searchlights at Cap Gris Nez, in order that his gunners could extinguish them with machine gun fire.

Wing Commander Dale, flying Wellington T2624, B, stayed at high level and dropped his bomb load from 10,700 feet. He saw his incendiaries burst along the western edge of the dock starting a dozen or so fires, one of which rapidly developed and could still be observed many miles away.

The flak continued to arc up into the night sky in its colourful but deadly manner. The heavy flak was reported as being accurate both in height and direction, but fortunately there were no losses to the squadron.

Pilot Officer Dove's aircraft, Wellington T2847, R, carried a 4.5 lb photographic flash in its bomb bay, amongst the seven 500 lb bombs and two SBCs. His aircraft was also fitted with a camera for the first attempt by XV Squadron at night photography.

A total of 220 aircraft attacked Hanover on the night of 10/11th February, but not all of them returned.

When the first wave arrived over the target the sky was clear, but later it became covered by 9/10th cloud which made observation difficult. Squadron Leader Menaul's crew, one of the nine detailed by XV Squadron, dropped their bombs from 13,000 feet on the flak and balloon defences, but were unable to see the results through the cloud. As if by way of retaliation a burst of flak came up and hit Sergeant Fougere's aircraft, but fortunately the Wellington remained airworthy. Sergeant Garrioch was not so lucky. Having sent a 'task completed' signal at 21.35 hours he and his crew were not heard of again.

A total of four aircraft were lost with a further three shot down by German intruder nightfighters, over England.

The oil plant at Sterkrade Holten was the target on the night of 15/16th February. XV Squadron detailed ten crews to participate, including Menaul's. Observation over the target was impaired by the combination of the large number of searchlights and the hazy weather conditions. These conditions however did not stop the squadron from performing its allotted task. Stewart Menaul dropped two sticks of bombs on the aiming point from 12,000 feet and saw them explode in the target area.

Wing Commander Dale having released his bomb load, was informed by his rear gunner that they were being followed by a twin-engined aircraft. The rear gunner fired a short warning burst and the unidentified aircraft peeled off to the starboard side, and dived away without attacking.

Sergeant Fougere was also followed by an unidentified aircraft, in fact five of them all at the same time. He had just bombed a concentration of searchlights, about two and a half miles north west of the target, when he was informed of the presence of the five aircraft stealing up from behind. The range was given as approximately 600 yards. One of the aircraft closed up to 200 yards, at which point Sergeant Fougere took evasive action and lost sight of all five aircraft.

During the time that Stewart Menaul had been with XV Squadron he had made many friends, two in particular were Pilot Officer Bob Raymond and Flying Officer Bob Gilmour. The trio were however split up when Bob Gilmour was posted to No 20 Operational Training Unit at Lossiemouth, on 21st February.

The last raid that Stewart Menaul participated in during February occurred on the night of the 24th, when eight crews were detailed to attack a German Hipper class cruiser at Brest.

Brest was a dangerous target. No less than fifty searchlights were reported in the area, with both heavy and light flak which proved fairly accurate. With the searchlights scanning the sky and flak bursting around them, at various heights, the Wellingtons flew in over the harbour. Squadron Leader Menaul dropped his bombs from 10,000 feet and saw them burst in the area adjacent to the dock where the German warship was berthed. Photographs taken the following day indicated that the cruiser had received two direct hits.

The first two weeks of March took Stewart Menaul on three trips to Germany. The first was on the night of the 1st, when he joined seven other crews, to attack Cologne. The second raid was on Kiel on the night of the 11th and the third raid was two nights later, when Hamburg was the target.

For the third raid XV Squadron detailed eight aircraft to join a total force of 139 bombers, which headed for the inland sea port. Conditions were good, the moon was full and the weather was clear. Some crews encountered a thin layer of cloud at 20,000 feet, against which their aircraft were silhouetted.

When the squadron arrived over the target they saw many fires already burning, mainly in the north and eastern areas of the city. The usual reception of searchlights were much in evidence and first latched on to Wing Commander Dale's aircraft, but by evasive action he managed to lose the blinding stick of light before the exploding shells from the gun batteries followed. Stewart Menaul ran the gauntlet of exploding steel from both heavy and light flak, the former being very intense. His bomb load rained down to the conflagration below, and exploded 600 yards north east of the northern end of the Aussen Alster. At that moment the tenacious beam of a searchlight engulfed his aircraft and shrapnel burst all around the Wellington, puncturing its fabric skin in several places. His experience as a bomber pilot enabled him to avoid further damage and evade the searchlight, which having lost its quarry meandered off across the sky in search of other prey. He then watched with concern as the same searchlight picked up another aircraft, onto which the gun batteries directed their attention. This Wellington buffeted about as the flak exploded all around it, until it slowly peeled over and dived vertically earthwards.

> Hamburg was always fierce for action, you could see the flak exploding just off your wingtip. Sometimes you could see it hitting an aircraft below or off to one side of you.

It was later revealed that all of XV Squadron's aircraft had been caught by the searchlights, and that six of the eight Wellingtons had been hit by shrapnel.

The raid was considered a success however, with damage inflicted on the Blohm and Voss shipyard, a timber yard, a main fire station and many other buildings.

Squadron Leader Menaul only flew on two other operations during March. One on the night of the 15th, when the squadron attacked the submarine base at Lorient and the other on the 31st when he flew against Bremen. He participated in two raids against Kiel on the nights of 7th and 15th April. Although the searchlights and flak were much in evidence, his aircraft returned to Wyton unscathed on both occasions.

It was during this period that XV Squadron began converting to the Short Stirling. The first of these four-engined bombers to reach the squadron was a dual-control machine, which arrived from No 7 Squadron on 10th April. The following day Flight Lieutenant Best arrived from Oakington, where No 7 were based, to give instruction in handling the aircraft.

The Stirling, being a new breed of aeroplane with more flying controls and defensive armament, called for the addition of two further crew members. A flight engineer, to assist the pilot, and an air gunner to man the additional mid-upper turret.

An order was received on 16th April ordering seven of XV's crews to Malta immediately, where experienced Wellington crews were needed urgently. The selected crews arrived there safely the following day. This change in the state of the squadron's strength did not hamper the conversion programme. Wing Commander Dale, with the assistance of Squadron Leaders Menaul and Morris, had the squadron ready for operations in their new aircraft by the end of the month.

The first operation in which XV Squadron participated with the Stirling was a raid on the 'Big City' – Berlin – on the night of 30th April. Unfortunately, it was somewhat of an inauspicious start for various reasons.

A total of ten Stirlings took part in the raid but only three managed to reach the target; one of which was N6018 flown by Flight Lieutenant Raymond.

Wing Commander Dale piloting N3654 experienced problems with his port outer engine. Excessively high oil temperatures and low engine revs gave him cause for concern. Not wishing to waste his bomb load, he dropped it on a searchlight battery at Hamburg, before returning to Wyton. Cloud prevented Wing Commander Dale from observing any results.

Squadron Leader Morris was using fuel at such a rate that he abandoned his primary task and bombed Kiel, from a height of 16,000 feet. Menaul also experienced problems. He had to contend with failure of not one but both starboard engines! After jettisoning the bomb load in the sea five miles north of Borkum, he turned for home. On the return journey the starboard outer engine picked up, which enabled him to keep better control of the aircraft, even though it wasn't giving full power. However, he eventually landed safely at Wyton.

Stewart Menaul did not hold a good opinion of the Stirling:

> The Wellington bomber was slow and vulnerable, its successor the Stirling was probably worse. It was an aeroplane built by a committee from bits of other aircraft. It had part of the wings of a flying boat, a ghastly gangling undercarriage and the first of the exactor throttle controls, which were inherited from the Empire flying-boats. These exactors were a constant cause for concern, as they would not stay in place, but would move to the 'closed throttle' position.
>
> Another problem was its climb rate, the bloody thing just refused to climb, but my method of getting the Stirling to climb was to take her up, which took an awful long time, then lower the nose and go into a short descent. Having gained speed in the dive I would open the throttles wide and then pull up again. The momentum gained in the dive could give as much as a thousand feet extra height. Some of today's military aircraft use a similar method to gain extra altitude.

A Wellington bomber R1498, still operated by XV Squadron and piloted by Sergeant Leggate, was detailed to join three Stirlings for a raid on Hamburg on the night of 6th May. The four aircraft joined a total attacking force of 115 bombers, but due to inclement weather only 81 of them reported having reached the target.

Wing Commander Dale flying Stirling N6004 located and bombed the Kiel Canal, where he encountered a barrage of flak. Pilot Officer Campbell also experienced problems finding the target, so when a hole appeared in the cloud he turned Stirling N3656 towards it and bombed a flak battery near Elsfeth, some miles to the south-west of Hamburg.

Squadron Leader Menaul also experienced problems with the weather. For a brief moment, through the cloud, he saw one or two small fires burning which he took to be dummies. Suddenly flak came up through the cloud and exploded in the vicinity of his aircraft. Without further ado Stewart Menaul ordered the release of the bomb load, which rained down to detonate below the clouds. Although the crew were not able to see the explosions, the rear gunner reported the reflection of a terrific glow on the clouds after the first stick had exploded. Sergeant Leggate, unable to locate the target, returned to Wyton with his bomb load still in the belly of the ageing Wellington.

Menaul's friend Bob Gilmour, who back in February had been posted to Lossiemouth, returned to XV Squadron on 9th May with the rank of flight lieutenant.

The night of 10/11th May was a bad one for the squadron, when it detailed two aircraft to join an attack on Berlin. Flight Lieutenant Raymond's Stirling N6018 was mauled by accurate and intense flak over the target area, and was severely damaged. The other aircraft, flown by Wing Commander Dale, was intercepted and ferociously attacked by an Me110 as it crossed the Dutch coast, on the inbound journey. The Stirling refused to die easily and sustained eight separate attacks, before the crew baled out and the bomber, with two engines ablaze, succumbed and dived to its destruction. Dale's position as commanding officer of the squadron was filled by the appointment of Wing Commander Patrick Ogilvie DSO, who arrived at Wyton on 16th May.

His duties as a flight commander prevented Stewart Menaul from flying operationally until 27th May, but on this date he joined four other crews for an attack on the German cruiser *Prinz Eugen*. Although the search for the ship covered a wide area no trace of the potential target could be found, and the bombers returned to base.

On 7th June, Pilot Officer Peter Boggis, whose name was to be long associated with the squadron, and who was to become one of its most well known characters, joined XV from Bassingbourne.

Two targets were selected for Bomber Command's attention on the night of 11th June, Düsseldorf and Duisberg. XV Squadron detailed six aircraft to attack the former, over which the crews found a mixture of weather. The first main force wave of aircraft reported 3/10th cloud, whereas the second wave reported the cloud had increased to 10/10ths. The third wave however reported the weather as clear.

Squadron Leader Menaul finding solid cloud over Düsseldorf, turned his attention to the secondary target at Duisberg. He was able to report bombing a large building in the dock area, which burst into flame instantly.

The trip was a relatively quiet one, but they were not always like that, as he recalls:

> The Ruhr was one of the most disliked target areas, it was always fierce for action. You were being shot at from the moment you crossed the Dutch coast on the way in, until you crossed the coast again on the way out. It was a never ending barrage of bursting flak. The Ruhr really was most heavily defended.

On 13th June Squadron Leader Menaul, flying Stirling N6015, led a formation of four aircraft away from Wyton for a daylight attack on the German pocket battleship *Lützow*, which was off the Norwegian coast. About one hour after take-off he and his companions, Flight Lieutenant Gilmour, Pilot Officer Thompson and Flying Officer Campbell, received a signal recalling them back to base. Later the same day the same four crews were detailed to join an attack on three cruisers anchored at Brest.

Finding 10/10th cloud at 16,000 feet Menaul took his formation down to 13,000 feet, but found the target obscured not only by haze but also a heavy smoke screen. Pinpointing the target proved impossible, Menaul therefore dropped his bombs in two sticks, taking photographs to ascertain where they fell. The first stick fell into the sea just off Lanvéoc, where there was a seaplane base. The second stick fell inshore in the Anse de Morgat.

Nine days after Pilot Officer Boggis joined the squadron another experienced pilot was posted in, when Acting Squadron Leader Piper arrived from Lossiemouth. Stewart Menaul has reason to remember Piper:

> I took Tim Piper on his first trip with the squadron, as second pilot. Unfortunately he didn't last very long, he was shot down by flak a month later over the French coast. I remember only too well, as I had to go and break the news to his wife.

Although Stewart Menaul's name appeared on the battle order for a raid against Hanover on the night of 17th June he took off too late to join the raid. Instead, he dropped his bombs on an airfield eight miles north-west of Osnabrück, where he saw the second stick explode across the runway.

Three nights later he participated in a raid on Kiel, with six other crews from XV Squadron. The weather was much as it had been in previous raids with heavy and persistent clouds, but this did not prevent the defences from opening up. An intense barrage of steel penetrated the clouds and exploded angrily around the invading bombers.

Sergeant Needham, flying Stirling N6021, was attacked by a twin-engined fighter which broke off the attack when Needham's rear gunner opened fire. The fighter withdrew to search for a different victim, which it found in the shape of Stirling N6015 flown by Squadron Leader Menaul. Using the same tactics the fighter crept up behind the Stirling, but to the German's misfortune Menaul's rear gunner was also alert and saw the fighter approaching. Opening fire, the rear gunner claimed hits on the fighter, which was last seen diving earthwards with flames trailing fiercely from one engine.

In January 1941, Air Marshal Sir William Sholto Douglas, C-in-C Fighter Command, instigated the idea of 'Circus' operations. A 'circus' was a daylight raid carried out by a small formation of bombers, escorted by a large number of fighters to a target within the escort's endurance. The object was to entice Luftwaffe fighters into the air so that RAF fighters could destroy them. Blenheims had been used as the bombing force but later Stirlings were used.

On Saturday 5th July, Squadron Leader Menaul was detailed to lead Flight Lieutenant Gilmour and Flying Officer Thompson on Circus No 33, to the Fives-Lille steel works.

The day was bright with good visibility, and Menaul had no difficulty joining up with the close escort, from Northolt and Kenley, at 10,000 feet over Scotland. The Biggin Hill and Tangmere Wings were flying as target support, with Wing Commander 'Sailor' Malan leading the operation. The target support aircraft arrived over Lille ahead of the bombers as planned and circled the target until the Stirlings arrived. Me109s could be seen some distance away forming into small groups, ready to pounce.

Stewart Menaul led Gilmour and Thompson over the French coast at Dunkirk, where the flak immediately burst into life, peppering the blue sky with shrapnel. It was strange to see the bursts in daylight; at night one mostly only felt them. As they

On Saturday 5th July Squadron Leader Menaul led Flight Lieutenant Gilmour and Flying Officer Thompson on Circus Operation No 33 to the Five-Lilles steelworks. Stirling N3658, LS-E, is shown (*above*) escorted by two of the many fighters and (*below*) running the gauntlet of bursting flak as Flight Lieutenant Gilmour crosses the French coast.

approached the target area the Me109s dived into the attack. Malan raced after two 109's and opened fire at one of them, at a range of 300 yards. Both cannon and machine gun fire racked the Messerschmitt's fuselage before it dived away.

The German fighters endeavoured to draw the close escort Spitfires away by diving between the Stirlings. The Czech 312 Squadron gave chase and claimed an Me109 as it made a stern attack on the bombers, whilst 610 Squadron stayed in position to protect its charges.

Owing to the target being obscured by 5/10th cloud, Menaul declared the first run a dummy one. Leaving their escort to take care of the German fighters, the three Stirlings ran the gauntlet of the intense flak for a second time. With exploding steel peppering the sky around them, the three bombers dropped their loads comprising of fifteen 1,000 lb and thirty 500 lb bombs. The steelworks shook as the bombs detonated on impact with the target, which was left severely damaged.

The following afternoon six Stirlings attacked the same target in two formations. Squadron Leader Menaul again led Gilmour and Thompson in the first formation, whilst Squadron Leader Piper led Sergeants Jones and Needham as the second. On this occasion, 'Sailor' Malan's squadrons provided the close escort.

As the main force, flying at 20,000 feet, approached Lille, Malan saw a number of Me109s. His section of Spitfires broke into two pairs in anticipation of the forthcoming dog-fighters, but in the ensuing battle all four Spitfires got separated.

While Malan went on to extricate himself from the mêlée and shoot down a Me109, the bombers continued towards the target at 14,000 feet. The German fighters again dived down through the formation in an effort to destroy the bombers. Sergeant Ward, Flight Lieutenant Gilmour's front gunner, drew a bead on one of the 109s and opened fire. Strikes were seen to hit the fighter, which was later claimed as damaged. Sergeant Needham's Stirling N6021 was attacked by another of the fighters, but Needham's rear gunner was unable to return the fire due to two of the escorting fighters being in his line of fire.

As the heavy barrage of flak rose angrily into the sky, twenty-four 1,000 lb and fifty-six 500 lb bombs whistled down to explode on the steelworks. Although many direct hits were claimed some sticks of bombs fell in the adjacent marshalling yards.

On 7th July Squadron Leader Menaul, Flight Lieutenant Gilmour and Flying Officer Thompson flew another daylight circus to attack the Kuhlman chemical works at Chocques. The lack of fighter activity against the bombers was compensated for by the heavy and intense flak thrown up around the bombers.

Stewart Menaul remembers this operation.

> The raid I distinctly remember was the one during which we got some good photographs. It was a daylight attack against the Kuhlman Chemical Works, on 7th July 1941. There was flak bursting all over the place, as a series of pictures taken at the time show. In one of them you can see flak bursting around the tail of my Stirling, whilst another shows it bursting around Bobby Gilmour's aircraft. He seemed to get more of it than I did, and some of it was pretty damn close. However we hit the factory fair and square, and left it burning like hell. It was still burning when the results of our work was later photographed by a Spitfire.

Almost every bomb of the total fifteen 1,000 lb and forty-two 500 lb HE load struck the target, creating large clouds of smoke.

The raid was such a success that the following day Stewart Menaul was able to read about it in the newspapers. He was later awarded the Distinguished Flying Cross, for his part in the raid. Having completed thirty-two operations with the squadron, Stewart Menaul was declared 'tour expired' and posted, on 19th July, to No 3 Group HQ.

During the period mid-July 1941 to the first week of December 1942, Stewart Menaul not only instructed novice pilots in the art of flying Stirlings, at a conversion unit, but also took them and their crews on their first operational missions. This work eventually earned him the award of the Air Force Cross.

Squadron Leader Menaul relates how he returned to flying with an operational squadron:

> I was sitting in the 'ops' room one morning, about half past eight. I had been on 'ops' the night before, but as it was a

Stewart Menaul photographed on the day of promotion to Wing Commander, 7th December 1941, when he returned to and took command of No XV Squadron.

reasonably short trip I was back before midnight and had managed a good night's sleep. Air Vice Marshal 'Jacky' Baldwin, the No 3 Group Commander strode into the room, after his morning ride across Newmarket Heath, pointed his riding crop at me and said, 'You! You're going to take over a squadron'. And that was that.

On 7th December, with the rank of acting wing commander, he returned to XV Squadron – this time its commanding officer. It was his third posting to the squadron, which was now based at Bourn, but still operating Stirling bombers.

His first mission, ten days later, was successfully carried out but almost came to grief at the last moment. Seven aircraft had been detailed for mine-laying operations, two in the Friesians and five in the Bay of Biscay. Wing Commander Menaul was flying with Squadron Leader Faulkner in Stirling BF356, which was one of the original Mark I's. During the flight, which lasted just over four hours, the port outer engine cut out due to the exactor throttle going u/s. At 21.20 hours, as the aircraft was approaching to land back at Bourn, Wing Commander Menaul found he was unable to throttle back. Without hesitation he opened up the throttles with the intention of going round again, but as he did so the port inner engine also cut. With the Stirling settling onto the runway, Menaul throttled back. The aircraft continued to roll, it overshot the end of the runway and burst into flames after colliding with a tree. Fortunately, only one injury was sustained.

On his second mission, another mine-laying operation on 14th January 1943, Stewart Menaul was forced to return early due to heavy icing. The following night he participated with seven other crews in a raid against Lorient. He took off at 17.40 hours, flying Stirling BK611. XV Squadron delivered its attack at 20.09 hours from 16,000 feet, and all crews claimed to have hit the target.

Three weeks later Wing Commander Menaul returned to Lorient as part of an attacking force of 323 bombers. XV Squadron detailed fifteen aircraft, which included three of the new Mark III Stirlings.

Despite the heavy German defences, a devastating attack was carried out which left large fires burning. Although the flak managed to shoot down seven bombers, all XV Squadron aircraft returned safely to Bourn. As it turned out, this was Stewart Menaul's last operation with XV Squadron.

After this raid he was engaged in preparing to transfer the squadron and its equipment to RAF Mildenhall, which had recently re-opened after having concrete runways laid.

The actual move was made on 14th April, with the assistance of two Armstrong Whitworth Whitleys and two Airspeed Horsa gliders, which airlifted some of the personnel and ground equipment. The Stirlings were flown in by their crews, who were then stood down and given twenty-four hours to settle into their new quarters, before commencing operations.

Stewart Menaul's long association with XV Squadron came to an end on 7th May, when he was appointed to the rank of acting group captain and posted to command RAF Station Bourn.

Air Vice-Marshal Stewart Menaul DFC, AFC served throughout the entire war. Even as a group captain he continued to fly on operations, including a tour of duty with the Pathfinder Force. His distinguished career with the Royal Air Force continued into post war years, the defence of his country ever present in his mind.

CHAPTER TWO

MacRobert's Reply

Squadron Leader Peter J.S. Boggis DFC

The recommendation for the immediate award of one Distinguished Service Order, seven Distinguished Flying Crosses and two Distinguished Flying Medals, by the Air Officer Commanding-in-Chief, Bomber Command to His Majesty King George VI read:

> On the 18th July 1941, in daylight, a strong force of Stirling and Halifax bombers carried out a determined attack on the German warships *Gneisenau* and *Scharnhorst* at Brest. The operation was carried out in the face of extremely heavy and accurate anti-aircraft fire and determined attacks by enemy fighters. Nevertheless, the aircrews engaged pressed home their attacks to the utmost and succeeded in scoring direct hits on their objectives. Many enemy aircraft were shot down. The success of the operation, which demanded the highest degree of skill and courage, reflects the greatest credit on the efforts of the following officers and airmen who participated in various capacities as leaders and members of aircraft crews.

Amongst those men listed were four from No XV Squadron, including its CO, Wing Commander Patrick Ogilvie DSO and Flying Officer Peter James Somerville Boggis.

For Peter Boggis this raid, his 55th operation, marked the completion of his second operational tour with Bomber Command, but not the end of his service career. His association with the Royal Air Force began when he was accepted for a Short Service Commission in June 1937.

By the time Peter Boggis reached No XV Squadron he was already an experienced bomber pilot. He held the rank of pilot officer and had completed a tour of operations with No 38 Squadron, on Wellingtons. He had also completed a spell as an instructor at a conversion unit at Bassingbourne.

Peter Boggis recalls:

> When I joined XV Squadron on 6th June 1941, there were only two Stirling squadrons in service with the RAF, one at Oakington (No 7) and the other, No XV, at Wyton. Naturally, there was rivalry and friendship between the two and, unlike later in the war, when an aircraft went missing there was sorrow at both stations. The odds were that the crew would be known to both squadrons: this was especially so with me, because prior to going to XV Squadron I had been an instructor at a Wellington conversion unit and many of the pilots that passed through there went on to Stirlings.

He was obviously pleased with his new surroundings and found the base well-situated.

> Wyton was a nice station with good pubs in the area of St Ives and Huntingdon, and Cambridge within striking distance. Cambridge in those days was a bright city and the Mecca for all aircrew within a reasonable radius. Every 'night out' was a virtual reunion with our chums.
>
> Wyton was fairly easy to find from the air because of two parallel canals that ran from the Wash almost to Huntingdon – a great asset when returning from 'ops' in claggy weather. These canals were also part of our official low flying area. Looking back, we must have frightened no end of farmers, locals and cattle with our Stirlings roaring over their heads only a few feet up!

Apart from the main base, Wyton also operated satellite fields.

> We operated a satellite airfield, for dispersal and training, at Alconbury on the old Great North Road. For a few weeks in

> September 1941 the squadron also operated from a second satellite airfield at Warboys, whilst runways were being laid at Alconbury.
>
> We used to be a bit apprehensive about operating from these fields because with all the activity going on (air tests, arming up with bombs and ammunition and general coming and going of transport, etc) everybody in the vicinity knew 'ops' were on that night. It was a standing joke that if you wanted to know the target for that night the barman or barmaids in the local pubs would tell you. It was not an uncommon sight to see cars stopped on the main road whilst Stirlings were being bombed up.

And of the Stirling itself Peter had mixed feelings.

> My memory of the Stirling aircraft was of a huge aeroplane with the pilot's cockpit a long way off the ground, due to a massive undercarriage that created a lot of drag, especially with a full load on board. It had a very poor heating system and an operating height that compared very unfavourably with that of Halifaxes or Lancasters. However, once airborne, with the undercarriage safely up, I found the aircraft pleasant to fly and quite manoeuvrable. Fortunately, it could also take a lot of punishment from flak.

This was the picture that presented itself to Peter Boggis as he was about to start his second tour of operations during the summer of 1941.

His first mission took place on 20th June, when a total of 115 aircraft set out in an attempt to locate and bomb the *Tirpitz* at Kiel. However, the German battleship was not identified and the city itself was attacked. Although the flak was heavy, Pilot Officer Boggis returned to Wyton without incident.

On 7th July, Bomber Command detailed three Stirlings to attack Frankfurt, the main raid being on Cologne. XV Squadron supplied all three aircraft, one of which was N6030 'P' piloted by Peter Boggis. The two other Stirlings were flown by Pilot Officer Leggate and Sergeant Jones, both of whom dropped their bomb loads on the target whilst Pilot Officer Boggis attacked Hochheim, fifteen miles to the west. Again he returned to Wyton without incident.

Four days later, XV Squadron again detailed three aircraft for a daylight raid. On this occasion, the target was the steel works at Fives-Lille in France and Peter Boggis found his name on the battle order. For this mission he was accompanied by Pilot Officer Leggate and Squadron Leader T. Piper.

A thunderstorm over the target precluded the trio from performing their allotted task, so they turned their attention to the secondary target at Hazebrouck. Direct hits were obtained by two of the three sticks of bombs which fell on the marshalling yards, and the station was also badly damaged.

Of these operations Peter Boggis recalls:

> We did a few daylight raids in the summer of 1941, usually three Stirlings with a very large fighter escort of Spitfires and Hurricanes. We didn't appreciate the fact at the time but in hindsight these raids were presumably part of the general plan to obtain air superiority, and the Stirlings were the bait! It was nice to see so many of our fighters around and crossing the Channel one felt like the King of England with an escort of Life Guards. We flew in at 15,000 feet which must have been an easy height for the German flak and on each raid our Stirlings came back with flak holes, though I'm glad to say we had no casualties in men or aircraft. We would watch, with baited breath, as the German fighters attacked from above, diving down through the fighter escort and being pursued by the Spitfires and Hurricanes as they passed through the formation. It was difficult to sort out who was who.

The daylight raids continued until 25th July, when the squadron returned to night operations, the first of which was a raid against Berlin. Five crews were briefed for the attack, including that of Peter Boggis, who had recently been promoted to the rank of flying officer.

The weather during July 1941 left a lot to be desired. Thunderstorms, ten tenths cloud and poor visibility had hindered many of the operations. However, on this particular night it was the aircraft which caused problems. On the outward flight faults developed in both the front and rear turrets. With his defensive armament lost Peter Boggis had no option but to turn Stirling

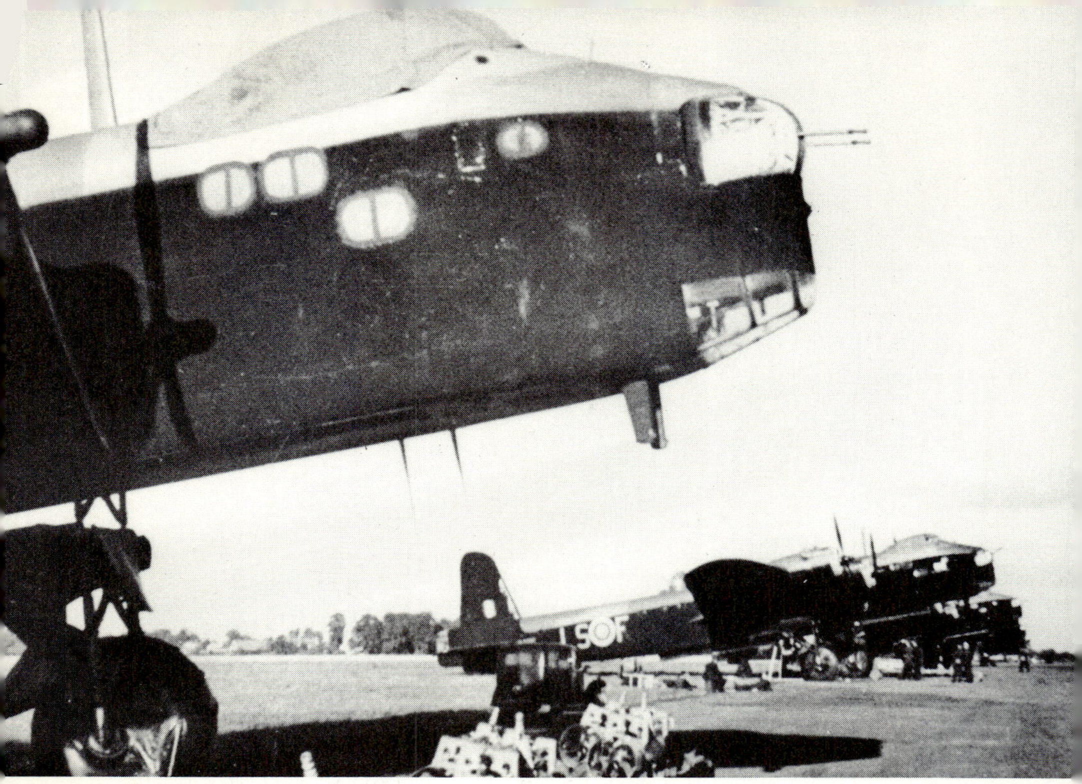

A line-up of No. XV Squadron Stirlings at Wyton in 1941. Stirling N6086, LS-F 'Freddie', was the aircraft donated by Lady MacRobert. It carried the MacRobert family emblem and the name 'MacRobert's Reply'.

The original crew of MacRobert's Reply: *L to R* Sergeant Watson, flight engineer, Sergeant Wilson, rear gunner, Sergeant Soned, mid-upper gunner, Pilot Officer King, 2nd pilot, Flying Officer Peter Boggis, captain, Pilot Officer Ryan, navigator, Sergeant Clark, front gunner, Sergeant Allen, wireless operator.

W7429 for home. As they crossed Münster a battery of searchlights came on, criss-crossing the night sky in search of the lone intruder. Peter took the opportunity to lighten his aircraft and dropped the five 1,000 pound and seven 500 pound bombs which were stored in the bomb bay. The crew were relieved that they experienced no opposition from either fighters or flak.

Operations against targets in Germany continued through August and September with raids on Berlin, Karlsruhe, Essen Frankfurt and Hamburg.

A somewhat unusual and moving ceremony took place at RAF Wyton on 10th October 1941, when a Stirling bomber bearing the name 'MacRobert's Reply' was officially taken on charge by XV Squadron.

Lady MacRobert, the widow of Sir Alexander MacRobert the first Baronet of Cawnpore and Cromar, who had died on 22nd June 1922, had three sons. Sir Alasdair, her eldest son, was killed in a flying accident near Luton in 1938. Her two younger sons, Sir Roderic and Sir Iain, who were both pilots, were killed whilst flying on active service with the Royal Air Force during 1941. In memory of her sons, Lady MacRobert donated a sum of money to purchase four Hurricane fighters. She also gave £25,000 for the purchase of a Stirling bomber which was to carry the MacRobert family crest and was to be known as 'MacRobert's Reply'.

The aircraft, a standard Mark B1 Stirling, had been allotted to XV Squadron on 15th September. It carried the serial N6086 and the squadron indentification LS-F Freddie. During the ceremony, which was photographed by an Air Ministry photographer, Wing Commander Ogilvie formally handed over MacRobert's Reply to Flying Officer Peter Boggis. With the aircraft came a letter signed by Lady MacRobert, the content of which wished the crew good luck and asked them to strike hard, sharp and straight. The letter went on to thank all those who had care of her 'Reply' and to prepare the aircraft for her missions.

Of the occasion, Peter Boggis comments:

> I do not know why I was chosen to fly 'MacRobert's Reply'. As I understood it, Lady MacRobert wanted a Scotsman to fly the aircraft.

MacRobert's Reply's introduction to operations came two nights later on 12th October, when she headed with a formation of 151 other aircraft for Nuremburg.

By the time XV Squadron had arrived over the target area a considerable number of fires were burning. Flying Officer Boggis circled the city for 35 minutes before taking N6068 in on the bombing run. At 01.15 hours five 1,000 lb and seven 500 lb bombs fell from MacRobert's bomb bay to the burning city 16,000 feet below. The crew watched as the shimmering orange and red carpet of flame below emitted clumps of black cloud as the bombs detonated and added to the carnage.

MacRobert's Reply returned safely to Wyton, landing at 03.50 hours.

The squadron paid a small price for its night's work when one aircraft, N3667, overshot and hit an obstruction on landing and another failed to return.

Two nights later Peter Boggis took MacRobert's Reply back to Nuremburg, but on this occasion they were unable to locate the primary target owing to the bad weather conditions. All eighty aircraft participating in the raid, including the four Stirlings detailed by XV Squadron, were hampered by ten-tenths cloud and severe icing.

Remembering the attack of two nights before, the enemy search-lights and flak batteries were taking no chances. The cold icy beams of light groped stiffly around the cloud as the flak burst in its all to familiar pattern.

The formation turned for home, still with the bomb loads intact in the bomb bays. As on previous operations, Peter Boggis released his bombs onto the searchlights, which on this occasion rose up from Mannheim.

During the rest of October and early November Flying Officer Boggis took MacRobert's Reply to Bremen, the Skoda Works at Pilsen in Czechoslavakia and Cologne.

On the night of 23rd November, a raid was scheduled against the docks at Brest. The five Stirlings, detailed from XV Squadron, set out in poor weather conditions, which did not improve over the target area. Once again, due to ten-tenths cloud and low visibility the crews had to abandon their task and turn for home.

Peter Boggis was flying Stirling N6098, G, on this raid and recalls:

> In those days we were instructed to take the bombs home if we could not identify the target. However, on this trip I dropped a 2,000 pound bomb on the estimated position and decided to take the remainder home.
>
> On the return journey, I had trouble with one of the engines and decided to feather it; I was also running low on petrol. Considering my plight I suddenly remembered a fighter pilot I had met somewhere saying we could always land at Exeter in an emergency. (Exeter was a nightfighter station). I called them on the R/T and, although there was a raid on at the time, they gave me every assistance including putting their searchlights into a cone so that I could home onto it. They also turned on the minimum number of landing lights when I was overhead, warning me that as soon as I had landed the lights would go off. I turned the Stirling on to finals and lowered her onto the runway, easing the brakes on as I felt the aircraft touch down. As pre-warned, the runways lights were switched off and the Stirling rolled to a halt in the dark. I shut down the engines and waited for the tractor which, I was previously told, would tow N6098 to a dispersal area.
>
> Fortunately the airfield escaped the air raid, but the city took a lot of punishment.

The Stirling was grounded for three days whilst repairs to the defective engine, and servicing were carried out, but Peter did not mind. Having been born forty miles away at Barnstaple, Peter knew Exeter fairly well and was able to show the crew some of the local scenery, including a pub near the airfield, where they added their signatures to those already on the ceiling of the bar, before returning to Wyton.

Brest was again the target on the night of 14th/15th December. The squadron despatched six aircraft to attack the German warships *Scharnhorst* and *Gneisenau*. Yet again, the operation was hampered by ten-tenths cloud, the tops of which rose to over 16,000 feet. Thunderstorms and severe icing created further problems for the crews, who were forced to abandon the mission and return to base.

Peter Boggis recalls:

> I decreased height down to 12,000 feet over the French coast and was still in cloud. There was some ack-ack activity, but not enough to bother us. I dropped four flares but was still unable to see anything. On the basis I must hit something, I jettisoned one 2,000 lb bomb over the area and turned for home with the rest of the load still on board.

Three days later, on 18th December, another attempt was made on the same target. Forty-seven aircraft comprising Halifaxes, Manchesters and Stirlings participated in a daylight attack against the warships. It was the operation for which Peter Boggis was to be granted the immediate award of the Distinguished Flying Cross.

XV Squadron detailed nine Stirlings, which took off just before 10.00 hours led by Wing Commander Ogilvie. Once airborne they formed themselves into three vic formations and headed towards St Ives, near Wyton, where they were to rendezvous with No 7 Squadron, who had also provided nine Stirling aircraft.

The two squadrons flew west towards Lundy Island where the Halifaxes and Manchesters, from Nos 35, 76 and 10 Squadrons, were to join the formation for the flight south, over Lands End. The weather had changed dramatically; the cloud had dissipated and presented a clear blue sky with bright sunshine and clear visibility.

As the bombers approached the target the enemy fighters pounced. No 7 Squadron took the brunt of the initial attack. The German fighters, who had been warned of the raid by the incoming plots on their radar screens, shot down two of No 7 Squadron's aircraft and damaged many more, some of which crash-landed at their home base.

The raid had been planned so that each flight would be over the target at one minute intervals, and XV Squadron were detailed to be the second wave. Each flight was to approach the target at 17,000 feet, dive to 14,000 feet in order to release its bombs and climb back to regain formation. The enemy fighters were determined this would not happen and peeled over to attack the

Flying Officer Peter Boggis DFC (*left*) and Wing Commander P.B. Ogilvie DSO, DFC, Commanding Officer No XV Squadron, at Wyton a few days after the attack on the German warships at Brest, on 18th December 1941.

bombers as the latter dived. A thick barrage of flak whirled up into the sky and burst indiscriminately as pursued and pursuer dived down.

The bombers pressed home their attacks even though there was intense fighter and anti-aircraft opposition. Most of the bombers were attacked by the fighters including MacRobert's Reply.

Of the raid Peter Boggis later reported:

> We bombed from 14,000 feet at 12.37 hours. Bursts of 250 lb bombs in the middle of stick, believed seen just short of the dry dock. Black smoke was also seen rising from *Gneisenau* after the bombing. We were attacked by three Me109s one of which is claimed as damaged.

The fighters were successful in their endeavours and shot down two of XV Squadron's aircraft. Flight Lieutenant Heathcote flying N3665, B, failed to return and Flying Officer Bunce, whose Stirling W7228, Z, had been attacked by five Me109s, was last seen diving into the sea with flames trailing from the port wing.

In the confusion of diving aircraft, anti-aircraft fire and black smoke rising from the bombed warships, Peter Boggis became separated from the rest of the squadron. Having completed the bombing run he put down the nose of MacRobert's Reply and headed north out towards the Channel.

With so many enemy fighters around, Peter warned the gunners to be vigilant. A short while later the rear gunner reported a formation of aircraft behind them. Instinctively, the crew tensed and waited for the impending fight which to them was inevitable, but before the gunners could get their sights on the aircraft they were recognised as a formation of Halifaxes who had the same idea of flying low out over the sea. As the formation reached the lone Stirling it opened sufficiently to allow MacRobert's Reply to join its ranks and together they flew back to England.

Behind them lay the results of a successful raid. The bombs were dropped with great accuracy, and the ships were left billowing black smoke high into the air. Two enemy fighters were claimed as shot down and others damaged.

The following day a signal was received from the Chief of the Air

Staff. It conveyed his thanks to all those who took part in the raid. It went on to state that he had the greatest admiration for the skill with which the raid was planned and the gallantry with which it was carried out.

This operation completed Peter Boggis' second tour of duty. The recommendation for his Distinguished Flying Cross was granted on 31st December 1941.

On 26th January 1942, Flying Officer P.J. Boggis DFC was posted to a Heavy Conversion Unit where, whilst acting as an instructor, he carried out a further six operations, including the first two 1,000 Bomber Raids on Cologne and Essen. In all he completed 61 operational sorties.

Peter Boggis ceased flying in 1953, but MacRobert's Reply was not so fortunate. Stirling N6086 F-Freddie was severely damaged when it collided with a Spitfire, whilst taking off from Peterhead, in January 1942. The aircraft was repaired, but was written off after crashing, through engine failure on 14th March 1943.

CHAPTER THREE

0.75 of an Operation and Five Days in a Dinghy

Group Captain T.H.B. 'Brian' Tayler

The blackness of the night that had protected them for the last few hours, began to recede as the morning light gradually filtered across the distant horizon, announcing the arrival of a new dawn. As the sky brightened that July day, and the features of the earth below began to take shape, the crew looked out anxiously from their Stirling. To their concern and disappointment they saw beneath them not the grey waters of the North Sea, but land. Having taken in that sobering fact, the question then was, where were they?

The trip to Berlin had been a long one, but then they always were long trips. A check of the compass and charts revealed their problem; their bomber was off course, a problem the pilot, Flying Officer Thompson, quickly rectified by turning onto a south-westerly heading, following a course correction by the navigator, Sergeant Beechcroft.

They began to feel vulnerable in the dawn's light. They were night bombers, used to the fragile protection of darkness and the sense of security, however tenuous, it gave them. A coastline slipped past underneath the Stirling. The rear gunner, Sergeant Guymer from New Zealand, watched as the waves broke on the beach. Whilst watching the sky for fighters he felt sure must soon appear, he occasionally glanced down, until the distant waves became an unbroken continuous white line of surf, as the bomber flew out over the sea.

The flight engineer, Sergeant Day, had been watching the fuel gauges closely. He was concerned, as the needles flickered alarmingly fast towards the zero reading. He had kept the pilot informed about the critical fuel situation, but about thirty miles out from the hostile coast the fuel tanks finally ran dry.

The bomber began to sink towards the vast expanse of water below, flying only on the vapour left in the tanks. As the sea grew nearer, Thompson ordered the crew to their ditching positions, whilst he became engrossed with 'landing' the strangely silent Stirling onto the water. It was an eerie feeling tinged with apprehension and fear. The slipstream made strong sounds as the air whistled through the bomber, to which was added unusual knocking and clinking sounds as bits of equipment rattled about, sounds that were usually masked by the roar from the engines.

Thompson did a good job and managed a successful ditching. Each man was able to scramble through the escape hatches and climb aboard the dinghy, wet, but without injury. After the initial reaction of ditching and ensuring each man was all right, they sat quietly in the gently bobbing life raft. They looked at one another and wondered how long it would be before they were rescued – and by whom!

*

The seven men who sat in that dinghy were the Australian pilot, Flying Officer Thompson; Sergeant Beechcroft, navigator; Sergeant Smith, wireless operator; Sergeant Titlerton, front gunner; Sergeant Day, flight engineer; Sergeant Guymer, rear gunner and Flight Lieutenant Tayler, the second pilot. Their experience ranged from thirty trips, completed by Sergeant Guymer, to Brian Tayler, who was completing only his second trip, as second pilot, before taking his own crew on operations.

Flight Lieutenant T.H.B. 'Brian' Tayler had benefited from a peacetime training, as he recalls:

> At the age of twenty-two I qualified for a Short Service Commission in the Royal Air Force.
>
> I was posted to Hatfield as a pupil pilot and carried out my first flight in a Tiger Moth on 24th May 1937.
>
> After some 68 hours of all manner of flying, I was posted to the RAF Depot at Uxbridge where I was commissioned, kitted out and drilled. This took a fortnight.

My next stop was No 10 Flying Training School at Tern Hill, Salop, where the drill was advanced flying training in Hawker Harts and Avro Ansons – the latter, as I was scheduled for heavy bombers.

On 26th March 1938, I was posted to No 148 Squadron, at RAF Stradishall to fly Vickers Wellesleys.

The squadron retained its Wellesley bombers until August of that year, when these aircraft were sent to the Middle East. No 148 was then re-equipped with Handley Page Heyford Mk III bombers, some of which came from No 99 Squadron. Brian Tayler remembers the Heyford:

The Heyford was a very old twin-engined, open cockpit biplane, which at that time was still a front line aircraft! We kept all the aircraft bombed up throughout the period of the Munich Crisis, although we knew they would not have lasted five minutes against the lastest German fighters.

During March and April 1939, No 148 Squadron re-equipped with the more modern Wellington bombers. On 4th September, the day following the declaration of war, it took these aircraft to RAF Harwell in Berkshire, where it became a training squadron within No 6 Group Bomber Command. Exactly seven months later, on 4th April 1940, No 148 Squadron merged with No 75 Squadron to form No 15 Operational Training Unit. Twenty-six days later, the squadron was re-formed in its own right as a bomber squadron, only to be disbanded on 23rd May 1940.

Whilst the future of No 148 was in some doubt, Brian Tayler made plans for his own future; he married his fiancée on 12th October 1940.

Brian Tayler stayed with No 15 OTU for some sixteen months, as an instructor, giving dual instruction to a large number of pilots that came through the unit, both on Wellingtons and later on Stirlings, telling them, as he put it:

What to do on 'ops' although I had not been on one myself. Eventually, I decided it was time I practised what I was preaching so on 22nd July 1941, I was posted to No XV Squadron, which flew Stirlings from Wyton, a No 3 Group Station.

As one of his closest friends, Squadron Leader Tim Piper, was already based at Wyton with No XV, Brian Tayler was, therefore, happy with the posting and he looked forward to seeing his friend again. However, his feelings turned to sorrow when on arriving at Wyton when he was informed that Squadron Leader Piper had been shot down during a daylight raid over France three days earlier and was 'missing'. Flight Lieutenant Tayler found the set-up before him most depressing, especially as the squadron commander, Wing Commander Ogilvie, informed him he was to take over Squadron Leader Piper's flight.

The following day Brian Tayler's name appeared on the battle order. He was detailed to fly as 'second dicky' to Pilot Officer Needham on a daylight operation against the German battle-cruiser *Scharnhorst*. The German warship had slipped her moorings at Brest and sailed south to La Pallice. Three crews from No XV were detailed to join three crews from No 7 Squadron for the attack.

Unfortunately for No XV, the raid was a failure. Sergeant Jones bombed a ship at Fromontine, instead of La Pallice. Flying Officer Campbell having bombed the target was forced to ditch some fifty miles from Milford Haven on the homeward journey. Pilot Officer Needham, unable to raise the undercarriage of his aircraft, was forced to jettison his bombs and fuel and return to base.

Although Flight Lieutenant Tayler was passed fit to fly solo, after a duel conversion flight on 24th July, he was still required to fly his first operation as a second pilot to an experienced crew. The next opportunity arose the following night when seven Stirlings and two Halifaxes were detailed to bomb no less a target than Berlin, as a diversionary raid whilst main force aircraft attacked Hanover and Hamburg. Two of the Stirlings came from No 7 Squadron while the other five were detailed by XV Squadron.

A raid on Berlin was bad enough for an experienced crew, but for a novice, it could be a daunting prospect. Brian Tayler, however, was not unduly worried; he had been assigned to fly with Flying Officer Thompson, an experienced Australian bomber captain.

Stirling N6029, K – King, in which Tayler was flying, took off from Wyton and set course for Berlin, with five 1,000 lb and seven 500 lb bombs in the bomb bay:

> We were briefed to fly over and bomb the city at ten minute intervals. This was asking for a lot of attention, which we duly received.

Nevertheless, damage was caused to military establishments, two railway station and an armaments factory, which was still burning the following day.

The inevitable searchlights swept the sky as a barrage of hot steel exploded around the bombers. Fortunately, N6029 escaped unscathed.

Flying Officer Thompson sent the 'Operation Completed' signal and headed for home.

> We got safely away from Berlin, but something went wrong with the navigation on the homeward journey. As dawn broke, we were still over land and not the North Sea. A quick check of the compass showed were the fault lay, so we turned south-west. The night fighters had all gone to bed, but we attracted our fair share of flak. We were by this time down to about 7,000 feet, thinking we were approaching the English coast.

The situation was now very serious. The petrol started to run low. Then N6029 lost the use of one of its engines.

Flying Officer Thompson informed his crew of the dilemma before them, whether to bale out now or risk the petrol gauges being inaccurate. After a brief discussion, they decided to press on and risk it, but some thirty miles out to sea, their luck deserted them. The engines, starved of fuel, stopped and they were forced to ditch. It was an experience that Brian Tayler would not forget.

> We arrived in the North Sea at dawn on 26th July, four days after my arrival on the squadron. We immediately transferred to the dinghy and there we sat, cold and miserable, watching the aircraft which floated for three hours.

Before they ditched, Flying Officer Thompson had sent a signal informing Wyton that his aircraft was short of fuel. When the Stirling failed to return to base, a search was ordered on the last reported line of bearing.

Wing Commander Ogilvie immediately took off in a Lysander, whilst two Hawker Hurricanes hurriedly departed from the fighter airfield of Martlesham Heath. Squadron Leader Oakeshot, piloting a Beam Approach Training Flight (BATF) Wellington, searched for two hours together with three other Wellingtons from No 40 Squadron. Although there were a few local rainstorms, the sea was calm and visibility was good, but nothing was seen.

At 13.00 hours the men in the dinghy heard the sound of aero-engines, and their hopes rose. Scanning the sky they spotted three aircraft flying in a wide 'vic' formation about half a mile away. To their dismay they identified the aircraft as German Dorniers, but nevertheless fired off a rocket flare, to which there was no response.

The dinghy drifted with the currents of the sea, thwarting the mens' attempts to paddle towards a buoy. The sea roughened and during the night it rained heavily, soaking the men to the skin.

The rough seas and rain continued into the next day accompanied by low scudding clouds, which prevented the downed airmen from sighting any aircraft when they again heard aero-engines just after dawn. The inclement weather remained with them all through the day, into the night and continued into the following day. Brian Tayler recalls: 'The dinghy rode the waves very well, and only small quantities of water were shipped.'

At approximately 19.00 hours on the evening of 29th July, the men's morale was boosted by the sight of two ships with fighter escort about three miles away. The escort flew to within half a mile of the dinghy, but failed to see the crew's restricted attempts at waving. The remaining flares were inoperative due to the soaking they had received over the previous few days. The fighters flew on protecting their charges, and the men sunk back into their state of cold misery.

On the morning of the 30th, the crew realized the thin dark strip they could see on the horizon was land. Brian Tayler takes up the story:

> On the fifth day, at approximately 07.30 hours, we sighted land. We were drifting in towards it so didn't bother to paddle. An hour later we were two miles away from the shore line, but then lost ground. We started paddling to keep land in sight, but the currents were strong and we drifted away. We paddled flat out until 16.00 hours, when we arrived safely at Haamstede on the island of Schouwen, off the Dutch coast. A party of German troops had seen us and awaited our arrival. We were wet through, cold and weak around the knees, otherwise OK. For us it was a case of, 'For you the war is over'!

During their five day ordeal, the crew of Stirling N6029 had survived on rations consisting of one biscuit, two Horlicks tablets and a piece of chewing gum, per person per day. Due to a shortage, they drank no water until the fourth day, when each man consumed only one mouthful, although they did partake of a tot or two of rum.

Brian Tayler remembers their welcome on Schouwen:

> On landing we were given sweets, cigarettes, coffee and bread. We were then taken to a Luftwaffe aerodrome and given a change of clothing and some more food and coffee.
>
> After spending the night in the Luftwaffe barracks, we were sent, by lorry, to Amsterdam gaol where we stayed for four days in solitary confinement.

In order to try and extract information from their new prisoners, the Germans would send bogus Red Cross officials into the cells with cigarettes for their reluctant guests. They also gave the airmen forms to fill in, advising them that their names could then be sent home quickly to their respective families and the authorities. But, as Brian Tayler points out, 'Questions such as CO's name, time of take-off and place of take-off were all too obvious to catch us out.'

At 08.30 hours on 2nd August, the crew were moved, by way of Utrecht, to Dulagluft at Frankfurt, where further interrogation took place. It was here that Flight Lieutenant Tayler heard the news that his friend Squadron Leader Tim Piper had survived being shot down, and had in fact only left Dulagluft interrogation centre the previous day.

Flight Lieutenant Brian Tayler (*second from left, back row*) at Oflag XXIB, Schubin, Poland, in November 1942. Also in the photograph are Hugh Falkus, (*fifth from left standing*) who later became a BBC broadcaster and Chris Cheshire, (*sixth from left standing*), brother of Leonard Cheshire VC.

Flight Lieutenant Brian Tayler (*second from left*) at Oflag XC, with his friend Squadron Leader Tim Piper (*third from left*)'

Ten days later Brian Tayler was moved to Oflag Xc, the first of many POW camps in which he was to be interned, (amongst them the famous Stalag Luft III at Sagon). His arrival at the camp, in the late afternoon, was heralded by a welcome from his chum Tim Piper, with whom he was able to share a room. Of his time in these camps, Brian Tayler recalls:

> Our main hobby was trying to escape and I had several attempts foiled. One tunnel we dug got through, but the second man out, got up and walked away instead of crawling, thus alerting the guards.

Flight Lieutenant Brian Tayler remained a POW until released by the advancing British Army in May 1945.

His first sight of England came as the Lancaster bomber, in which he was flying, crossed the English coast on its journey from Rheine to Dunsfold airfield, where most of the repatriated prisoners were being taken.

After the war Brian Tayler received a permanent commission and stayed in the RAF. He retired from the Service in 1958, with the rank of group captain.

CHAPTER FOUR

The Diary

Sergeant Frederick Stevens

His eyelids flickered once or twice, then slowly opened. Equally slowly his eyes focused, but it took Frederick Stevens a few minutes to understand what had happened to him. He felt as though he was upright, but he was not standing on anything solid. He glanced down to see the ground a short distance below his dangling feet; turning his gaze upwards he perceived that he was hanging by a parachute from a beech tree.

In his mind he heard the sounds of battle. The staccato rattle of machine gun fire, the crackle and roar of flames fanned by the rush of air, the screaming of tortured aero-engines as the aircraft dived to earth and the feeling of fighting for survival before oblivion. As the recollections came flooding back, Frederick Stevens remembered the horror and nightmare of being shot down.

*

Steve, as he was known to his friends, had joined the Royal Air Force in February 1940. He was mustered as a clerk, General Duties, and sent to Manston for basic training before being posted to the RAF Records Office at Ruislip. When the department was transferred to Gloucester in 1941, Steve went with it.

It was at Gloucester that Steve purchased a diary in which he recorded his RAF career to date. Thereafter, he wrote in his diary every day.

As time went by and the war progressed, Steve thought about the future and made a decision:

> During 1942, I felt I could be more useful to the war effort. Therefore, without warning my parents, I applied to remuster to aircrew. My application was approved and on 20th September I reported to the Aircrew Selection Board at Weston-Super-Mare, where I was accepted to train as an air gunner.

Training took place at Hereford, Dalcross, Inverness and then Marham near King's Lynn, where Steve joined an Operational Training Unit.

The OTU at Marham was equipped with twin-engined Wellington bombers, but on Monday 1st February 1943 Steve was surprised to see, for the very first time, one of the four-engined Stirling heavy bombers, which had flown into Marham.

Two weeks later, Steve Stevens reported to No 1657 Heavy Conversion Unit at Stradishall where he renewed his acquaintance with the Stirling. The HCU flew Stirlings and Steve was initiated into the mysteries of the inner working of the huge bomber, with the aid of various lectures on the aircraft, which took place during the first week.

By the third week of February, he had been assigned to 'B' Flight, and crewed-up. His pilot, Pilot Officer Jim Stowell, was a New Zealander. The rest of the crew consisted of Sergeant Pattison, wireless operator, Sergeant Jim Banyer, bomb aimer, Sergeant Ted Kirby, flight engineer and Sergeant Jennings, mid-upper gunner. The navigator, Sergeant Jackson, joined the crew a week later.

On Tuesday 2nd March, the crew were declared combat ready and received a posting to No XV Squadron, based at Bourn. However, the actual order to move was not received for a further two days.

Even though he was going operational, Steve had still not informed his parents that he had joined the more dangerous occupation of aircrew. This was an omission that was to give them a double shock two months later.

Having arrived at Bourn at 16.00 hours on the afternoon of Friday 5th March, Steve spent the rest of the day settling in. The following day he travelled, with the rest of the crew, to Oakington to draw flying clothing from the stores.

They made their first cross-country flight, from Bourn, on

Sunday 7th March. Stirling BK6111, U – Uncle, took off and headed north, via King's Lynn, to Whitley Bay. Pilot Officer Stowell then turned out over the North Sea in a wide sweeping turn, before recrossing the coast and overflying Lincoln, with its magnificent aerial views of the Cathedral. BK611 then retraced her flight plan south, landing back at Bourn a couple of hours later.

The following day Jim Stowell took charge of Stirling Mk I EF345 M – Mother, which the crew took on a night cross-country later that day. They got to know their aircraft inside and out, on the ground and in the air, before taking it on its first operational mission on the night of 11th/12th March. Steve wrote in his diary:

> Did an air test on M – Mother over the Wash, tested guns.
>
> Took off at 19.00 hours to lay mines in enemy waters. Took six mines, saw them float down. Flak ship opened fire on another aircraft, apart from that no excitement. Took three hours.

The following night another mine laying operation was undertaken, among the Frisian Islands. As with the previous raid Steve was able, from his rear turret, to watch the mines go down and saw one explode soon after hitting the water.

Three attempts were made, by No XV Squadron, to bomb St Nazaire during March; each time the operation was scrubbed due to inclement weather. The mission finally took place on the night of 2nd April.

Stirling EF345 took off at 19.30 hours and set course towards the Bay of Biscay. The aircraft was sluggish and Pilot Officer Stowell experienced problems maintaining height. When out over the sea, off the south coast of England, he ordered Jim Banyer, the bomb aimer, to jettison a 1,000 pound bomb. EF345 crossed the French coast at 8,000 feet and had only managed to climb another 1,000 feet by the time the target was reached. Although Jim Stowell experienced trouble maintaining height, he had no such problem maintaining speed. EF345 arrived at the target ahead of ETA as Steve recorded in his diary:

> Arrived at target early, at 9,000 feet. The defences opened up. Stooged around until PPF dropped flares. Going in AA had our

> height to a 'T'. We dropped our 6 x 1,000 lb and 1 x 500 lb bombs and scrammed.

The ground defences opened fire and EF345 was buffeted and tossed around as flak exploded about them, hitting the aircraft several times, but fortunately not damaging any vital parts. Sergeant Kirby felt unwell, as the aircraft buffeted up and down, and was eventually air sick. Steve, sitting in the claustrophobic confines of his rear turret, later confided to his diary that he also felt unwell.

The aircraft continued to fly and having left the target area, headed north towards the south coast of England. Apart from having to fly a damaged bomber, Jim Stowell also had to contend with a navigator of inferior quality, who got confused over the aircraft's actual position. This resulted in the Stirling landing at the grass fighter airfield of Middle Wallop, Hampshire.

The crew had breakfast and lunch at Middle Wallop while the Stirling was patched up and refuelled, before flying it back to Bourn. Their arrival back at Bourn was an unhappy one for Sergeant Kirby, who was grounded. His place as flight engineer was taken by Sergeant Pete Sharman.

An operation against Kiel was undertaken on 4th April in Stirling BF475, T – Tommy, due to EF345 being unserviceable. They took off at 20.30 hours and headed for the target in 10/10th cloud, which stayed with them for the length of the journey. As they crossed the coast on the way in, two searchlights endeavoured to penetrate the cloud in search of the raiders. Flak rose into the night sky in a very haphazard, and almost lazy, manner. The raid was not considered a success, possibly due to a number of decoy fires drawing the bombers away from the real aiming point. The flak was more intensive on part of the route out, but did not create any problems for Jim Stowell. Fortunately, neither did the fighters, for Steve later wrote in his diary: 'Aircraft T – turret not up to scratch'.

Pilot Officer Stowell and his crew were to have participated in a raid on Duisberg on 8th April. EF345 took off with the rest of the squadron, but as the Stirling headed towards the North Sea the navigator informed the pilot that he had mislaid his navigation charts. Jim Stowell continued his track out to sea, where he

Five members of Pilot Officer Jim Stowell's crew. *L to R* Sergeant Jim Banyer, Sergeant W. Jennings, Sergeant Ted Kirby, Sergeant L. Patterson and Sergeant Frederick 'Steve' Stevens.

The six other members of 'Steve' Stevens' crew lie side by side in the Reichswald War Cemetery, near RAF Laarbruch. Jim Stowell, the pilot, is buried in the grave on the extreme left.

jettisoned the bomb load before returning to base. The following day the pilot informed the members of his crew that the navigation charts had been found; they were in the navigator's bag. As survival depended very much on each man carrying out his duties to the best of his ability, Jim Stowell had no alternative but to replace his navigator; thus it was that Pilot Officer Dave Murray joined the crew.

A raid on Frankfurt on the night of 10th/11th April was the last mission No XV Squadron made from Bourn prior to transferring to Mildenhall. Unfortunately, one of their number was not destined to make the move to Mildenhall, as Steve recorded:

> Operations Frankfurt. Saw nothing on way in. Flak not very heavy near us, plenty of dummy fires. PFF late. Wimpey came up close to us on way back. ... We lost 18 kites, one from our squadron.

During the afternoon of 13th April Steve, along with other members of the squadron, watched the arrival at Bourn of two Armstrong Whitworth Whitley bombers and two Airspeed Horsa gliders. These aircraft were to be used to transport equipment to the new station. Later that day, Steve returned to his billet and packed his kit in preparation for the move.

On the night of 16th April, No XV Squadron flew its first operation from Mildenhall. The target was Mannheim and a total force of 271 aircraft were to carry out the attack, eighteen of which were detailed from XV Squadron.

EF345 took off from Mildenhall at 21.26 hours and climbed to 9,000 feet. As the aircraft crossed the French coast, Jim Stowell reduced altitude to 1,500 feet and skimmed, at low level, over the French countryside which was bathed in the silvery blue moonlight. A burst of flak which suddenly lit the sky died as quickly as it appeared, leaving a black smoke drift to signify its presence.

Approaching the target Pilot Officer Stowell increased height to 12,000 feet in order to mke his bombing run. The flak was now bursting with vengeance, and could be heard above the constant drone of the four Hercules engines and whistling of the bomb load as it fell to earth. The aircraft vibrated as a flak shell exploded close to the bomber, shrapnel ricocheting along the fuselage and shattering the astro-hatch. Fortunately, nobody was injured. They breathed a sigh of relief as they escaped the flak barrage, but their troubles were not yet over. In the glow of the moonlight, Steve spotted a Ju88 nightfighter stealing up from the rear starboard quarter. He yelled a warning to the captain who, on receipt of the instruction, 'Port go', began evasive action. The Ju88 did not follow but was seen to fly over the top of EF345 and away.

Their bombs went down on the TI markers at 00.55 hours. They then flew home without further trouble, landing back at Mildenhall at 03.54.

During the following week, Steve Stevens was feeling a little fed-up. The entry in his diary for Monday 19th April read:

> On battle order for Turin. Scrubbed at 19.00 hours. Went to bed early as I was feeling very 'cheesed'.

For some reason Pilot Officer Murray had suddenly left the crew. His place as navigator was taken by Pilot Officer D. Spooner. Spooner had a chance to prove his capabilities the following night when the squadron joined an all Stirling raid against the Heinkel Works at Rostock.

EF345 took off from Mildenhall at 22.30 hours and flew at very low level out over the North Sea. Jim Stowell steadily climbed to 8,000 feet as he approached the industrial port situated eighteen miles from the Baltic coast. The attacking force found the target concealed by a smoke screen, but many crews bombed on their ETA positions. Others, seeing the glow of fires burning beneath the smoke, unleashed their bomb loads to add to the conflagration.

The searchlights and flak were much in evidence and, as EF345 flew over the target, Steve saw another Stirling 'coned' by searchlights with flak bursting all round it. Having released their deadly cargo, Pilot Officer Stowell dived out of the target area and flew north at low level, over the coast towards Denmark. Several flagships around the Danish Islands opened fire as the Stirling skimmed overhead. Steve depressed his guns and returned the fire from the rear turret.

Over Denmark, Spooner, the navigator, gave his pilot a new course to fly. Stowell, still flying very low, banked EF345 onto the new heading, only to find a factory chimney directly in his path. Avoiding the chimney, Stowell continued across Denmark and out across the dark expanse of the North Sea. EF345 landed at Mildenhall at 06.30 hours, having been airborne for eight hours.

Eight Stirlings were lost including BF476 P – Peter, of XV Squadron, flown by Acting Flight Lieutenant C. Lyons. He and his crew were shot down by flak at 02.46 hours, some twenty kilometres south-west of Ringkobing, Denmark. Two of the crew, Sergeant R. Howland, the wireless operator, and Sergeant M. Huggett, the rear gunner, were wounded.

Low cloud, wind and rain between 20th and 25th April cancelled all operations, but the weather improved sufficiently for a raid to take place on the night of the 26th/27th against Duisberg.

The raid was not considered totally successful, as the bombing was scattered over a wide area. Nevertheless, over 300 buildings in the city were destroyed. The searchlights were very active, sweeping the sky in criss-cross patterns. They were successful many times in locating the bombers, including EF345 which was coned in the blinding glare. Steve later recorded in his diary:

> Coned in searchlights for six to eight minutes, got everything including the kitchen sink. Very lucky, about sixteen holes in all some just missing vital spots.

Flak came up thick and fast, bursting all round EF345. Sergeant Bill Jennings, the mid-upper gunner, had a lucky escape when a large piece of shrapnel entered his turret, shattering the perspex and just missing him. But the Stirling remained airworthy and survived to fight another day.

Sergeant Tom Malcolm was a new pilot who had only just been posted to No XV Squadron. Before going operational with his own crew, it was mandatory for him to fly two missions with an experienced pilot and crew. For the first of his 'second dicky' trips Tom Malcolm was detailed to fly with Pilot Officer Jim Stowell on a raid against Dortmund on the night of 4th/5th May.

The flight to the target was uneventful. The night sky was clear,

Flight Lieutenant Charles Lyons (*centre*) and his crew consisting of Pilot Officer Roy Lockwood, BA, (*far right*), Sergeant James Marshall, navigator, Sergeant John Shaw, mid-upper gunner, and Sergeant Hugh Hipwell, flight engineer. Missing from the photograph are Sergeant Howland and Sergeant Huggett, both of whom were injured when shot down.

Stirling Mk III BF476, LS-P, which crashed near Kragelund, 15 km north of Vejle on the night of 20th/21st April 1943. Most of the damage was sustained when the crew set fire to the aircraft, prior to making their escape. Five of the crew were captured the following afternoon.

with a new moon, and the crew of EF345 could see the green markers on which they were to bomb quite clearly when they arrived over Dortmund at 01.20 hours. The shimmering sea of fire was well concentrated and punctured by the occasional explosion which tossed clouds of black smoke and orange flame high into the air. Pilot Officer Stowell joined the bomber stream and prepared for his bombing run. Each man was at his respective station, including Sergeant Banyer, the bomb aimer, who was directing the pilot on his run-in.

Then suddenly, a couple of minutes from the aiming point, night turned to day as the searchlights found them. Jim Stowell immediately pushed the control column forward in an effort to evade the groping beams. The blinding rays stayed with the Stirling as it dived and twisted from 16,000 feet to 4,000 feet. The angry black bursts of flak, guided by the searchlight beams, exploded around the diving aircraft. The controls were wrenched momentarily from the pilot's grip as EF345 lurched through the air as a shell exploded under the wing, setting fire to the port inner engine and wingroot.

As the stricken Stirling plunged down, Stowell gave the order to bale out. Steve clambered hurriedly from his rear turret and unhooked his parachute from its storage rack above the rear escape hatch. He clipped the 'chute onto his harness, jettisoned the hatch and with one hand on the release handle of the parachute, and the other steadying himself, prepared to leave the aircraft, then …

… Then he came-to in a beech tree. Steve Stevens had landed near the village of Anholt, Westphalia in West Germany near the Dutch border. He was captured immediately and held in custody by the Burgomaster, until he was handed over to the authorities. Sergeant Stevens spent the next two years as a prisoner of war.

Sergeant Tom Malcolm had evacuated the doomed aircraft from the forward escape hatch, and also floated down to land near the Dutch border.

The blazing Stirling fell at 02.00 hours, with the rest of the crew still on board. It penetrated deep into the ground in the common grazing land on the outskirts of Anholt. The remains of four members of the crew were recovered from the wreckage and buried with full military honours, in the parish cemetery on 6th May. The following day a further body was found and buried by the side of the four already interred. Although the grave was marked 'Unknown' the airman was accorded the same respect as his comrades. One member of the crew was, at that time, not accounted for, but was found later.

Steve's parents were still not aware that their son had remustered to aircrew; as far as they were concerned he was still a records clerk. Their feelings can be imagined when they received a telegram, from the Air Ministry, informing them that their son was listed as 'Missing in action'.

*

Forty years later, almost exactly to the day, Frederick Stevens joined a group of ex-XV Squadron members on a weekend visit to RAF Laarbruch. On Sunday 8th May 1983, with the rest of the group, Steve attended a Memorial Service at Reichswald War Cemetery, where many RAF aircrew are buried. After the service, he ambled slowly amongst the headstones of the 7,000 airmen resting there. Suddenly, he stopped and remained motionless, staring at the names on six headstones which caught his eye. Steve read them and then stood, with head bowed, in silent tribute for the names were those of his crew; the names recorded in the pages of his diary.

CHAPTER FIVE

The Permanent Reminder

Pilot Officer Graham 'Mick' Cullen

The room at No 11 Operational Training Unit at Westcott, near Aylesbury, was full of flying personnel. Some wore pilot's 'Wings' on their tunics, others wore the half wing brevets of wireless operators, navigators, bomb aimers or air gunners.

The purpose of the gathering was for these men to form themselves, voluntarily, into groups ready to train together as operational aircrews. It was normally the pilots who took the initiative and spoke to the other members of aircrew, deciding instantly whether the navigator, bomb aimer or gunner he was talking to was the sort of chap he wanted on his crew.

One pilot had an advantage over the rest; he had already completed a tour of operations and wore the ribbon of the DFM beneath his 'Wings'. Having recently completed a period of instructing in Canada, Robert Megginson had returned to England with a promotion to flight lieutenant, to begin a second tour of operations.

As Flight Lieutenant Megginson wandered amongst the uniforms, his experienced eye looking for a wireless operator, he met a slight, handsome man whom he engaged in conversation. As they talked, it became obvious to Megginson that the young sergeant came from the Antipodes, New Zealand to be precise. The sergeant gave his name as Graham Cullen, adding that he was always known as Mick. When invited to join Megginson's crew, Mick Cullen did not hesitate to answer in the affirmative. The opportunity of flying with an experienced pilot was too good to miss.

During the first week at No 11 OTU, the rest of the crew was formed. It consisted of Pilot Officer H. (Bunny) Burrows, navigator; Pilot Officer Andy Haydon, bomb aimer and Pilot Officer D. Mitchell, rear gunner.

From the very outset they trained hard. Megginson knew the value of a good team and therefore did not let up. When they were posted to No 1657 Conversion Unit for training on four-engined Stirling Bombers Megginson did not relent.

Mick Cullen remembers:

> As a crew we were highly trained, probably more so than other crews and, therefore, hopefully stood a better chance of survival.
>
> Our skipper insisted that we practised all aspects of crash drill, ditching procedure and the very important one of fighter control.
>
> Whenever the chance arose we would be in the air with fighters from the nearest airfield, practising fighter affiliation. The fighters were fitted with camera guns, and the nature of the exercise was to prevent the attacker from getting a bead on our bomber, thus preventing the fighter from 'firing' his camera guns. This was achieved by the gunners watching the attacking fighters and relaying instructions to the pilot as to which direction to break and when. Although the procedure was great fun, it was of course more important to our survival. Too many crews were lost for lack of knowing what to do at the right time.

Sergeant P. (Joe) Woollard and Sergeant E. (Geordie) Soulsby joined the crew at No 1657 CU as mid-upper gunner and flight engineer respectively. They too were encompassed into the training.

Having completed their conversion course Flight Lieutenant Meggison and his crew were posted, on 17th May 1943, to XV Squadron at Mildenhall. The crew were allotted Stirling BK818, O – Orange, as their own aircraft, on arrival at the squadron. Their operational tour started four days later on the night of 21st/22nd May. Being an experienced pilot Megginson did not fly the obligatory 'second dicky' trip, but went straight on to ops.

Seven aircraft were detailed for a mine laying operation, in the

L to R Pilot Officer D. Mitchell, (killed night of 23rd August 1943), Flying Officer Andy Haydon, Flight Lieutenant Megginson, Sergeant Soulsby, Sergeant P. Woollard. *Seated L to R* Pilot Officer Burrows and Sergeant Mick Cullen.

The size of the Stirling is evident in this picture, thought to be of a Mk III BK818, LS-O, flown by Flight Lieutenant R.R. Megginson.

Frisians, and BK818 appeared on the Battle Order. All aircraft planted their loads, as ordered, and returned to base without incident.

Two nights later, BK818 was on the Battle Order for a raid on Dortmund. The squadron despatched fifteen aircraft, two of which returned early. The remainder flew on and dropped their mixed loads of high explosive and incendiary bombs on the German town. The raid was reported as good with concentrated fires, the glow of which could be seen from the Zuider Zee. One aircraft failed to return.

During their free time Mick and the crew would often visit one of the local hostelries, including the Bird in Hand Hotel. Mick got to know Brenda Jaggard, a local girl from Beck Row, who was originally a waitress at the 'Bird' but later became a barmaid. A friendship grew between Mick and Brenda, which came to the attention of George Ashley, the landlord of the hotel. In due time, George got to know Mick and the crew and afforded them certain privileges, such as allowing them credit when they wanted to dine at the 'Bird', but found they were short of funds.

The crew continued operations on the night of 25th/26th May when they participated in a raid on Düsseldorf. For No XV Squadron it was a bad night. Two aircraft failed to return, two aircraft returned early and two returned with battle damage, one of which was BK818. Over the next few days, the stalwart ground crews set about repairing the battle-damaged aircraft. They made good severed hydraulics and replaced defective instruments.

Mick Cullen recalls his ground crew:

> Our ground crew were first class chaps. We spent many hours of our standby time out at dispersal talking and clowning with them.
>
> Having seen us off on a mission, one of them would always be at our dispersal point to welcome us back. We as a crew had great faith in their ability to keep our aircraft airworthy.

Whilst BK818 was being repaired Megginson continued the training of his crew. Ever mindful of the perils of operational flying, Megginson continually practised his crew in the dictates of ditching procedure and dinghy drill. The North Sea could be a long and lonely expanse in a crippled bomber and Megginson wanted his crew prepared for any eventuality.

BK818 was airworthy in time for a raid against Wuppertal on the night of 29th/30th May. The squadron detailed eighteen aircraft for the operation, seventeen of which took off.

Sergeant Cullen remembers the Ruhr raids:

> Raids over the Ruhr, I think, were the worst. The towns in the valley were so close together they just passed you from one group of defences to the next. The bombers could therefore be under continuous fire. The situation was aggravated by the searchlights; once in their cone it was very difficult to evade them, for as you flew out of the range of one set, the next would take over. The real danger was the blue master beam, for once this locked onto an aircraft the other beams homed in on it to form a cone.
>
> Andy Haydon, our bomb aimer, would lie in the perspex nose of the Stirling and inform Megginson of the position of the master beam. If and when it approached our aircraft the skipper would pull back on the control column for a steep climb then roll over the beam and away.
>
> I remember one occasion when Flight Lieutenant Megginson carried out this manoeuvre and held back on the control column a fraction too long and all four engines cut out. The experience was amazing; one moment the noise of four throbbing Bristol Hercules engines combined with the bursting flak. A second or two of deathly silence followed as the Stirling stalled and tailslid into a dive. As the aircraft went down the engines, with a shattering crescendo, roared back into life.

Wuppertal was left burning with large explosions being reported by the rear gunners as the invading force left the target area. The textile producing and light engineering areas of Barmen were devastated. Many factories and public buildings were also severely damaged.

When the crew returned from leave, Flight Lieutenant Megginson was informed that he has been promoted to the rank of acting squadron leader, with effect from 18th June 1943.

The rest of June saw the crew participating with XV Squadron in raids on Krefeld, Mülheim, Wuppertal and Gelsenkirchen. Cologne was raided twice, first on 28th/29th June and again on 3rd/4th July.

On the night of the latter raid Megginson had left Mildenhall at 23.25 hours flying a different aircraft, BK805. The route out over the east coast and North Sea was clear, as was the target area. Having discharged his load of incendiaries, Megginson was turning away from the target area when the port inner engine was set ablaze by a hit from the ground defences. The engine was immediately feathered, which rendered the front and mid-upper turrets u/s. BK805 landed at the small fighter airfield at Manston in Kent.

Further raids on German towns and cities prevailed throughout July and into early August.

On the night of 12th/13th August 1943, Bomber Command switched its attention to Turin, Northern Italy. No XV Squadron detailed 9 aircraft to participate in the raid, including the BK818.

Mick Cullen recalls:

> Trips to Northern Italy were regarded as the best of the lot, very little flak and not too much interference from fighters.
>
> These raids were usually carried out during the full moon period and the magnificent sight of the snow covered Alps had to be seen to be believed. On one occasion, as the Stirling droned its way towards the target flying about 1,000 feet above the mountains, the crew marvelled at the brilliance of the moonlight reflecting its silver rays on the snow covered backcloth. Suddenly, a pyrotechnic scene erupted ahead of us as the green and red marker flares cascaded down marking the death of a pathfinder aircraft. As we watched in awe we clearly saw the mushrooming canopies of the parachutes as some of the crew floated down.
>
> I must admit that even our sorrow and concern for the crew could not override the beauty of the scene.

Mick and Brenda's friendship blossomed and they were by now engaged. One night they went to a dance on the base, accompanied by other members of the crew and their respective partners. At the end of the evening, the eight of them in the party made their way, in the blackout, to the Bird in Hand. It was decided that as Brenda was the smallest she should climb through the ground floor window of the hotel in order to open the front door for them. Having found one of the windows it was quietly opened and Brenda was unceremoniously pushed in. As she crashed to the floor a startled sleepy man's voice came gruffly across the darkened room demanding to know who was there.

In the blackout the party had not reached the hotel as they thought, but had only got as far as the Officers' Mess, which was adjacent to the hotel. Needless to say, Brenda made a hurried departure.

Turin was visited again by Bomber Command on the night of 16th/17th August. Megginson's crew were accompanied by Air Commodore H. Kirkpatrick from Group HQ, who had decided to go along for experience.

Mick Cullen recalls:

> Crossing the South of France, we began to experience trouble with the engines which has started to heat up. Climbing to gain more height to cross the Alps, one of the engines deteriorated to the extent that it seized up completely. It was impossible to maintain height so we meandered our way through the mountains, watching carefully in the light of the full moon for the peaks that towered above us.
>
> Having safely negotiated the Alps we finally arrived over the target area, which in our case was a small factory. However, due to low cloud we could not locate the building and so attacked the main target. Owing to our engine problems we bombed at a lower level than the other crews. We unloaded our cargo and left the area as quickly as possible.
>
> The skipper debated with the rest of the crew as to whether we should carry on and land in North Africa for repairs, but it was decided to try and get our VIP passenger back to Mildenhall.
>
> Once again we successfully negotiated the valleys through the Alps, but this caused a strain on the already overheated engines. As we crossed out over France, a second engine had to be stopped. We were now in an emergency situation.
>
> We decided to forget Mildenhall and land at the first available

airfield which turned out to be Tangmere on the south coast. Unfortunately, fog had closed our bomber bases in East Anglia and all aircraft were diverted to fighter airfields along the same coastline.

As we were preparing to land an aircraft with a strange callsign came on the air requesting priority for an emergency landing, saying he had only two motors going. The runway was cleared and a rather old and battered Wellington bomber with, of course, only two engines going, touched down.

Our situation was now critical and as Megginson put BK818 on the runway another engine seized completely.

An inspection the following day revealed that two of the engines had completely melted the pistons to the block. We had a couple of days' unexpected holiday while Mildenhall flew down two new engines together with our ground crew to fit them. We then all returned to base aboard BK818.

I was looking forward to getting back to Mildenhall, but my welcome was a cold one. Being young and not very thoughtful I had, in the excitement of the situation, neglected to notify Brenda that I was all right.

Not being detailed for ops on the night of 22nd August, Mick ventured down to the Bird in Hand for a drink with Brenda, as it was her birthday. The rest of the crew decided to go with him and they all spent the evening together. After closing time, Brenda invited them back to her parents' home, where they were always made welcome. The rest of the evening was spent with 'Mitch' Mitchell, the rear gunner, seated at the piano playing the popular songs of the day, with Mick, Brenda and the others happily singing along. The evening came to an end with much laughter and happiness.

By contrast, the following evening brought sadness to the crew. They were detailed to participate in the first raid, for many months, against Berlin.

BK818 left Mildenhall's runway at 20.40 hours and struggled into the air. The Stirling crossed the coast at Cromer and headed east. The weather was clear and visibility excellent; it was obvious that the enemy nightfighters would be active.

Mick Cullen remembers that night with great sorrow.

Having reached the turning point 30 miles south of Berlin, our navigator, Pilot Officer Burrows, gave Megginson the new course. We carried out our bomb run without any problems and when Andy Haydon called 'bombs gone' Megginson turned onto the course for home. It was at this point we were attacked by a nightfighter, which fired aggressively before losing us. The skipper called for a damage report, and one by one the crew responded from their respective stations that all was well. That is except for Pilot Officer Mitchell. There being no reply, Megginson instructed me to investigate. I made my way down the fuselage towards the rear turret, feeling slightly apprehensive. The turret was jammed but with the aid of an axe I managed to break open the doors. The nightfighter had turned the turret into a twisted mass of tangled steel and shattered perspex and there, slumped over the gun butts, lay Mitch. I gently eased him back and found he had been killed by a solitary bullet through his left eye.

I informed the skipper of the situation and then proceeded to remove Mitch's body from the turret. I struggled for a few minutes and then called Andy Haydon on the intercom to come down and assist me and between us we managed to extricate Pilot Officer Mitchell from the wreckage.

Although the guns were useless, Megginson requested me to occupy the shattered turret to watch for nightfighters on the homeward journey. With no heating it was a cold, uncomfortable and unenviable trip.

On return to Mildenhall the rest of the crew were given a few days' leave. We all travelled to Rugby to attend Mitch's funeral.

By coincidence, there was at that time on the squadron a rear gunner without a crew. Sergeant G. Fell had been taken off operations due to illness, his crew had continued with their tour and failed to return from a raid. It was therefore agreed that Sergeant Fell would complete his tour of operations as Megginson's rear gunner.

Celebrations returned to Megginson's crew when Sergeant E. 'Geordie' Soulsby got married.

Mick Cullen remembers with amusement:

Right) Sergeant Mick Cullen, ·ireless operator to Flight ieutenant Megginson's crew, t his station on Stirling K818, LS-O.

Below) Pilot Officer Mick ullen marries Brenda aggard at St John's Church, eck Row, Mildenhall on 7th ugust 1944. The Air Force adre officiated at the edding, which was attended y over 100 guests.

The wedding was a quiet affair with a reception held at his mother's house. All the crew, with the exception of Andy Haydon, attended. After the formal proceedings and toasts the guests went up to one of the bedrooms to view the wedding gifts.

One of the crew members suddenly held up a large chamber pot he had found. Much joking and laughter ensued, including a suggestion that it should be filled with beer. Geordie said he would willingly pay for the beer if the others carried the chamber to the local pub. Without further ado the chamber pot was ceremoniously conveyed with military escort to the local pub. The landlord was instructed to fill the receptacle with beer, prior to it being passed round. Bearing in mind the colour of the ale one or two people were hesitant in drinking from the chamber.

On the night of 8th September, Acting Squadron Leader Megginson and his crew participated in a raid on Boulogne. Flying Stirling EE974, Megginson took off from Mildenhall at 21.00 hours. There was no cloud over the target and the crew reported seeing their bombs bursting 14,000 feet below. EE974 touched down at 23.10 hours the same night. This raid was the only occasion that Megginson and his crew bombed a target in France.

On 25th September 1943 Air Vice-Marshal R. Harrison, Officer Commanding 3 Group, signed a recommendation for the immediate award of the Distinguished Flying Cross to Acting Squadron Leader Megginson who had by this time completed 51 operational missions.

Further celebrations came on 12th October when Sergeant G. Cullen was commissioned to the rank of pilot officer.

Mick Cullen recalls:

Whenever one of the crew was commissioned a celebration was called for. This involved an initiation ceremony whereby the new cap was escorted to the Bird in Hand and on its arrival was duly filled with beer. It was then passed round for each of the crew to drink from.

The crew's last operation took place on the night of 19th November, when they were detailed for a raid on Leverkusen, north of Cologne. The mission was successful and Megginson landed at 21.46 hours.

The crew that has trained, worked, played and stayed together was split up on completion of their tour.

On 7th August 1944 Mick crewed up with Brenda on a permanent basis when they married at St John's Church, Beck Row. The Air Force padre officiated at the wedding which was attended by over 100 guests.

The local schoolmaster's wife made a three tier wedding cake, with ingredients secured from various sources. One tier of the cake was sent to Mick's family in New Zealand. Ration coupons were donated and gathered together to provide the food at the reception. Everybody gave willingly and joined in the preparations.

Mick returned to New Zealand and took Brenda with him, a loving and permanent reminder of his time at Mildenhall.

CHAPTER SIX

The Biter Bitten

Sergeant Douglas Fry

He glanced down from the mid-upper turret and saw flames flickering in the fuselage below him. Quickly, he clambered down in an effort to tackle the fire which had started on the port side of the Stirling. As he was stepping off the ladder, from his turret, an AA shell exploded outside the aircraft; at the same moment he felt what seemed to be a hefty kick in the stomach. He doubled up in pain and crumpled in a heap to the floor, close to the flames.

The aircraft lurched as a huge explosion ripped into the nose of the Stirling, causing it to fall in a near vertical screaming dive to earth.

The wounded gunner found himself floating, literally floating, as if in space. Sundry items from the aircraft drifted effortlessly around him. It was like a dream but he knew it wasn't. Below his floating body the flames danced, flickering up towards him. It was at this moment that Sergeant Douglas Fry, mid-upper gunner, resigned himself to the fact he was about to die.

Momentarily, his thoughts turned to his family and the events that had led to him being in his present predicament.

*

Douglas Robert Fry was fourteen and still at school at the time of the Munich Crisis in 1938. It was with his mother's agreement that he decided not to put his name down, with the other youngsters, for evacuation. As it turned out the crisis was averted, albeit temporarily; the inevitable had only been delayed. So it was that around this period many young men decided to make some attempt

(*Left*) 19-year-old trainee air gunner Doug Fry at Dalcross AGS in 1943.

(*Below*) Stirling MkIII EF427, LS-A, at Rochester, Kent, prior to delivery to No XV Squadron. Flown by Pilot Officer George Judd EF427 was shot down by flak over Remscheid on 30/31st July 1943.

to prepare themselves for future events. To this end they joined such organisations as the Queen's Cadets, which was an army cadet force, the Territorials, the Sea Scouts or Sea Cadets. Doug was beginning to show an interest in aircraft and so joined the Air Defence Cadet Corp. He remembers:

> I was in 9F/Islington Squadron and we were affiliated to No 54 Fighter Squadron based at Hornchurch, Essex. A flight lieutenant would sometimes come and give us a talk, as did people from Handley Page, the aircraft manufacturers.

When war eventually came, the Air Ministry took over the ADCC which became the Air Training Corp. Doug went to two summer camps with the ATC, Both at RAF Halton, where he received his first 'taste' of flying, in a De Havilland Rapide.

He had started work in the City of London at the age of fifteen, in May 1939, and so when the blitz on London started towards the end of 1940, it was very close to home, especially as he lived only a short distance away in Islington. Doug recalls:

> Hardly a morning went by when I didn't have to walk to work, usually the long way round to avoid blown down trolley-bus wires, craters, fires and unexploded bombs. Once I saw about five feet of wing-tip of a Dornier Do17, lying in the road in Shoreditch.
>
> I must confess to being scared in the blitz with a feeling of helplessness, and I had thoughts of being on the delivering end instead of the receiving end.

His chance came when Doug joined the Royal Air Force as a direct entry air-gunner, having received a certificate of service from the ATC when he was about eighteen. His training went smoothly and followed the usual course; St John's Wood Receiving Centre, ITW at Bridlington, Air Gunnery School in Scotland, OTU at Chipping Warden where he crewed up with a pilot by the name of George Judd, and then on to No 1651 Conversion Unit at Waterbeach, Cambridgeshire.

George Judd's crew, apart from Doug Fry, consisted of Sergeant

D. Brown, navigator, Sergeant W. Wells, wireless operator, Sergeant Syd Long, bomb aimer, Pilot Officer Ken Banks, rear gunner, and Sergeant 'Dick' Richard, flight engineer. This was the team that reported for duty at RAF Mildenhall during the middle of June 1943.

Before operating as a crew, George Judd was required to fly his first mandatory trips as a second pilot, which meant the rest of the crew were in effect 'spare'. Doug Fry recalls an incident which occurred during this period:

> I was sitting in the crew room one morning, chatting to another mid-upper gunner, when the gunnery leader entered the room. The latter asked for a mid-upper gunner to join Flying Officer Hawkins' crew. Apparently, they had been on leave and their MUG had not reported back for duty, and Hawkins' crew was listed on the Battle Order for that night. I volunteered to join the crew. I was not allowed into the briefing, so I waited around with my flying kit at the ready. When the briefing was over, Flying Officer Hawkins told me it was alright and I was not needed as his mid-upper had turned up. He had apparently cut across the airfield direct to his billet without reporting in at the guardroom.
>
> The target was Mulheim and Flying Officer Hawkins and his crew were killed that night. How lucky can you get?'

George Judd completed his two 'second dickie' trips and was declared fully operational. Their first mission as a crew occurred on the night of 22nd/23rd June when, accompanied by two other aircraft flown by Squadron Leader Martin and Sergeant Grundy, they carried out a mine-laying operation in the East Frisians. Between 22nd June and 3rd July Doug Fry flew on five raids, including two against Cologne.

With five operations recorded in their respective log-books, these 'veterans' of XV Squadron were given six days' leave. Doug of course went home to see his family in North London.

Whilst Doug was enjoying the wartime comforts of home, Sir Arthur Harris, the Commander-in-Chief, Bomber Command, was putting the finishing touches to the plans for a major operation. It was on the morning of Thursday 22nd July that he decided to launch Operation Gomorrah, the Battle of Hamburg, which was to commence two nights later. Doug and the rest of the crew returned to Mildenhall to find their names on the Battle Order for the first of these raids on the night of the 24th/25th.

During the course of the day, their Stirling was prepared for the forthcoming operation that night, along with seventeen other aircraft from No XV Squadron. At each dispersal the ground crews worked feverishly away, pumping high-octane fuel onto the aircraft's tanks, whilst armourers winched a 2,000 lb bomb and 6 x 4 lb and 7 x 30 lb incendiary canisters into each bomb-bay. A vast quantity of paper wrapped bundles were placed in the fuselage of each Stirling. As these were deposited near the flare chutes many 'erks' thought propaganda leaflets were to be dropped with the bomb loads.

The bundles were in fact strips of aluminium foil, each of which was cut to half the wavelength of the German radar. They were to be dropped by all the participating aircraft in an effort to confuse the enemy radar screens. The principle was that the foil acted as a resonating dipole aerial and reradiated more of the radar pulse than an aircraft, thus giving a stronger 'echo' on the German radar screens. The codename given to this secret weapon, which was to be used for the first time on this particular night, was 'Window'.

As the first of the bombers approached the north German coast, the bundles were cut open and the strips of foil were pushed out of the aircraft, mainly via the flare chutes. Within minutes hundreds of strips of aluminium foil were fluttering and snaking gently earthwards on the night air.

The German radar operators who had been watching the bombers approach, were suddenly confused by the display on their radar screens. A 'snowstorm' of blips obliterated the screens giving the impression that a vast aerial armada was on its way to Hamburg. In reality only 791 aircraft of Bomber Command were heading for the north German port. So successful was Window that the defences only managed to claim twelve RAF aircraft that night.

The action on board most of the bombers was the same, with wireless operators and flight engineers pushing bundles of Window out of their respective aircraft every two minutes. The scene on Stirling EF427, A – Apple, piloted by Pilot Office George Judd, was no different. Sergeant Wells had cut open the bundles and, at the allotted time, started to feed them down the flare chute.

With German fighter controllers unable to direct their charges into the bomber stream, it meant a relatively quiet trip for the gunners, but nevertheless both Doug Fry and Ken Banks had to keep constant vigil for the nightfighter who struck lucky.

Of this period Doug Fry remembers:

> Between 24th and 29th July we operated against Hamburg on three nights – Operation Gomorrah, and Essen, all of them highly successful raids. The only trouble my crew met was when we were coned over Hamburg on the second raid of the series. However, the flak came nowhere near us to do any damage, so we were able to bomb, withdraw and get back to base safely.

However, had it not been for the keen ear of Sergeant Wells, the wireless operator, their next trip to Hamburg could have ended differently, as Doug Fry explains:

> On the way back from our third Hamburg raid, we did have a brush with a Ju88 nightfighter, but we were already alerted to the possibility of attack by Bill Wells our wirelss operator. He had tuned into the German radio frequency and let us hear their chatter through our intercom.
>
> We were over the North Sea and flying a somewhat parallel course to the Dutch coast, but were several miles therefrom, at the time. Thus, Ken Banks, the rear gunner, and I were not too surprised when a fighter flare burst above and slightly astern of us. Incredibly, the German pilot flew past the flare at roughly our height, but slightly to starboard and was also well illuminated. I was somewhat unsighted by the fin and rudder of our Stirling, so could not get a bead on the Ju88. I suggested, over the intercom, to Ken that he 'open up' to let the German know we were awake. Ken fired off a long burst, and although I could see the tracer falling short – the range was about 700 – 800 yards – it had the desired effect. The fighter sheered off without firing a shot. The flare disappeared into the mist below, thus returning us to the safety of the night.

Having operated almost continuously over the past week, it came as a surprise when, on ambling into the crew room in 'A' Flight hangar on the morning of 30th July, Doug Fry saw the names of his crew on the Battle Order for that night. They had been hoping to spend the evening in the local, the Bird in Hand, or go dancing in Cambridge, but Bomber Command had other ideas as to how they should spend their evening.

> Briefing was scheduled for eight o'clock that evening, and when we arrived we found that arc-lamps had been set up and there was an RAF film unit preparing to film the briefing. We then recalled that a few weeks previously 'Butch' Harris had visited the squadron and given us a chat. He told us that Churchill wanted a film made about the work of Bomber Command and that it should be called *The Biter Bit*. It seemed that they were now making this film. In fact later, whilst we were waiting for the crew bus to take us out to our 'kite', and standing around chatting trying to control our nerves, I noticed a cameraman busily filming us. Subsequently, my mother saw the film at the local cinema; incidentally, whilst I was still posted as missing. The Ministry of Information gave her some 'stills' from the film showing yours truly in close-up.

The target that night was to be Remschild, south of Wuppertal on the edge of the Ruhr. A total of 273 aircraft were detailed for the raid, including twelve from XV Squadron.

XV's participation in the raid began at 22.35 hours when Pilot Officer Gabel took off from Mildenhall. The rest of the squadron aircraft followed at regular intervals. Stirling EF427 A – Apple, took off at 22.42 hours, with Pilot Officer George Judd at the controls. In the bomb bay was a full load of 30 lb and 4 lb incendiaries, which were destined to be dropped during the second wave of the attack.

Apart from some desultory flak and a few searchlights after they had crossed the enemy coast, they did not encounter any problems and eventually arrived at the point near Cologne, where they altered course to bring them onto the final leg before their bombing run.

Naivety of a nineteen-year-old expressed in a cartoon drawn by Doug Fry, as he was about to start operations as a mid-upper gunner.

A still from the film *The Bitter Bit* shows Doug Fry (*centre*) with pilot George Judd (*left*) prior to take-off on the night of 30th July 1943.

Pilot Officer George Judd, who died at the controls of Stirling EF427, A-Apple, on the night of 30/31st July 1943.

Riding high in the mid-upper turret on the back of the Stirling, it was not long before Doug Fry saw the target:

> I saw the glow of the target dead ahead, and the usual hell of bursting shells, searchlights and photo-flashes going off. We were now preparing for the imminent bombing run and Syd Long, our bomb aimer, was already in position. We, the gunners, were desperately trying to look into every corner of the sky at once.
>
> 'Bomb doors open', Syd's quiet voice, and the skipper's response, 'OK'.
>
> By this time we were into the outer defences of the city; the searchlights were probing, although the barrage of flak was not all that heavy. The target was already well alight.

Suddenly, as Doug was searching to the starboard side of the aircraft, a blue master beam flickered across the mainplane wingtip. Even as he was reporting it to George Judd, the beam swung back and 'locked' onto A – Apple. Doug continues the story:

> I kept up a running commentary as to the position and number of other beams which were trying to cone us, as we pressed on with our bombing run. The flak began to get our range. 'Bombs gone – let's get out of here,' I heard Syd's quiet voice say.
>
> 'Let's get our picture first', replied the skipper, which meant another ten seconds or so of straight and level flying. A fatal ten seconds, because we were now being hit quite a lot.
>
> I then heard a different sort of sound over and above the noise of the engines and the bursting shells. I glanced down and saw the flickering light of flames, and as I was not doing much good in the turret by this time, I decided to get down and see if I could do something about the fire which was well underway and appeared to have started in the priming boxes on the port side.
>
> The flames had already burned through the bulkhead and were consuming my 'K' type dinghy, which was hanging thereon.
>
> As I was stepping down from my turret, with one foot still on the ladder, there was a shell burst astern and I felt what seemed

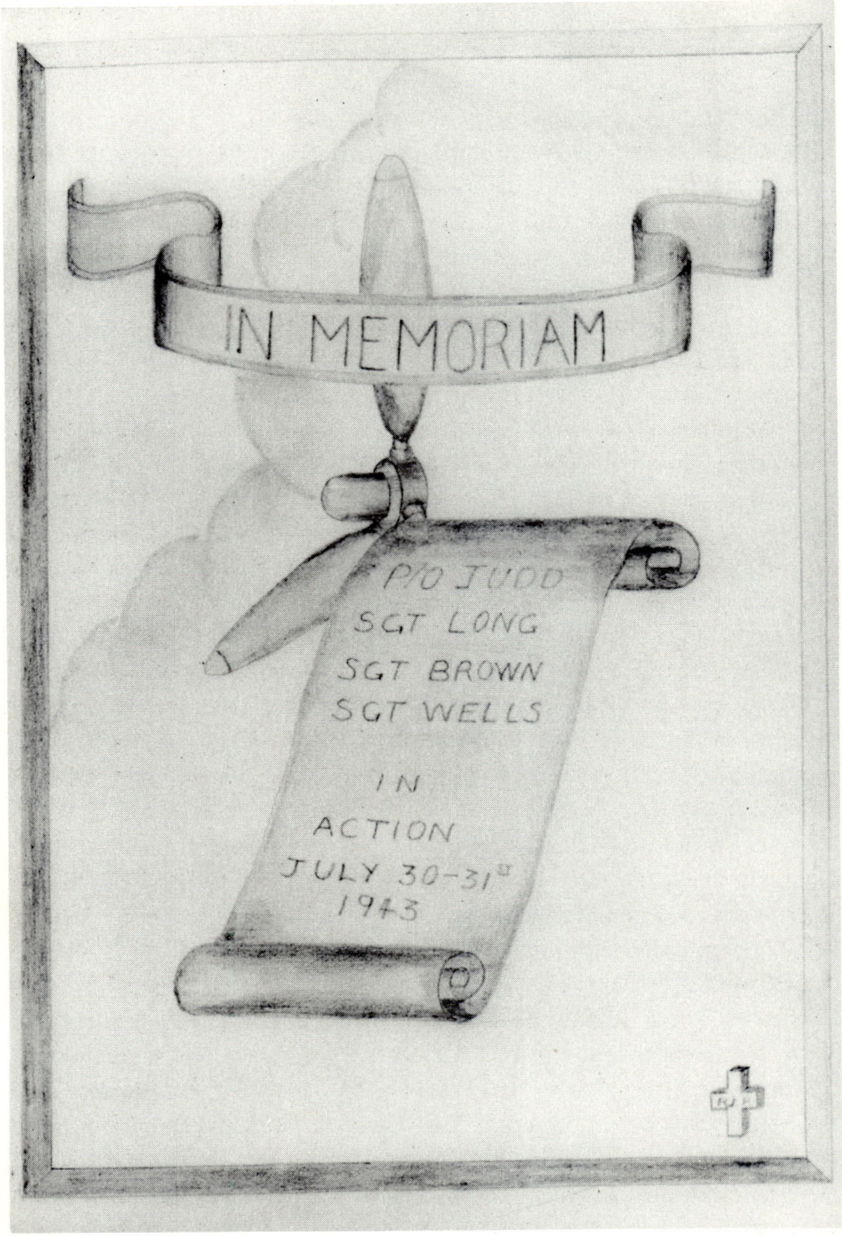

Doug Fry's personal tribute to those members of his crew who did not survive the events of the night of 30/31st July 1943.

> to be a hefty kick in the stomach. I doubled up and fell to the floor, very close to the flames, and then there was an almighty explosion up in the nose of the aircraft – a direct hit.

The Stirling went into a near vertical dive as the pilot lost control of the aircraft. The mid-upper gunner found himself floating, but even in his dazed condition he knew it wasn't a dream. Doug Fry continues:

> At that moment I resigned myself to death, because how could we possibly pull out of such a dive? However, George Judd, our skipper, who must have been badly wounded by that shell burst did pull the Stirling out with what must have been a super human effort and thus gave me a chance of survival.
>
> I fell to the floor once again, only half conscious and whilst lying there, vaguely saw Dick Richard, our flight engineer, go past. He baled out of the rear escape hatch which had already been opened by the rear gunner, who made good his escape.
>
> Although I felt pretty ropey, I decided that I now had a chance to get out, but when I went to get my 'chute from the rack it had gone, presumably breaking free when we had gone into the violent dive. Just when I was thinking, 'Well this is it', I saw the 'chute which had slid along the floor and had come to rest at the small step which was part of the bulkhead.

Doug crawled past the flames, retrieved his parachute and clipped it on. He removed his flying helmet and slowly made his way to the rear escape hatch, where he dangled his feet over the edge and rolled out in the prescribed manner. He gave no thought as to the altitude.

> I had no idea what altitude we were when I left. As we had lost a lot of height since we were first hit, we may have been about fifty feet up for all I knew.
>
> However, I never gave this aspect a thought, I just went. My 'chute opened perfectly and I saw poor A – Apple flying away – nose down – with flames streaming from her, and unhappily four members of our crew still on board, dead or wounded.

> I think we must have been at about 5,000 feet when I jumped. As I drifted down I saw what I thought was a vast lake, by virtue of the way it shimmered and moved, and so I pressed the 'gas button' on my Mae West in order to inflate it, as I thought I would come down in what I took to be water. It turned out to be a field of wheat or some such crop, undulating and swaying in a ground breeze.

Although there was no moon, it was a clear starlit night and Doug watched as the ground rapidly came up to meet him. He was drifting forward and noticed a wall right in his path. He lifted his feet to miss the wall by inches and made a good landing in what turned out to be the back garden of a small house, but this gave Doug some cause for concern.

> I immediately released my harness and took off my Mae West, as my first thought was to be on my way and try to escape.
>
> However, I had been wounded and was not feeling quite myself and thus, firstly, I failed to retrieve and hide my parachute which was hanging over the wall and into the road; and secondly, I'm damned if I could find any way out of the garden. In the event, I collapsed and lapsed into semi-consciousness, soon to be aroused by the sound of the 'all clear' siren, and then somebody calling 'Halloo, halloo', from somewhere at the rear of the garden – back in the shadows. So that's where the door was!

A man in uniform, whom Doug took to be a soldier on leave, stepped out of the darkness. He helped the injured airman to his feet, and with the assistance of two other men who had appeared, carried him into the house, where a lady shook her fist at him before pointing to a chair, into which he was lowered.

The room soon filled with villagers, who all looked very pale and apprehensive. Some of them loosened his clothing and lifted his shirt and sweater to inspect the wound. Doug had been hit by a chunk of shrapnel which had left a jagged hole about an inch in diameter, as it penetrated into his stomach. The biter had been bitten.

The two young men, who had assisted in carrying Doug Fry into the house, produced a stretcher on which he was conveyed to the local doctor's house. Here the wound, which was on the right side of the body close to the liver, was cleaned and dressed prior to Doug being given an injection. He was then carried out and placed on the back seat of a car, which then sped off into the night.

As the car travelled towards its destination, Doug lapsed into a state of unconsciousness on more than one occasion. He had no knowledge of the arrival of daylight, until he was helped out of the car and between semi-conscious eyes realised the sun was shining. The injured airman was half carried up a flight of steps and into a hallway, where, as he sank to another bout of oblivion, a woman asked him if he wanted a cigarette.

He was awakened into semi-consciousness by the movement of a stretcher on which he lay, as it was being carried down the steps at the front of the house, towards a waiting ambulance. As the stretcher was being loaded onto the bottom shelf, Doug heard a familiar voice emanating from the top deck. It was the Canadian rear gunner from his crew, Ken Banks, who had also been wounded.

Apart from seeing the tops of bombed-out buildings through an open window in the ambulance, Doug Fry knew little about his journey or where he was going. Oblivion was his companion during much of the journey.

He regained consciousness to find people undressing him in a brightly lit room, and remembers,

> I was lying on some sort of table, and in what seemed to me to be the far distance, but was only a few feet away, was another person lying on a table. It was in fact our rear gunner who later told me that when they undressed me, I looked as though I was made of marble and well on the way to becoming a corpse.
>
> Somebody in a white coat bent over me and by way of sign-language, asked me if I had false teeth; I shook my head. A pad then came down over my nose and mouth and I was gone again.

Doug's state of health was a cause for concern to many of the other 'patients' for several days. When he regained consciousness three or four days later, he found a saline drip entered into his back passage with the bottle hanging from a wooden pole, fixed to one corner of the bed. Although he was not aware of it, Doug had also been hit in the right hand; this he found firmly supported by a wire frame.

During this troubled time, Doug made many friends, which included the Polish doctor who operated on him, a Yugoslav, an American and two Frenchmen. He received many acts of kindness from these men, who were in a similar situation as his own. The memory of their humanitarian acts remain with him to this day.

As Doug recovered and took note of what was happening, he learned he was in a small camp approximately three kilometres from Düsseldorf. There were a number of shot down flyers who were recuperating from their wounds, as he recalls:

> There was Pete Saunders, a Halifax pilot shot down over Wuppertal, with a broken leg and facial injuries sustained when he was blown out of the starboard side of the cockpit, when the port wing exploded. There was a Canadian who lost a foot when he crashed through the roof of a monastery in Holland and an American, Luke Wilson, who had his left elbow shattered by flak. There was also 'Chuck' Johnston, another American, who had half slipped out of his parachute harness and landed upside down, head first. He had a split pelvis and facial injuries. There were, of course, myself and Ken Banks.

One night, Pete Saunders, whose bed was under a window, glanced out and reported a reddish glow over the compound. He looked up and saw a red sky marker about to drift out of ten-tenths cloud. The inmates had not heard any aircraft, but assumed that the Pathfinders had dropped the marker. They were concerned as to whether it was a spoof raid, or a turning indicator or a preliminary to an attack on the Ruhr. Slowly, the throbbing drone of aero-engines could be heard, growing louder as the main force passed almost overhead.

The bombs started to fall and the inmates all hit the deck, dragging their bed clothes on top of them. Doug Fry remembers:

> I learned that 'cookies', 4,000 lb and 8,000 lb bombs, made a horrible tumbling, rushing noise as they fell. Some bombs and

incendiaries fell fairly close, but we suspected these were undershoots.

The raid, which lasted about forty minutes, was against Leverkusen, on the night of 22nd/23rd August. A force of 462 bombers attacked the I.G. Farben factory but the attack, which took place in thick cloud, was unsuccessful with bombs falling over a wide area.

The time came for those POWs fit enough to travel to move on, and this included Doug, Ken Banks and the one-footed Canadian. They were taken first to Dulag-Luft at Frankfurt, the transit and interrogation centre for shot-down aircrew. Two armed guards escorted the three prisoners on a public transport bus to Düsseldorf, where they caught a train to Cologne. To complete their journey it was necessary to change trains at Cologne and Koblenz, and whilst waiting on the platform at Cologne Doug had a good opportunity to view the damage caused by Bomber Command, remembering that he had been involved in two raids against Cologne.

They arrived at Frankfurt in the evening, just as it was getting dark, and were taken to a large room over the station. The three POWs were confronted by an assorted group of RAF flyers, all recently shot down, including a fighter pilot whose head and hands were swatched in bandages and whose battledress blouse was badly scorched.

The following morning, the whole group was herded down the stairs and out into the street, where they boarded a street car. Their German fellow-travellers shouted abuse at them as the tram rattled its way out to the suburbs of Frankfurt, but the fliers ignored it; they were tired and hungry, they hadn't eaten for a couple of days.

After they had disembarked, the party was split into two groups, those going direct to Dulag Luft for interrogation and those recovering from wounds, who were sent to Hohmark Sanatorium. Doug Fry joined the latter group.

At the sanatorium, the POWs were given a bath, the first in weeks, issued with long white night shirts and told to get into bed. Doug's bed was one in a room of four, which also boasted a hand wash-basin. Soon a doctor arrived to check the various injuries.

When he got to Doug, he inspected the wound, which was healing quite well, and then changed the dressing.

A couple of days later, Doug was ordered out of bed and escorted to the end of the corridor where a Luftwaffe officer was sitting at a small table by a window. He remembers:

> Feeling a bit of a twit prancing along in my long night shirt, but I sat down and waited for the inevitable questioning. The officer merely asked me to fill in the so called Red Cross form. However, we knew all about these forms, so I just filled in my name, rank and number and then put on a blank uninterested look. The interrogation officer tried to persuade me to complete all the other details such as squadron number and other pertinent information, but I refused. He then left and I went back to my room.

It was not long before another Luftwaffe officer arrived, this time for the real interrogation. He started by saying that he knew and liked England, having been educated at Oxford:

> He then showed me a large file he had with him and this contained details and information on XV Squadron, there was even a picture of the squadron crest on the inside cover of the file. The top page listed all my crew and against four of the names were marked small crosses. He told me they were dead and I told him that I already suspected they had been killed, thus letting him know that he was not telling me anything that I was not already aware of. He then went on to tell me when I went into the RAF and where I had been trained, etc. This news presumably to lead me to believe that they knew all and that there was no point in keeping anything from them. They merely wanted confirmation of certain facts. I was asked the position of the runways at base, when we took off, where and when we crossed the coast and what sort and colour of markers were used. I was also asked the circumstances of our being shot down. After pretending to rack my brains, I humbly confessed that as I had been somewhat badly wounded and it was several weeks ago, I could remember nothing of what happened and that as a gunner,

> I had no idea of what colour the markers were, etc. In short, I played dumb and uninterested and although I suspect he knew what my game was, he calmly gathered up his file, said goodbye, and cleared off.

Some two weeks later a number of the inmates were taken to Dulag Luft to await transfer to a permanent camp. At Dulag Luft they were photographed, each with their respective POW numbers round their necks, and finger printed. It was from here that Doug Fry wrote his first card home to his mother.

A short while later, when a sufficient number of prisoners had been gathered together, they were herded into cattle trucks for the five day journey to Heydekrug on the Memel Peninsula, in Lithuania.

The floor of the cattle trucks was inches deep in a fine brown dust so they were very soon in a pretty dirty state. However, after a day or so into the journey, they were given some straw to put on the floor. Before boarding the train Red Cross food parcels had been issued, but only one between two men.

Occasionally, as the train steamed northwards towards its destination, some of the men peered out through the apertures and knot holes in the sides of the timber cattle wagons. An air of excitement suddenly permeated throughout the wagon. Doug, like many of his fellow prisoners, pressed one eye against the nearest knot hole to see the cause of the excitement. There, sitting quite majestically and apparently intact, in a field alongside the railway track was an American Army Air Force B17 Flying Fortress. It gave the men aboard the train something else to talk about for a while.

Eventually, the train pulled into the sidings at Heydekrug, where the prisoners de-trained and began the march to the camp – Stalag Luft VI. They arrived in the outer compound, where they were stripped and searched before going through into 'K' Lager. This was a new compound which consisted of two huge blocks which were divided into twelve barrack rooms; six rooms to a block.

There were approximately 30 two-tier bunks in each room, and Doug settled himself into a lower bunk at the far end of one of the rooms, away from the door and the winter draughts which were blowing through.

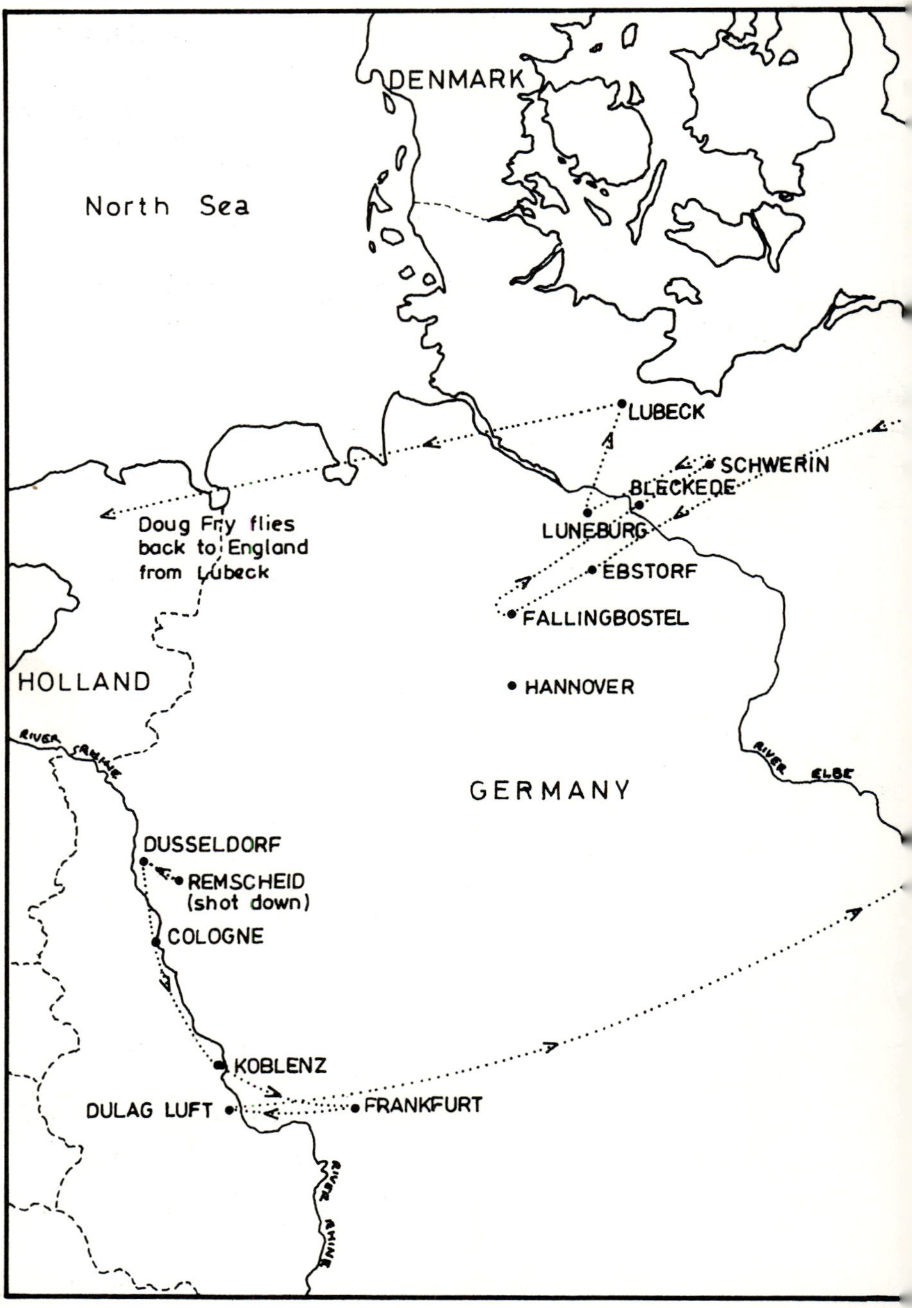
DENMARK
North Sea
LUBECK
SCHWERIN
BLECKEDE
LUNEBURG
Doug Fry flies
back to England
from Lubeck
EBSTORF
FALLINGBOSTEL
HANNOVER
HOLLAND
RIVER RHINE
RIVER ELBE
GERMANY
DUSSELDORF
REMSCHEID
(shot down)
COLOGNE
KOBLENZ
DULAG LUFT
FRANKFURT
RIVER RHINE

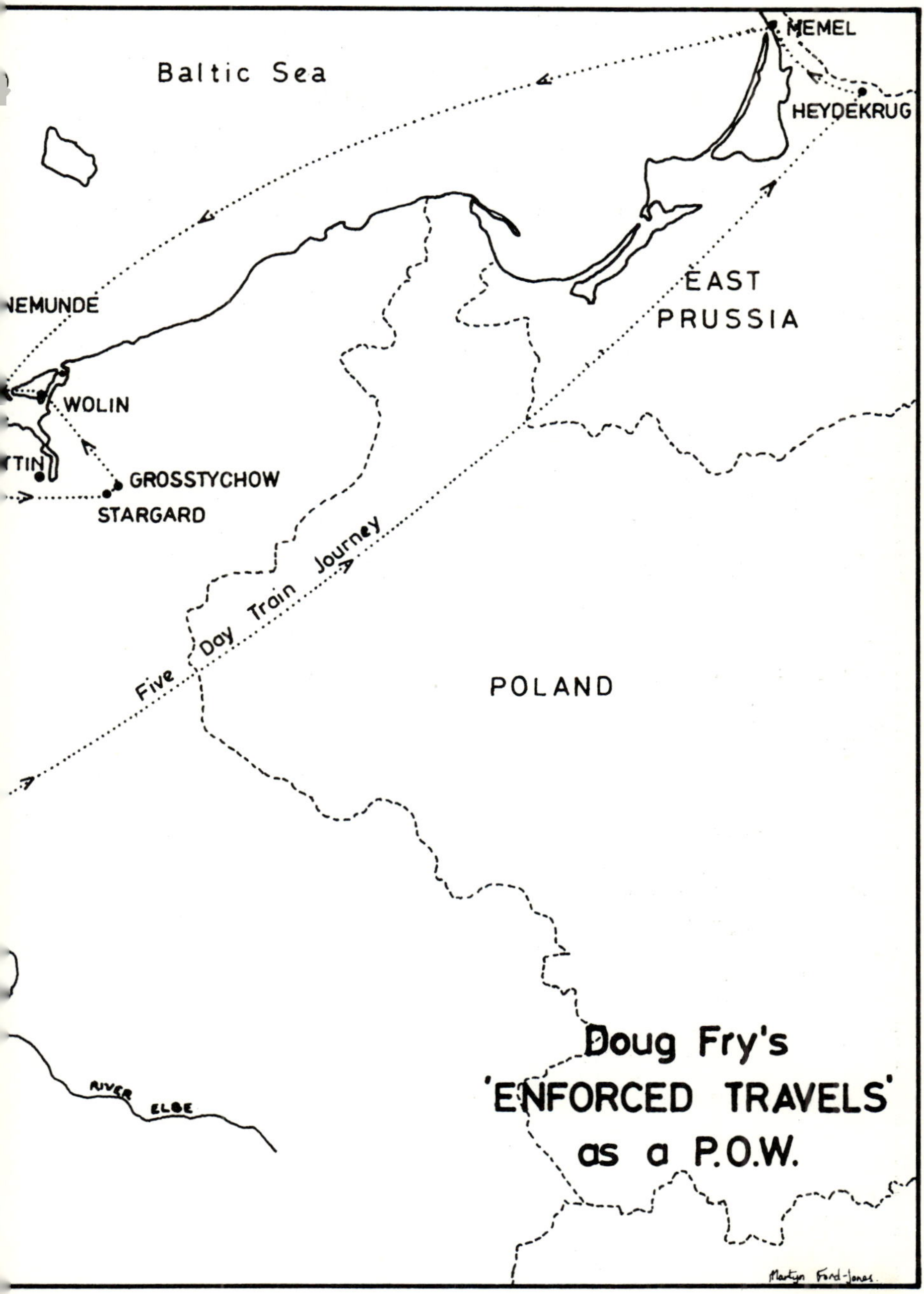
MEMEL
Baltic Sea
HEYDEKRUG
EAST
PRUSSIA
NEMUNDE
WOLIN
TIN
GROSSTYCHOW
STARGARD
Five Day Train Journey
POLAND
Doug Fry's
'ENFORCED TRAVELS'
as a P.O.W.
RIVER ELBE
Martyn Ford-Jones

The new 'Kriegies' were kitted out from the store according to their immediate individual requirements and Doug received a pair of boots, a great-coat and some underwear, all of which was RAF issue and provided by the Red Cross.

The food situation was another matter, as Doug Fry recalls:

> We received one eighth of a loaf of bread a day each, this was about five slices cut very thin, although it became quite an art cutting bread as thin as possible in order to get the maximum number of slices.
>
> At this particular time, 1943, Red Cross parcels were in good supply so at Luft VI we received a regular once a week issue of one food parcel each.

This first intake of prisoners had arrived at the camp during the first week of October. A couple of weeks later another group of some 700 prisoners arrived from Stalag Luft 1 at Barth, on the Baltic coast. Amongst their number was Dick Richards, the flight engineer from Doug's crew. He expressed surprise at seeing Doug alive and well, and then apologised for not helping him. Seeing the prostrate figure of the mid-upper gunner lying face down on the floor of the stricken bomber, with flames flickering towards him, Dick Richards naturally thought that Doug Fry was past all help.

The prisoners settled into their new surroundings and put their various talents to good use. Soon an empty hut had been converted to a theatre and recreation room, with a stage, seating and lighting. Others, like Doug, turned their talents to 'Goon-Baiting'.

> Occasionally, if the ground was dusty, we would quietly fall-in behind a guard as he was leaving the compound after a roll-call and pour dust down his rifle barrel; sometimes a cigarette end went down the barrel; they were just the right calibre for the old German rifles which were always slung so that the barrels pointed skywards. T'was just a bit of fun.

One night the weather was very bad. Very low scudding clouds raced across the sky and squally rain beat like a drummer beating tattoo, against the side of the wooden huts. Doug Fry lay awake in his bunk listening to the sound of the elements when he became aware of another, familiar sound. Above the noise of the wind and rain he heard the uneven drone of aero-engines. Some of his fellow Kriegies heard the engines too, and on looking through the top of the shutters which were closed outside the windows, they were able to see landing lights reflected on the clouds. A discussion ensued and the conclusion reached that the aircraft was in some kind of trouble, and had mistaken the camp perimeter lights for an airfield. The aeroplane circled the camp a couple of times and then veered off. The engine 'note' suddenly changed to, what was for Doug, a familiar high pitched scream and as he watched through the gap in the shutters he saw the landing beams descend straight down followed by a dull explosion as the aircraft struck the ground.

Those Kriegies who had witnessed the event or heard the crash gave a loud cheer. The following day, the German Camp Commandant sent a note thanking the prisoners for cheering when the German crew baled out. As Doug remembers, 'We cheered merely because the Luftwaffe had lost another aircraft and, as we thought, a crew. After all, they were our enemies!'

The severe East Prussian winter gave way to spring and new hope surged amongst the prisoners with talk of being home for next Christmas. The talk continued as spring became summer, and with it some news they had all been waiting for. One wet morning in June the camp 'canary' (the prisoner's secret radio) announced that Allied Troops had landed in Normandy. The prisoners went wild with jubilation, and ran round the compound in a state of joy and exhilaration. The cry was, 'It's only a matter of time'. The prisoners were confident the invasion forces would succeed in their endeavours, and began speculating as to how long it would be before they were liberated. They still reckoned to be home for Christmas.

Unfortunately for the Kriegies, the Russians were advancing steadily on Estonia and Latvia, which meant that East Prussia was threatened. After approximately nine months at Heydekrug, the Germans decided to evacuate the camp. The inmates were split into two groups, the first group being sent by rail to another camp whilst the second group which included Doug Fry were sent by rail to Memel, where they boarded a ship; the infamous *Insterburg*.

Doug Fry has reason to remember the voyage.

> We were battened down in the hold where one dim bulb provided light, and toilet facilities consisted of a bucket lowered down on the end of a rope. As I was one of the last into the hold there was no room left on the deck, so I found myself a spot on a strake, a small girder, about twelve inches wide and three feet long and about four feet above the deck. I spent three days and nights, squatting on my little shelf.

After three days at sea, the ship docked at the port of Swinemunde. The POWs were disembarked, relieved of their footwear, and herded into the familiar wooden cattle wagons. Suddenly, the wailing of the air-raid sirens penetrated the air, followed a few minutes later by the heavy drone of many Wright Cyclone engines, as a formation of B17's of the 1st Bomb Division, American 8th Air Force flew over and prepared to bomb Peenemünde.

The Germans immediately started a smoke screen and the cruiser *Prinz Eugen*, which was berthed alongside, opened fire with her ack-ack guns. Three B17's were subsequently lost.

The train journey was not a long one and fairly soon they arrived at Stargard, some 35 miles on the Polish side of the border of what is now East Germany.

The men, having had their footwear returned, were then marched off to Grosstychow where their next camp Stalag Luft IV was situated. The scene which greeted the POWs when they arrived at Luft IV has remained in Doug Fry's memory:

> When we arrived at the camp, on 20th July 1944, we saw the first group to leave Luft VI milling about outside the camp. Some men were in a state of shock and some wounded. We soon learned that these chaps had been manacled together and forced to run up and down the road at bayonet point. Several of the men had been stabbed during this episode, some more than once. Later that afternoon we heard that an attempt had been made on Hitler's life.

Conditions in the camp were very poor and the accommodation severly cramped. Food was scarce and there was a feeling of foreboding and pending disaster. All thought of being home in time for Christmas were dispelled.

As time passed, some of the conditions improved. The Kriegies were moved into a larger compound where a pump supplied fresh cold water, and coal-fired boilers provided heat. Doug Fry volunteered to look after the boiler for his hut and thereby managed a few extra perks for himself, like first with the hot water for shaving and washing clothes. He also managed to get involved in a bartering system.

Nineteen forty-four passed into 1945 and the food situation was getting worse. There were no potatoes or bread and Red Cross parcels were in short supply.

The Russians were still advancing and even though there was two feet of snow on the ground the Germans decided to move the POWs yet again. On the morning of 6th February the men were awakened and told to be ready as soon as possible and paraded outside. It was just about 6 am, a blizzard was raging but the POWs were lined-up in the snow, where they were kept waiting for over two hours.

Eventually, the column trudged off. As they passed out of the camp gate each man was handed two Red Cross food parcels, the last of the supply it was stated. They marched doggedly on during the day, stopping now and then for a five minute rest. The roads were deep with snow and ice and rutted in many places. It was difficult for them to keep a hold and many a man took a tumble.

The column, marching by day and sleeping in barns or in the open at night, eventually reached its destination – Swinemunde. They crossed the estuary by bridge and ferry boat, and marched on to a farm where they rested for a couple of days.

As the days passed, the snow melted and the weather turned wet, but was still very cold. The march continued, with the Kriegies having to endure hunger as well as facing the elements.

One day having crossed the Elbe river the column entered a town full of wounded German soldiers, who watched silently as the prisoners passed through. Leaving the town a mile or so behind them, the POWs were about to cross some open ground when the distant drone of aero-engines became audible. The drone increased to a throbbing beat as a large formation of B17 Flying Fortresses passed overhead, escorted by a number of Mustang fighters.

As the prisoners moved on they cast a glance skywards and saw movement on the underside of the fuselages; the bomb bay doors were opening on the B17's. Almost immediately, dark cylindrical shapes began to tumble from the formation leader's aircraft, some of which trailed smoke. As the bombs and smoke markers rained down, whistling as if to announce their impending arrival, the other bombers released their respective loads. The ground shook as the bombs exploded on impact with the town, demolishing or damaging many of the buildings. The bombers flew over the town completely unhindered by either German ground defences or fighters. The Mustang pilots not having to worry about their charges looked for something else to do. The escort leader pushed forward his 'stick', kicked the rudder pedal and his Mustang banked and dived towards the ground, the rest of his unit followed close behind. Flashing lights flickered along the leading edges of the fighter's wings as they made their first strafing run the road, at tree-top height.

Although cold, hungry and exhausted the prisoners summoned the strength and, helping the less fortunate amongst their number to scatter into the woods, took cover amongst the trees. It was an experience Doug Fry hasn't forgotten:

> When the lead bomb aimer dropped his load in which there were bombs trailing smoke, the others in the formation dropped their bombs. There was no opposition from the Germans whatsoever, but seeing the smoke bombs go down, the German Commandant in charge of us Kriegies started shouting, 'New weapon, new weapon', thinking that the smoke was trailing from shot-down aircraft. As there were neither German fighters nor flak in evidence, he thought a new weapon was responsible for what he thought were crashing aircraft. He was, of course, sadly disappointed.
>
> The Mustangs then came down to tree-top height to do a bit of strafing; we, of course, beat a hasty retreat into the woods.
>
> Although it may have seemed the ideal opportunity to escape, we were tired, cold and hungry, and had no idea in which direction we were heading.

Their course took the POWs to another town where the Luftwaffe guards handed their charges over to the Wehrmacht, who immediately bundled the prisoners into the all too familiar wooden cattle trucks.

The train took them to Fallingbostal, near Hanover. Here, as he entered the camp, each man was given a Red Cross food parcel, the first for many weeks. Food was still short, the Germans providing only one bowl of turnip soup a day, but it was more akin to greasy water with one or two bits of turnip floating in it.

Owing to the rapid advance of the British 2nd Army towards Hanover, the Germans decided to evacuate the new intake of prisoners, even though they had only been at Fallingbostal for about two weeks.

As the column once again headed east, it was obvious that the guard's morale was somewhat lower than that of the prisoners. It was by this time April 1945; the days were beginning to draw out and the weather had turned mild. The prisoners knew that either way liberation was not far off. Some of the guards began talking to the POWs in a friendly manner, even showing them photographs of their respective families, but Doug Fry and the others were only too well aware of the Germans' motives.

Early one morning, having just crossed to the eastern bank of the river Elbe by ferry, the prisoners were given a sign of hope which literally came out of the sky. As they were tramping across a field, away from the river, two Spitfires appeared and whilst one kept top-cover at about a thousand feet, the other one executed several tight turns over them at about two hundred feet. Straightening out to rejoin his wingman, the pilot 'waggled' the Spitfire's wings in recognition and encouragement before flying off. The men, Doug included, stood and cheered and waved like mad, whilst the Germans dived to the ground in terror.

The boost to their morale allowed many of the men to sleep fitfully in a barn that night, which they reached at the end of that day's march.

The next day dawned bright and sunny and, as usual, the men were up early. They were assembling outside the barn when the quiet morning air was shattered by the roar of Merlin engines, as two Spitfires came screaming overhead, from behind them at tree-top height. Fire spat forth from the fighters' wings as the two aircraft opened fire at something behind the barn. Cannon and machine gun shells rained down amongst the men as they were ejected by the guns. The noise of battle increased as ground defences, concealed from the prisoners' view, retaliated. The only other indication of their presence was the smoke which drifted lazily over the roof of the barn. The Spitfires, having completed their first pass, came round again on the same course. Fire again spat out as on this occasion they flew through a hail of 20mm flak, but they continued on unscathed. The 'deep-throated' roar of an aircraft taking off made the POWs turn towards the direction of the sound. To their amazement, they watched as a FW190 climbed steeply into the air, engulfed in flames. It turned sharply over onto one wingtip and spun into the ground, killing its pilot as it exploded.

The Spitfires flew off totally unharmed having attacked a German airfield behind the barn in which Doug Fry and his comrades had spent the night.

The march continued. On the evening of the next day, they came to a farm which had two barns, both timber framed with brick infill and thatched roofs. The floors were concrete with the usual covering of straw. Doug remembers the events that followed:

> At about one o'clock in the morning, I was awakened by the sound of an aeroplane and then a loud explosion close by. At first I thought the aircraft had crashed, but then I heard it flying away. As I listened I realised it was coming back and, through an opening high in the wall opposite me, I saw the flash of guns and streams of tracer coming straight for the opening. I turned my face to the floor as all hell broke loose. Cannon shells exploded in and around the barn. The thatched roof caught fire and bits of burning debris dropped to the floor, where it immediately set light to the straw. I felt a dull thump on my back and knew I had been hit, although it turned out to be a small cut, probably from a shell splinter. I was lucky for the chaps either side of me were killed, one was an American and the other was Reg Brown, who had been a POW for about four years. Four others were injured, two seriously, one of whom died later.
>
> I knew I was not badly hurt but could feel the blood trickling down my back, and as I knew my body and clothes were

> somewhat dirty, I thought I should at least have my 'scratch' cleaned up.

It was decided that the wounded should be taken in a horse-drawn cart in search of a place where they could be cleaned up and suitably treated. They eventually arrived at a small POW camp just outside a town called Schwerin. Here they were treated in the camp sick bay by some of the inmates. The sick bay staff were quite competent and everybody was attended too.

Unfortunately, the camp, like the barn, was situated very close to a German airfield, as Doug recalls: 'A few kilometres from the camp was an airfield and judging from the number of aeroplanes in the air at any time, there must have been the equivalent of about five squadrons based there.'

Each morning four Hawker Tempest fighters would attack the airfield, thundering in at low-level with cannon fire blazing from the wings, as the aircraft strafed all within their path.

Doug Fry and the others often heard the siren wail as the Tempests approached, followed by the earth-shattering roar as a number of Daimler-Benz and Junkers engines burst into life. They heard the engine notes change as Focke Wulf 190's and Messerchmitt 109's scrambled into the air, and climbed away in tight climbing turns so as not to be caught on the ground. This did not deter the Tempest pilots who, in pairs as leader and wingman, would join the circuit and endeavour to send some of the German aircraft crashing back onto the airfield.

The RAF pilots sometimes got bitten themselves, as Doug remembers:

> On one occasion I saw a Tempest go down in flames, after being caught in intensive light flak. The pilot managed to bale out, but the Germans still continued firing 20mm stuff at him.
>
> Now and again a 20mm shell would hit the deck in the compound and explode, so it was not too healthy for us to be out watching the action.

On 2nd May 1945, a day before Doug Fry's 21st birthday and after they had been at the camp only about two weeks, an early-rising

Kriegie excitedly rushed into the hut shouting that the guards had gone, and that there were some broken rifles lying on the ground outside the wire.

It took an hour or more for the truth to sink in, and then only when assisted by the sight of a jeep, with a 5″ Browning machine-gun mounted on the back, crewed by two American soldiers, driving past.

It was not long before the Americans arrived with ample supplies of food and drink, more than these men had seen for a number of years. Unfortunately some had forgotten that over a period of time their stomachs had shrunk, and that they couldn't eat all they could see.

Due to the number of refugees and fleeing German servicemen blocking most of the roads, chaos and confusion reigned in and around Schwerin. It was about a week later that the ex-POWs were taken to Lüneburg, where they were billeted in a German barracks, in preparation for their repatriation.

Good food with white bread was the order of the day, closely followed by showers under a copious supply of hot water.

The proposed flights home, in Dakota aircraft, from Lüneburg airfield were postponed in favour of evacuating many wounded soldiers. Although eager to return, the ex-POWs realised that to a severely wounded soldier a day could mean life or death. They, they reasoned, had been away so long a day or two would make no difference.

In the event, arrangements were made for the ex-Kriegies to fly home from Lübeck airfield, to which they were transported in British Army trucks. At Lübeck the men were divided into groups ready for their flights home, which Doug Fry will never forget:

> We met the crew of the Lancaster in which we were to fly home. As the mid-upper gunner of the crew had nipped off home for a quick '48', the skipper allowed me to ride home in my old position – the mid-upper turret. Thus, events had come full circle. I had flown to Germany in the mid-upper turret of a Stirling of XV Squadron, and eventually returned in the mid-upper of a Lancaster.

CHAPTER SEVEN

The Darkness of Pain

Flight Sergeant 'Gil' Marsh

It was an eerie feeling heading towards Berlin with no sign of the expected searchlights, nightfighters or flak. The only consolation was that out there, in the night sky, 726 other bombers were heading for the same target.

The crew of Stirling BK816 'X' – X-ray remained silent. Each man was preparing himself for the coming battle over the German capital. The gunners traversed their respective turrets alternately in opposite directions to scan the sky for nightfighters which on this night, 23rd/24th August 1943, seemed almost elusive. The pilot, Flight Sergeant Gil Marsh, peered out through the cockpit, and saw the marker flares indicating the final turning point for the run-in to the target.

The attacking force comprised 335 Lancasters, 251 Halifaxes and 124 Stirlings. The route to the target was being marked by 17 Mosquitos.

As the force turned onto the final leg, all hell broke loose. Searchlights penetrated into the darkness and lit up the sky, which revealed the presence of German nightfighters waiting at a higher altitude, waiting to pounce! Taking advantage of their height, the German pilots dived into the attack, cutting through the bomber formation with cannons blazing.

Many bombers succumbed to the attacks and fell in flaming masses to the ground. In all, by the end of the raid, 56 RAF aircraft were lost. BK816 continued towards Berlin, but it was not going to be an easy trip.

*

For Gil Marsh, his journey to Berlin effectively began when he volunteered to join the Royal Air Force at Cardington, Bedfordshire, at the beginning of 1941. Having thus enlisted he was promptly sent home and waited six months before receiving his call-up papers.

He was instructed to report, on 14th July, to the Aircrew Receiving Centre at Regent's Park, London, where he was billeted until being transferred to Torquay on 2nd August for six weeks basic training, with No 5 Initial Training Wing. The third week of September saw Gil back in Liverpool, where he was born on 23rd January 1922. He spent a week at the West Kirby transit camp prior to being sent overseas for flying training.

The troopship SS *Empress of Russia* sailed from Liverpool on 25th September and headed for South Africa, arriving at Durban at the end of October. After spending a week at the Clarewood transit camp in Durban, Gil Marsh moved on to the Initial Training Wing at Bulawayo and then to No 26 Elementary Flying Training School, Guinea Fowl.

Training at No 26 EFTS commenced immediately and on 31st January 1942 LAC Marsh made his first flight in Tiger Moth T6128 with an instructor, Sergeant Chamberlain, at the controls. The flight lasted 50 minutes and consisted of straight and level flying in order to show Gil the effects of the controls.

Flying almost every day with Sergeant Chamberlain, Gil Marsh learned the rudiments of flying until 13th February, when after a 55 minute dual flight in Tiger Moth T7924 he was sent off on his first solo which lasted ten minutes.

From 29th March to 10th September 1942, Leading Aircraftman Marsh flew Harvards with No 22 Service Flying Training School based at Thornhill. During this period, he spent a week in August, living under canvas, at the Kabanga Operational Training Unit emergency landing ground.

Returning to England at the end of October, Gil was posted, on 17th November, to No 14 (Pilots) Advanced Flying Unit at Ossington where he converted to twin-engined aircraft and flew the Airspeed Oxford. Then, on 2nd February 1943, with the rank of sergeant, Gil Marsh was sent to No 26 Operational Training Unit where he crewed up and converted to Wellington Bombers.

Stirling BK816, LS-X, from a painting owned by Gil Marsh.

Flight Sergeant Gil Marsh (*right*) with Sergeant Art Hynam, rear gunner.

His crew consisted of Pilot Officer A. Richards, navigator; Sergeant H. Hynam, rear gunner; Sergeant George Wright, wireless operator and with a Canadian, Sergeant Jack Bailey as bomb aimer. As they flew and trained together they got to know each other well, which was to stand them in good stead later in their operational career.

After a week's leave, at the end of May, the crew re-assembled and on 3rd June reported to No 1651 Conversion Unit based at Waterbeach, Cambridgeshire, where they joined 'B' Flight. The crew increased as Jimmy Meaburn, the flight engineer, and Sergeant W. Smith, the mid-upper gunner, joined them. Now with the crew at full complement Gil Marsh was ready to convert to the big four-engined Stirling bomber.

Fourteen days later, on 17th June, Sergeant Marsh took off in Stirling BK622 on his first solo on this heavy bomber; the flight lasted 1 hour and 40 minutes.

By the end of June the crew, having satisfied the instructors as to their competence, were declared combat ready and posted to an operational squadron reporting for duty with No XV Squadron at RAF Mildenhall on 1st July 1943.

They were attached to 'C' Flight, commanded by Squadron Leader J. Martin, a powerfully built man who had been a farmer before the outbreak of war. Two days later, Gil Marsh went on his first war operation. On this occasion, he flew, as was usual, as a second pilot to an experienced bomber captain, Flight Lieutenant Norris, who took him on a raid against Cologne, giving Gil an insight into what he could expect on a bombing raid. His crew had yet to find out! He later wrote in his log-book, 'Fighters and searchlights very active. Flak medium to heavy'.

The crew were initiated into war operations on an easier mission, on 5th July, when they flew on a 'Gardening' sortie, a mine laying operation.

Gil Marsh lifted Stirling EF351, 'L' – Love, off the runway at Mildenhall at midnight and set course for the Frisian Islands. They planted their mines at 01.56 hours from a height of 2,000 feet. Gil Marsh's log-book recorded, 'Quiet trip. No troubles at all'.

The crew's second mine laying operation, on 8th July, in the Bay of Biscay, had to be abandoned shortly after take-off due to rear turret hydraulics failure. A total of 1,500 gallons of fuel were jettisoned over Cambridgeshire before Gil Marsh was allowed to land with the three mines still aboard.

Practice bombing and fighter affiliation exercises were carried out over the next few days in Stirling BK816 'X' – X-ray, which was to become Gil Marsh's regular aircraft.

On 13th July, he took BK816 and his crew over Germany for the first time when they participated in a raid on Aachen. The flak was light and the searchlights few which was probably due to the very active presence of German nightfighters. BK816 was not attacked but was fired upon by a flakship as it flew over the enemy coast on the homeward journey. Gil Marsh manoeuvred the Stirling away from the danger area and concentrated on crossing the North Sea, whilst the gunners kept a watch for any marauding nightfighters or night intruders.

BK816 crossed the east coast at Lowestoft where it was immediately coned in the blinding glare of the searchlights, the dazzle of which the crew found troublesome. Gil Marsh however managed to extricate them from the beams and landed at Mildenhall without further trouble.

Further practice bombing and fighter affiliation exercises were undertaken until the night of 24th July when they went to Hamburg. The raid was significant on two accounts; it was the start of a ten-day battle against the city, during which the RAF made four heavy night raids and the American 8th Air Force two daylight raids; it was also the first time that the RAF used 'Window', the anti-radar strips of aluminium foil which confused the enemy radar.

At 08.30 hours that Saturday morning, Air Vice-Marshal Harrison, AOC-in-C 3 Group, ordered a maximum strength of heavy bombers to carry out the raid. No XV Squadron responded with a full complement of aircraft participating, including Gil Marsh and his crew.

Carrying six 4 lb and seven 30 lb incendiary canisters, a 2,000 lb bomb and loaded with fuel, BK816 lumbered into the air at 22.00 hours. Marsh set course with the rest of the squadron and headed out over the North Sea. Ahead of them the Pathfinders marked the city with their target indicators (TIs) at exactly 57 minutes past midnight. Sixteen minutes later BK816 was over the target area.

The probing beams of the searchlights and the prowling nightfighters were, as usual, very active, but Marsh kept 'X' – X-ray steady at 13,000 feet as he made his bomb run over Hamburg in accordance with Jack Bailey's instructions. At 01.13 hours, Bailey pressed the 'tit' and their deadly load cascaded down from the bomb bay to the moving sea of flame below. As the lightened aircraft lurched upwards, free of its loads, Gil Marsh pulled back on the control column and turned the Stirling onto a new course which he received from Pilot Officer Richards. Having been the first crew from XV Squadron to bomb Hamburg on this raid, they landed back at Mildenhall at 04.20 hours.

The following night, Gil Marsh took BK816 and his crew to Essen where they acted out the same drama as the previous night, with much the same results. As July gave way to August, Gil Marsh flew nothing more strenuous than fighter affiliations and air tests.

On the morning of 10th August 1943, No 622 Squadron was formed at RAF Mildenhall. The personnel, equipment, transport and seven Stirlings of 'C' Flight, No XV Squadron, were taken as the nucleus to form 'A' Flight of the new squadron. Squadron Leader Martin acted as its first commander until 20th August when Wing Commander G.H.N. Gibson DFC assumed command. With his transfer to No 662 Squadron, Gil Marsh was promoted to flight sergeant.

Being operationally experienced the crews were not allowed a settling in period but were detailed for a mission that night. The target was Nuremburg and, although all seven aircraft took off, two returned early.

Apart from being followed across the target area by an enemy nightfighter, luckily with no adverse effect, the raid for Gil Marsh was a quiet one.

No 622 Squadron participated in two raids on Turin on the nights of 12th and 16th August respectively, and Gil Marsh flew on both operations. Both missions were recorded as successful, with all seven aircraft bombing their allotted targets. However, due to adverse weather conditions, all seven aircraft landed at Hurn on the night of the second raid.

The long summer days and short nights had precluded Berlin from being attacked by Bomber Command aircraft since the previous winter. Small forces of Mosquitos had been making nuisance raids on the city for some time in order to reduce the Berliners' morale to the appropriate state of tension for when the big raids resumed.

The first of these raids was scheduled for the night of 23rd August. A maximum effort was ordered and a total of 731 aircraft of Bomber Command participated, seven of which were provided by No 622 Squadron. The weathermen predicted the night sky over Berlin would be clear with good visibility, a condition of which the German nightfighters would take full advantage.

The day passed much the same as any other prior to a mission, with the customary preflight meal of bacon and eggs preceded by the briefing. As the day gave way to early evening, the crews made their way out to the aircraft. Some cycled but most rode out on the trucks driven by the WAAFs. At each aircraft the truck stopped and the seven man crew jumped off and made their way towards the rear access door situated on the port side of the Stirling.

As they approached Stirling BK816, silhouetted against the setting sun, Gil Marsh and his crew was not aware of the events which were awaiting them later that night. For Gil Marsh, in particular, it was to be a night to remember.

They climbed the four rung metal ladder into the fuselage and made their way to their respective stations.

There was one change in the crew that night. Gil Marsh recalls:

> Our normal mid-upper gunner, Sergeant Smith, had been stood down by the MO with some physical complaint and Flight Lieutenant Berry, who had just arrived to take over as Gunnery Leader of No 622 Squadron, said to me, 'That's OK. I'll come with you tonight as mid-upper'. I don't know if he subsequently regretted that decision.

Although a flight test had been carried out during the day, each man checked his instruments or controls and then settled down to await the start of the raid.

The seven Stirlings stood at their dispersals. The peace of the Suffolk airfield was broken only by the occasional call of an 'erk' shouting to a colleague and the chirping of a few birds as they settled down at the end of the day.

A cough, a splutter and a cloud of blue exhaust smoke rose as the first propeller came to life, turning slowly at first and gathering speed as the three other engines raced to catch it up. The peace of Mildenhall was shattered by the roar of 28 Hercules engines as the aircraft of No 622 Squadron started up.

Using the outer engines for manoeuvring the Stirlings taxied out one by one and lined up for take-off. When his turn came, Gil Marsh swung BK816 onto the runway. With brakes on he opened each throttle until the engines were running at approximately 2,000 rpm. On receipt of the green light from the Control Caravan's Aldis lamp, Flight Sergeant Marsh released the brakes and opened the throttles slowly with the starboard levers slightly forward to counteract the tendency of the aircraft swinging to starboard on its take-off run. Armed and loaded for war, the Stirlings trundled down the runway at regular intervals and slowly lifted off the ground like ageing birds of prey.

The route was to take the force from Mildenhall across the east coast at Cromer flying at 8,000 feet over the North Sea and Zuider Zee, on a direct course to 30 miles south of Berlin. There a turn north was to be made for the run-in, bombing and run-out of the target area. The course was to be held until the Baltic, the Kattegat area, was reached when another turn was made across southern Denmark, followed by a run home back across the North Sea.

Flight Sergeant Gil Marsh recalls the journey:

> The weather was clear, but there was no activity of any kind during the outward journey. No fighters, no flak; a most eerie sensation which created a feeling that doom was looking over one's shoulder. Then, as we arrived at the turning point south of Berlin, the Pathfinders dropped their marker flares for the first wave of Lancasters; we Stirlings were usually fourth wave, or 'mid-field'. At that moment, masses of searchlights forming a circle probably 10 miles or so in diameter came on with beams directed vertically, like the bars of a huge circus cage. The whole sky over Berlin was as light as day and fighters were observed at higher altitudes, flitting about like moths.

Activity was now increasing, the fighters had swooped down to attack the intruders and a considerable number of bombers were logged as they fell in balls of orange and yellow flames, a contrast to the small silver strips of Window which fluttered down to confuse the enemy radar.

The Master of Ceremonies directed the bombers to drop their loads on the green markers layed by the Pathfinders. The fires on the ground began to increase in intensity and black smoke rose to a height of 10,000 to 12,000 feet.

Gil Marsh took BK816 over the target at 12,000 feet and held the aircraft steady as Jack Bailey instructed. Then Jack called 'Bombs gone' and Gil Marsh leaned forward and flicked the switch, situated to the right of the throttle levers, and closed the bomb doors. At seven minutes past midnight, as the bomb doors were closing, a Ju88 nightfighter crept out of the darkness into the ring of searchlights and attacked BK816, opening fire at 500 yards. Flight Lieutenant Berry in the mid-upper turret and Sergeant Hynam the rear gunner, replied as the Stirling, with its partially open bomb doors took violent, but sluggish, evasive action.

Gil Marsh:

> Once the rear gunner had sighted and reported the enemy aircraft I waited for the shout 'Port go' in order to start evasive action. When the instruction came I pulled back on the control column and hauled the aircraft over to port. As we went down and then over to the starboard side a hosepipe of different colours shot in through the canopy over our heads. This was followed by cannon shells slamming into the flight deck side from above.

Sergeant George Wright, the wireless operator remembers:

> We were attacked three times in all. The hydraulics of the rear turret were severed during the final attack thus putting it out of action, but not before the enemy aircraft started to fall away. It was later claimed as a probable.

The Stirling sustained damage to the tailplane, the port elevator was shot away and the port outer engine was hit by cannon fire and had to be shut down.

George Wright continues:

During the attack a cannon shell appeared to hit the edge of the armour plate to the pilot's seat and explode. Gil Marsh was hit by shrapnel in some six places around the groin and leg, cutting the sciatic nerve.

The aircraft fell rapidly as the pilot slumped over the controls. Jack Bailey was still in the bomb aimer's compartment and took a bang on the head as the aircraft went down and was temporarily stunned.

Gil Marsh continues:

> I remember a big bang, my hands covered in green luminous phosphorus and a 14 pound sledgehammer hit me with full force. The encounter with the enemy aircraft had left me in a considerable state of discomfort, as the sciatic nerve had been severed at the top of my right leg and a large hole made through my shattered right hip. I was instantly overwhelmed by the spreading blank blackness of shock, which started at my feet and rose upwards ending in oblivion when it reached the brain.

With Gil Marsh unconscious in his seat, George Wright and Dick Richards endeavoured to pull back on the control column until the aircraft levelled out at 1,500 – 2,000 feet.

Gil Marsh regained consciousness and summoning his strength managed to climb the Stirling back to a height of 4,000 feet, but owing to the damage could get no higher.

He recalls:

> I called Jack Bailey for assistance, but he had been rendered unconscious by hitting his head. I therefore asked Dick Richards, the navigator, to occupy the second pilot's seat and eventually we managed to get back on course for the Baltic, still at 4,000 feet.

Jimmy Meaburn, the flight engineer, called up to say the port outer oil pressure had gone and the engine was overheating; to avoid fire risk the engine was feathered. Sometime later, after a discussion with the flight engineer, it was decided to risk restarting the engine

Sergeant Jack Bailey (*left*) with wireless operator Sergeant George Wright.

L to R Gil Marsh, Joyce Wright, George Wright and Amy Marsh at St John's Church, Beck Row, at a recent reunion.

in an effort to increase the altitude. However, because of the necessary rich mixture setting required for restarting, the engine threw out sheets of red and orange flame which due to the low altitude were obviously visible from the ground. The engine was therefore quickly shut down again. It was, however, subsequently restarted during the North Sea crossing and the Stirling eventually landed on all four engines.

By this time, the pilot's strength was sapping rapidly. Pilot Officer Richards, assisted by Sergeant George Wright, lifted the severly injured pilot from his seat and placed him just behind it on the floor, propped up against the side of the fuselage.

Over the period of time, Pilot Officer Richards injected the pilot with all the morphine carried in the first aid kit. This made the injured man so thirsty that he drank all the coffee on board.

During this period, Jack Bailey had recovered and had climbed up onto the flight deck where he sat in the left-hand seat and took control of the aircraft.

Gil Marsh had passed out again: his next recollections were:

> As we approached the coast of Denmark from Kattegat the flackships below opened fire. At 4,000 feet we would be an easy target for the ack-ack. I ordered Jack Bailey to turn away and go further north before crossing the Danish coast. This obviously met with some success, for having receded back into the darkness of pain I came to to find we were flying over the North Sea.

A discussion ensued amongst the crew as to the possibility of ditching or bailing out, both ideas being decided against, except in case of dire necessity, due to the injuries sustained by the pilot.

George Wright obtained a first class fix 420 miles out from base followed by two others on route. BK816 crossed the North Sea in daylight and was fortunate not to be attacked by Luftwaffe day fighters.

Coming to from another bout of oblivion, Gil Marsh found the aircraft crossing the east coast and yet another discussion ensued. The crew were debating whether to land at the first available airfield or to try for Mildenhall. It was agreed that as BK816 had got them that far they should try for home base.

Once more, Gil Marsh descended into the cold grey blankness, only to re-emerge as the Stirling approached Mildenhall.

> As the aircraft descended in a steep nose down attitude, I was able to see past Jack Bailey's left shoulder and noticed the glidepath indicators were red. I told him to increase power and maintain height until they showed green.

Being very low on fuel, Jack Bailey received instructions to go straight in to land; everything had been cleared in case the undercarriage malfunctioned. All escape hatches were removed and the crew decided no one should leave the aircraft until the captain had been safely removed. Jack Bailey was talked down by control and made a very good landing, with only 75 gallons of fuel left in the tanks.

Gil Marsh remembered nothing about the landing, only vague memories of being bumped about on a stretcher as he was manoeuvred down the fuselage and placed in the ambulance. Although he survived, Gil Marsh never flew operationally again.

Jack Bailey had been on a pilot's course but, having cracked-up a Cessna, re-mustered as a bomb aimer. He had never before landed a four-engined aircraft. He received an immediate award of the Conspicuous Gallantry Medal, the highest decoration awarded to a member of No 622 Squadron. On 21st September 1943, Sergeant J.C. Bailey CGM was commissioned and posted to RCAF 'R' Depot, Warrington, prior to returning to Canada for pilot training.

Gil Marsh remained in hospital until June 1944. He eventually returned to Mildenhall with a caliper on his right leg and walking with the aid of sticks, to take up his duties as Link Trainer instructor.

CHAPTER EIGHT

A Squadron of One

Flight Lieutenant Oliver V. Brooks DFC

In the early morning of 23rd April 1944, Lancaster ND763, LS-W, crossed the Suffolk coast from seaward at a mere 500 feet, struggling to maintain altitude. To any observer on the ground it was obvious that the aircraft was in a great deal of trouble. Fire had ravaged the port inner engine which had rendered it u/s; the starboard outer was giving very little power and the wing flaps were jammed down at 10^0. To add to the pilot's problems he had been unable to close the bomb doors, nor could he now lower the undercarriage.

Inside, the aircraft had been damaged by fire, which had partially damaged three of the crew's parachutes. Many of the controls were u/s and four of the crew had been wounded; two fatally.

As he flew over the coastline, 21-year-old Pilot Officer Oliver Brooks could see his objective dead ahead – the emergency landing ground at Woodbridge. He was tired, his arms and legs ached and his body was bathed in perspiration from the arduous return flight. He had struggled with the crippled aircraft all the way back from Düsseldorf, but being aware of the plight of his crew was determined to bring them home.

Keeping the stricken bomber in line with the 3,000 yard long runway, Oliver Brooks had to contend with yet another problem; he was unable to close the throttles and the Lancaster sank towards the concrete runway at 120 mph, indicated air speed. The ground controller had been warned that an aircraft in distress was approaching the airfield and the emergency services were standing by ready, as always, to cope.

Once the aircraft had slowed to a halt, after what can only be described as an exceptional landing in the circumstances, they extricated the crew from the wrecked Lancaster quickly but efficiently. Brooks had got them home.

*

Oliver V. Brooks was born in December 1922 in Hampshire, where he was raised and educated. He left school at the age of seventeen and worked for a short while as a temporary civil servant at the Royal Naval Armament Depot at Corsham, near Bath, Wiltshire.

He was at that time interested in sports, particularly boxing, and when the war began Oliver considered joining the Royal Air Force as a physical training instructor, but he was advised otherwise, as he recalls:

> I didn't think I was a suitable candidate to fly as I thought my eyesight would let me down, but I was recommended to try for aircrew which I did and was accepted.
>
> I was not one of those people with a passionate desire to fly, but like most young men at that time wanted to be in action.

Young Brooks set out on the same road that many other young men had trod before him, when he reported to the Aircrew Selection Board at Weston-Super-Mare, which he passed in July 1941. Six weeks later, on 1st September, Oliver reported to the Aircrew Receiving Centre at St John's Wood, London. Having been passed medically fit for all aspects of aircrew he then moved onto No 10 Initial Training Wing at Scarborough, where he stayed until 16th December. From Scarborough he went north to Perth, Scotland, where No 11 Elementary Flying Training School was based. It was here that Oliver Brooks experienced his first flight and learned the rudiments of flying, in a De Havilland DH82 Tiger Moth.

In early 1942, his metaphoric road took him to the United States, by way of Canada. Here, in the strange peace of the State of Georgia, flying a varied assortment of American training aircraft Oliver learned how to fly and progressed to twin-engined aircraft – the Beechcraft AT-10.

By October, Leading Aircraftman Brooks had satisfactorily

completed his course. In a ceremony held at Moody Field Georgia, Oliver, along with the rest of his class, received his 'Wings'.

> At 9.30 am on the morning of 9th October, I actually got my 'Wings'. They were presented at a ceremony held in the Base Chapel, along with a diploma, by the Commandant Colonel Fred Nelson, Army Air Corp. I was also promoted to the rank of sergeant.

Back in the United Kingdom, Sergeant Brooks was sent to No 6 Pilots' Advanced Flying Unit at Little Rissington, Gloucestershire, where his training continued on Oxford aircraft.

April 1943 found Oliver at No 12 Operational Training Unit at Edgehill, a satellite airfield to Chipping Warden, which was equipped with the Vickers Wellington. The elementary part of the training took place at Edgehill and then one progressed to the main station later on.

Oliver Brooks formed his first crew at Edgehill. Their first flight together occurred on 12th May, when they carried out some circuits and landings. Unfortunately, their time together as a crew was to be short-lived owing to Oliver injuring himself.

> At the end of May I took part in a 'Wings for Victory' boxing tournament and fractured my hand. I reckon that may well have saved my life. The injury put me back about two months. Crews were being fed into No 3 Group which at that time was operating Stirlings, and the 'chop' rate was very high; only about one in five or six crews were getting through. I've no idea what happened to my original crew, I can only assume they got another pilot. Anyway, I went back after my hand had healed, and virtually started again with another crew who, for some reason, had lost their pilot.

Sergeant Brooks took his new crew, Ken Pincott, navigator, Harry Marr, air gunner, Les Pollard, wireless operator, and Allen Gerard, bomb aimer, with him when he resumed flying Wellingtons on 8th July.

With the completion of their course at Chipping Warden, Oliver

Darr Aero Tech Primary Flying School USA. *L to R* Eric Chalk, Bill Berry, Leslie H. Freye (Instructor), Doug Boards, Duncan Cameron and Oliver Brooks. Boards and Brooks both served with XV Squadron.

A line-up of Stearman PT 17's at Darr Aero Tech Primary School 1942.

and crew were posted to No 1651 Heavy Conversion Unit at Waterbeach, where 'Chick' Chandler and Ron Wilson joined the crew as flight engineer and mid-upper gunner respectively. The seven man crew was now complete and ready for all aspects of training on the four-engined Stirling bomber. After four weeks at Waterbeach, Sergeant Brooks and his crew were declared ready for combat and posted to No XV Squadron.

They arrived at Mildenhall on 1st October and were directed to 'B' Flight, commanded by Squadron Leader Megginson, a quiet reserved man but a bomber pilot of considerable experience.

The introduction into war flying was the same for Oliver and his crew, as it had been for the other crews who had gone before, with a mine-laying mission. In Oliver's case it was off Terschelling, in the Frisians Islands. They dropped their six 1,500 pound mines without hindrance from German flak or fighters. Their initiation into war operations had been a quiet one, as was the second mining sortie in the Bay of Biscay on the night of 8th October, when they planted their mines in the Gironde river.

After an abortive first mission over enemy territory on the night of 18th/19th November, when the starboard outer engine lost pressure due to a burst oil pipe on the way to Mannheim, Oliver Brooks participated in a raid on the 'Big City' four nights later.

This raid on Berlin, by the largest force to date, was significant to Oliver for two reasons. Firstly, it was to be the first full mission he completed and secondly his was the only crew detailed from XV Squadron. He was in fact a squadron of one.

> On 22nd November there was a big raid on Berlin. My crew were the only representatives of XV Squadron to participate. The reason for this was that the squadron had been out the night before and were, on their return, diverted to another airfield and couldn't get back in time the following day.
>
> My aircraft was unserviceable, but a replacement was found. I was briefed alone as to the target, timings, weather conditions and routes and then away we went.

The city was completely obscured by 10/10th cloud which kept most of the German night-fighters on the ground, although the AA defences put up a fair barrage of flak.

Pilot Officer Oliver V. Brooks photographed by his father, in Derby.

The crew, conscious of the fact they were over enemy territory for the first time, carried out their duties with zeal and assiduity. The rear and mid-upper gunners traversed their respective turrets in opposite directions quartering the night sky in search of the, on this occasion, elusive night-fighters. Oliver Brooks held Stirling EF177 S steady on its bombing run as Allen Gerard, the bomb aimer, directed him to the estimated aiming point from 16,000 feet. When the one 1,000 lb bomb and ten canisters of incendiaries had tumbled clear of the bomb bay Gerard called, 'Bombs gone'. He checked the switches to ensure there were no hang-ups and confirmed the fact to his pilot.

The pilot received a vector from his navigator and turned the Stirling onto a new course, and headed for home. Harry Marr, the rear gunner, watched the red shimmering glow of the burning city reflected on the cloud layer below the bomber, as it headed away from the target. The mission was a great success with large areas of Berlin devastated by accurate bombing.

As he landed back at Mildenhall, Oliver was unaware that this raid was to be the last occasion that Stirlings were to be used against the German Fatherland. It was also the last raid he flew as a sergeant, for he was commissioned as a pilot officer on 24th November.

During December, No XV Squadron stood down whilst it converted to Lancaster bombers which took place, for Oliver at least, at Lakenheath. Some crews from Mildenhall went to Feltwell for their conversion course.

After carrying out dual circuits and 'bumps', solo circuits and 'bumps', loaded climbs, cross-country flights, air to air firing and bombing on local ranges, Pilot Officer Brooks was deemed ready for operations, with the new aircraft, by the third week of January 1944.

His first operation in a Lancaster was on the night of 20th January, when he and his crew took ED628, O – Orange, to Berlin. As with Oliver's previous trip the target was obscured by cloud, but Allen Gerard released the bomb load consisting of one 4,000 lb and three canisters of 30 lb and seven canisters of 4 lb incendiaries on the skymarker positions. Although Oliver later reported the flak as less severe, the German night-fighters were vectored early into the bomber stream and managed to shoot down 35 RAF aircraft.

Throughout the rest of the month and into February and March,

Pilot Officer Brooks participated in a number of raids, all against German cities, including three trips to Stuttgart. It was during this period that Pollard, the wireless operator, left the crew; his place was taken by Sergeant L. Barnes. Barnes was with them on the night of 24th/25th March, when the crew was detailed to return to Berlin in a raid which was to become known as 'the night of the strong winds'.

Oliver Brooks comments:

> We were routed in to the north, via Denmark. The winds were stronger than forecast and were judged to be about 130 miles per hour. The main stream was spread out many miles to the south of the proposed track.

The wind blew the target indicators to the south-west area of the city, which took the brunt of the attack as the crews aimed at the markers. The patchy cloud reflected not only the burning glow from below, but also the exploding flak from the ground defences which shot down approximately fifty bombers, many of which stayed over the Ruhr and its deadly flak on the way home.

Of that night Ken Pincott, the navigator, remembers:

> The winds were considerably stronger than the forecast and reached 130 mph. In order to use the computers in use at that time, to calculate the triangle of velocities all speeds (i.e.) T.A.S./Wind velocities were having to be halved to solve the problems. The computer scales were not calibrated high enough to cope with those kinds of speeds being found. The resultant answer was then doubled to give the correct solution, thus enabling accurate navigation to stay on track and arrive on target at zero hour.

The nightfighters accounted for another 23 Allied bombers.

A week later, on the evening of Thursday 30th March, a force comprised of 572 Lancasters, 214 Halifaxes and nine Mosquitos took off from various airfields on the east side of England and set course for Nuremburg. Having crossed the coast over Suffolk the bombers headed out over the North Sea in a south-easterly direction. The gunners took the opportunity of testing their guns before reaching the point where the bomber stream was formed. The stream crossed the Belgian coast at Knokke, where light flak rose into the night sky but fell short of the bombers' altitude. Turning east over Charleroi, the stream continued in a long straight leg to the German frontier, where it turned due south for its run in to the target.

Unfortunately, however, incorrect forecasting of the weather at briefing, combined again with severe cross winds over the Continent, led to the bombers being blown to the north of their track. This was only the start of Bomber Command's problems. The German fighters, who had been ordered to circle the fighter radio beacon Ida to the south of the Ruhr, discovered the bomber stream and immediately swung into action.

Pilot Officer Brooks had taken off from Mildenhall at 22.19 hours flying Lancaster LL827, O. He followed the specified route and, until he approached the target area, had had an uneventful trip. Of that night, Oliver remembers:

> That night we reportedly lost 95 aircraft. The German fighter defences appeared well organised and seemed to know our route. They were able to see the bombers quite easily due to the light of a half moon reflecting on a layer of thin cloud.
>
> As we approached the target the rear gunner reported a twin-engined fighter out on our rear port quarter, high. The enemy aircraft turned in towards us and dived, passing underneath us.

'Chick' Chandler, the flight engineer, who had seen the fighter emerge on the starboard side of the Lancaster, quickly warned the gunners over the intercom of the enemy aircraft's position. Flight Sergeant Harry Marr, the rear gunner, rotated his turret to the starboard quarter and elevated his guns, as the night-fighter, which he identified as a Ju88, executed a climbing turn into the same area. The enemy aircraft closed in and opened fire with cannon, the beauty of the illuminated stars of light leaving the fighter's nose belying their deadly intent. The Lancaster dipped its right wing as Oliver Brooks flung the aircraft into a corkscrew manoeuvre to starboard, but not before some of the deadly stars danced along the mainplane. Oliver Brooks recalls:

> We were hit in the number three tank on the port side. That was the small capacity (114 gallons) tank outboard of the outer. A shell went into it and exploded. It was in fact a brand new tank and had not been filled. If it had the results could have been disastrous. The enemy aircraft made just the one attack and disappeared, no doubt to seek other targets of which there were plenty.

As the Lancaster dived to starboard, Harry Marr opened fire with his Browning machine guns. The Ju88 continued in towards the bomber, then broke away to port. Sergeant Ron Wilson, whose sighting of the attacking fighter had been obscured by the Lancaster's tailplane, saw the enemy aircraft as it broke away. He depressed his guns and fired off a short burst of fifty rounds before it disappeared from view; neither gunner saw the fighter again.

Ken Pincott remembers the raid for another reason.

> I remember on the Nuremberg raid that because of the large number of aircraft being shot down, I was advised by the skipper to stop recording them. I believe in fact that I had logged fifty such positions before reaching the target.

On the night of 22nd/23rd April, Bomber Command sent 596 bombers to attack Düsseldorf. The force comprised of nineteen Mosquitos, 254 Halifaxes and 323 Lancasters. Amongst the latter type was Lancaster MkIII, ND763, LS-W-Willie, piloted by Oliver Brooks.

ND763 took off from Mildenhall, with the rest of XV Squadron, at 22.49 hours. Ensconced inside the fuselage were her usual crew plus Flight Lieutenant John Fabian DFC, the squadron navigation leader, who as 'Y' operator was to operate the H2S 'blind navigation' radar. The eight crew members sat quietly at their respective stations, the silence broken only by the constant droning of the aircraft's four Merlin engines and the occasional exchange of necessary information over the intercom.

The aircraft undulated gently on the night air, as it crossed over enemy territory. Oliver Brooks cast a glance at the instrument panel and then looked up. Ahead he could see sticks of light penetrating the darkness as searchlights began to sweep across the sky. Then the red markers began to fall; the Pathfinders had located the target.

Allen Gerrard, the bomb aimer, was lying in the nose of the Lancaster. The top half of his torso propped against the bomb aimer's body rest. He had a clear view ahead through the nose blister with its optically flat bombing window.

Approaching the target at 22,000 feet, Oliver Brooks started his bombing run with Gerrard guiding him towards the red target indicators, which were now burning brightly on the ground. In anticipation of the bombs being released, Flight Sergeant Barnes, the wireless operator, left his station and made his way down the fuselage as Oliver Brooks recalls:

> On the run in to the target Barnes would make his way down the fuselage. It was his job to ensure that the photo-flash we were carrying was released at the same time as the bomb load. Sometimes it would hang up, so he would ensure it went by giving it a push.

Gerrard instructed his pilot to hold the Lancaster steady as they crossed the target; the time was approximately 01.16 a.m. He pressed the 'tit' and the bombs began to tumble out of the bomb-bay. Relieved of her load ND763 rose gently upwards, as a hail of cannon shells slammed into the port wing. Undetected, an Me109 'Wild Boar' night-fighter had crept in from dead astern and opened fire at a range of about 800 yards. In one continuous burst the shells homed in on the port engine, setting it ablaze and, as hydraulic power from this engine operated the gun turrets, it thus put both the mid-upper and rear turrets out of action.

At the same time, before Gerrard could call 'Bombs gone' there was an explosion underneath towards the rear of the aircraft. A predicted heavy flak shell exploded below ND763. The blast reverberated up into the bomb bay and along the Lancaster's belly, twisting the metal and shattering the bomb aimer's compartment.

Gerrard, who was due to be married two weeks later, only lived for another two or three minutes.

Unfortunately, Barnes was also caught by the blast, as Oliver Brooks remembers:

> Barnes was ensuring that the photo-flash didn't hang up when the flak shell exploded, severely injuring him. Despite his terrible wounds he crawled towards the rear turret calling for help.

Although shrapnel had almost severed one of his legs, Barnes remained conscious. Obviously in great pain and losing a lot of blood, he dragged himself along the floor of the fuselage, with every bump and jolt of the aircraft making its presence felt in his wounded body. Using what little strength remained Barnes attracted the rear gunner's attention to his predicament. Flight Sergeant Harry Marr clambered out of his turret in an attempt to assist his comrade, but realising the severity of the wounds called over the intercom for help.

All the while, Pilot Officer Brooks was battling with the controls of his aircraft, which was rapidly losing height.

In response to the rear gunner's call, Flight Lieutenant Fabian struggled towards the rear of the aircraft. With the first aid kit in one hand, and grabbing what handholds he could with the other to steady himself as the aircraft buffeted about, Fabian made his way aft.

Although both the mid-upper and rear turrets were out of action, it was felt that Harry Marr should remain in his turret to fire the guns manually should the Me109 return. Sergeant Ron Wilson was therefore called down from the mid-upper turret to assist Fabian. Wilson himself had been caught by a fragment of shrapnel and sustained a cut ear. The same applied to Ken Pincott, the navigator, who was hit by flak in the finger.

As he climbed from his turret Wilson found yet another problem. A 'short' in the electrical circuit sent out a shower of sparks, which ignited and started a fire in the fuselage. Having disconnected his intercom, Wilson was unable to inform his pilot. Oliver Brooks had enough problems anyway trying to contról the Lancaster, which was still going down, and he had already warned the crew that they

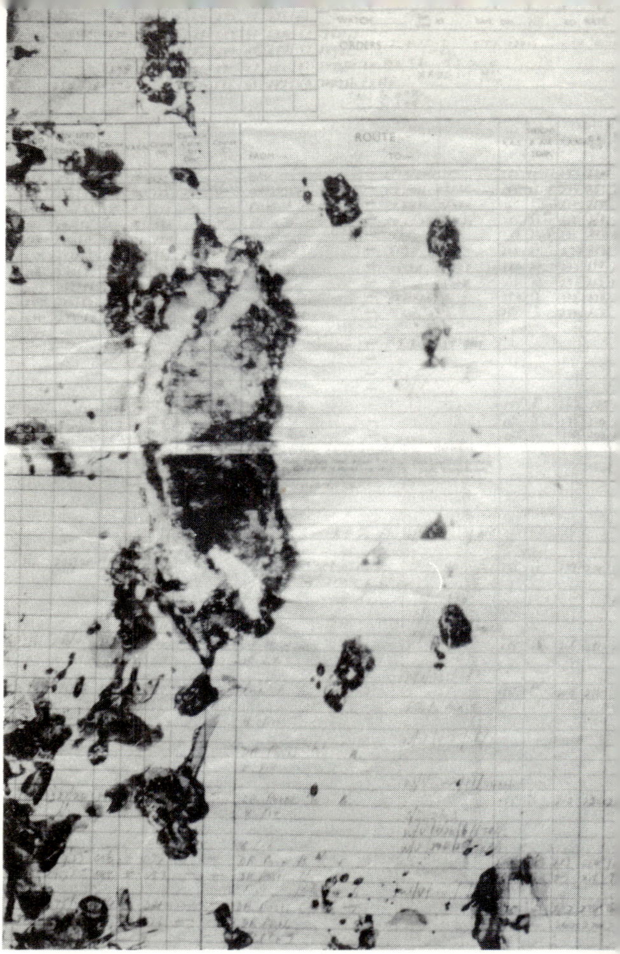

The blood splattered flight plan (*right*) and navigator's chart (*below*) still remind Ken Pincott of the night they were attacked by a German nightfighter.

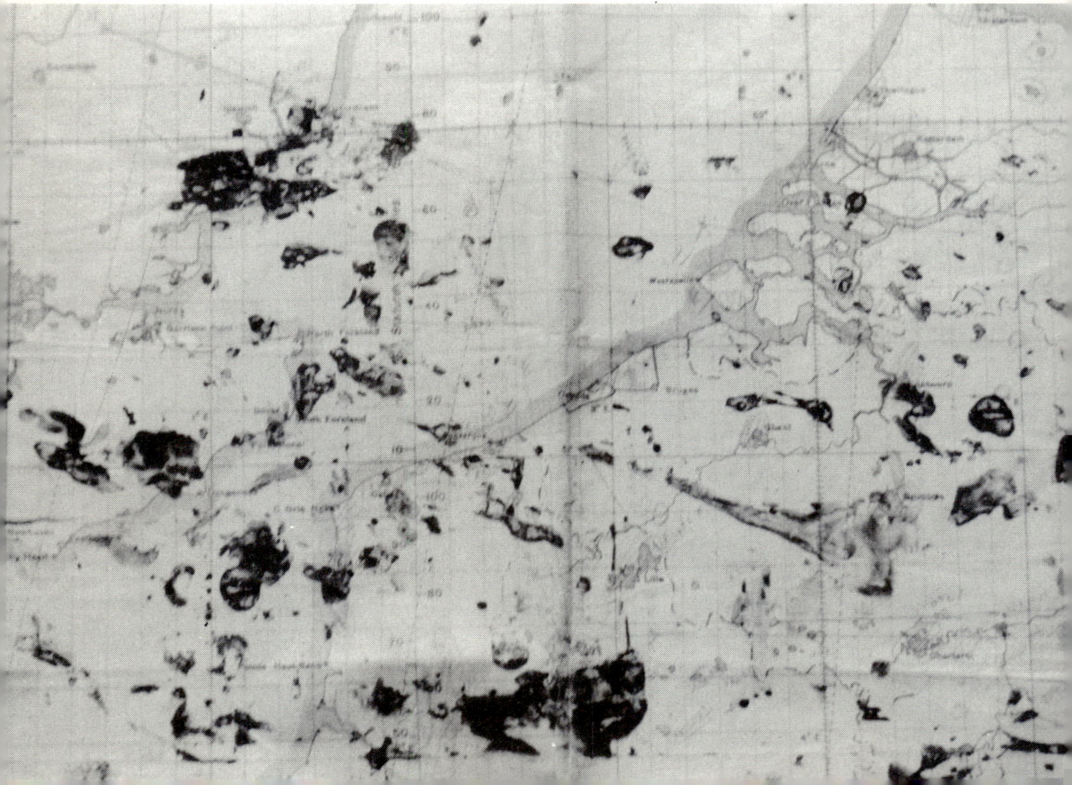

might have to bale out. Wilson set about extinguishing the fire on his own, which he eventually managed, but not before the fire had damaged three of the crews' parachutes.

Between them, Fabian and Wilson attended to the seriously wounded wireless operator. They cut away his clothing and injected him with morphine, but Barnes lay quite still, the life blood draining from him. A short while later in the undignified surroundings of a battle damaged Lancaster, lying in a pool of his own blood, Flight Sergeant Barnes, too, succumbed to his injuries and paid the supreme sacrifice.

ND763 was down to 4,000 feet before Oliver Brooks regained control of the aircraft. She was in bad shape. He knew it from the way she flew, and called for a battle damage report. That was not all the pilot called for, as Ken Pincott relates:

> Usually on the run in to the target, I would leave my navigation table and stand looking out of the astro dome. Another pair of eyes searching for fighters. When we were hit the aircraft dropped from 22,000 feet before pulling out at 14,000 feet! I had been thrown to the floor and found it difficult to regain my feet because of all the glycol, etc, all over the floor. I managed to get to my feet just as the aircraft dropped once more. Thinking that I didn't want to die just yet, having been married for only a fortnight, I was about to find my parachute and get out. I thought I was the only one still alive; then I heard the skipper's voice calling out for a crew check, followed by the comment. 'For Christ sake, navigator, give me a course for home out of here!'

They could not ditch in the sea due to the dinghy having been shot away when the aircraft was caught by the flak. Likewise, three parachutes were useless, having been damaged by fire. Then, as Oliver Brooks relates, there was Sergeant Chandler to consider.

> Chick Chandler had a bloody lucky escape. He was leaning slightly forward in his seat when the flak shell exploded. A lump of shrapnel came through the side of the fuselage and sliced through the back strap of his parachute harness. Had he been sitting three inches further back it would have taken his back out.

Calmly and collectively, Oliver assessed the situation, the qualities of his leadership coming to the fore. Although he still had trouble maintaining height, he decided their best chance was to try for one of the emergency landing runways in England.

Ken Pincott recalls:

> Having discovered that the aircraft was flying at approximately 90 mph ground speed, I calculated that we should head for Woodbridge, with an ETA of around 03.38. Once over the North Sea, I tried to operate the wireless, sending out SOS transmissions together with expected ditching positions, in case we should go down in the sea.

Having attended to the minor injuries of Wilson and Pincott, Fabian took over the navigation whilst Flight Sergeant Pincott took over the position of wireless operator.

The atmosphere aboard the Lancaster was highly charged. They all knew the crippled bomber was an easy target for both fighters and flak. By the time they got to the French coast, ND763 was below 3,000 feet and continuing to lose height. Then it seemed their worst fears were about to happen; they were coned by searchlights. The intense light of the multi-million candle powerbeams turned night into day. A lump in the throat, a restriction of breath as the chest momentarily tightened, the heart thumping as though trying to burst out of the body, and the dread that the other crew members could hear it over the noise of the engines. Each man alone for a few seconds waiting for the explosions of flak followed by the rattling of shrapnel against the aircraft, like heavy rain on corrugated iron; a repetition of what they had already experienced. The seconds increased; no flak. It must be fighters! The seconds turned into minutes; no fighters. What the hell was happening? Gone! Nothing but the blackness that immediately follows staring at a bright light. Was it a dream? No, each of the crew members knew that, for each man had offered a silent prayer. For reasons best known to themselves, after five to ten minutes the enemy dowsed the searchlights and allowed the bomber to fly on.

Oliver Brooks checked the altimeter as Chick Chandler, the flight engineer, gave him a run down on the fuel situation. They were now out over the North Sea and still losing height. In an effort to lighten the aircraft, Oliver ordered that all unnecessary equipment be jettisoned, a task which Fabian and Wilson immediately undertook. Everything removable went 'over the side', including the guns and ammunition.

Teamwork was essential to survival, and whilst Brooks and Chandler flew the aircraft, and Fabian and Wilson jettisoned the equipment, Pincott repeatedly sent out an SOS, together with a reference of the aircraft's position. Unbeknown to Pincott, due to their low altitude, his transmissions were not being received.

Slowly and almost unnoticeably, ND673 ceased her downward attitude of flight; in fact she was starting to climb. With the port outer engine u/s and the constant speed unit of the starboard outer engine being weak and giving little power, Oliver was reluctant to 'push' the Lancaster too hard. However, the wounded aircraft responded to this gentle coaxing and gained sufficient height to cross the English coast at 500 feet.

Although ahead of him Oliver could see the most welcoming sight of his young life, the threshold of the emergency runway at Woodbridge, he could not relax. The landing was by no means going to be easy. He had to make it first time, he could not chance having to go round again, even though there were approximately 100 gallons of fuel left in the tanks. The elevator and rudder trims were both u/s, he couldn't lower the undercarriage or close the bomb doors.

The crew, unable to take up their crash positions, remained at their normal positions during the landing, which they knew would have its own dangers.

With the throttle jammed open Oliver brought the Lancaster into Woodbridge at 120 mph IAS. Losing height, he held the nose up as the aircraft was eased towards terra firma. Lower and lower ND673 sunk until he felt contact with the ground. At 03.55 hours the emergency service swung into action and raced across the airfield, as the Lancaster slid along on its belly. In a shower of sparks, dirt, dust and debris and with the metal screeching on the concrete, the bomb doors buckled and collapsed under the weight of the aircraft and the propellers twisting as they struck the ground.

When the Lancaster slithered to a halt the bodies of Barnes and Gerrard were immediately removed from the fuselage, whilst the surviving crew members were taken to the station sick back for attention and check-ups. ND763, the Lancaster who had brought her crew home, was unceremoniously hauled from the runway by the crash crew in less than five minutes.

Pilot Officer Brooks, Flight Lieutenant Fabian, Flight Sergeant Pincott and Sergeant Chandler were not given time to ponder on the events of their experience, as Oliver Brooks recalls:

> The next night our names appeared on the Battle Order for a raid against Karlsruhe. The CO, Wing Commander Watkins, came as my bomb aimer to see how we got on.

Ron Wilson, who was still in the sick bay, was replaced as mid-upper gunner by Sergeant W. Walker and Barnes' place as wireless operator was taken by Sergeant J. Murphy.

Flying Lancaster LL827, O, Oliver Brooks took off from Mildenhall at 21.56 hours. The bomber laden with one 4,000 lb high explosive bomb, six 12 x 30 lb and two 90 x 4 lb incendiary canisters, lumbered into the air.

The strong winds returned and again pushed the bomber stream to the north of its allotted track. The target indicators, although fairly well concentrated, also fell victim to the winds and were blown off the actual aiming point. Cloudy conditions and heavy icing also hampered the attacking force.

Approaching the target at 15,000 feet, LL827 was attacked by an unidentified fighter. Creeping out of the darkness, it opened fire at the Lancaster but the illuminated stars of cannon fire missed their target. Oliver Brooks swung the bomber into a corkscrew as the fighter curved round for another attack. The German pilot pressed his gun 'tit' and the cannon spat forth another burst of shells at the Lancaster, but these too missed their intended victim. The enemy aircraft disappeared into the darkness never to be seen again.

Pilot Officer Brooks returned to the job in hand, bombing the target which he did without further hindrance. His aircraft was, however, coned twice on the way out, but on each occasion he managed to evade the unwelcome attention of the beams by corkscrewing out of them.

The raid was not considered a success, as many bombs are thought to have fallen outside the city.

Two photographs taken from Lancaster PB115, LS-W, flown by Flight Lieutenant Oliver Brooks, en route for a daylight attack against V1 sites at Domleger, on 21 June 1944.

During the first week of May, Pilot Officer Oliver Brooks was notified that he was to be awarded the Distinguished Flying Cross by His Majesty King George VI; he was also to receive promotion. At the same investiture, Flight Lieutenant John Fabian was to receive a Bar to his DFC, and Flight Sergeant Ken Pincott the Distinguished Flying Medal.

Ken Pincott DFM stayed with Oliver Brooks when the latter took over an experienced crew, whose pilot had been lost flying with a novice crew. They also took charge of a new aircraft, a Lancaster Mk111, ND955, W – Willie. Unfortunately, their association with ND955 was short lived, for it failed to return from a raid on the night of 24th/25th May when Flying Officer Mckay took it to Aachen.

Amongst the targets this new team attacked during May were the railway yards at Le Mans, coastal gun positions at Boulogne and the railway yards at Trappes. These raids were in preparation for the forthcoming invasion which took place on 6th June 1944. At 03.34 hours that morning Oliver Brooks took off from Mildenhall flying Lancaster LL889 W, and headed for the gun emplacements at Ouisterham. There, he and his crew unleashed the eleven 1,000 lb and three 500 lb bombs they were carrying in the bomb bay, after a timed run by instruments on the red target indicators.

Oliver flew his last 'op' on 21st June, the day XV Squadron resumed daylight operations. The squadron detailed twelve Lancasters to join a total force of 322 aircraft in a raid against a V1 flying bomb site at Domleger. The crews found 10/10th cloud over the target and could not see the target indicators. Due to the conditions, the attack was abandoned after only seventeen aircraft had dropped their loads.

His tour of operation finished as it had started, on a quiet note. Oliver was proclaimed tour expired and sent on leave for a well earned rest. His leave, however, was interrupted, as he recalls:

> I had been on leave about a week when I received a telegram ordering me to report back immediately to Mildenhall. The King, accompanied by Queen Elizabeth and Princess Elizabeth, was visiting the station where an investiture was to be held on 5th July.

ght) *L to R* Sergeant Ken
ıcott, Sergeant Harry Marr,
rgeant Oliver Brooks,
rgeant 'Chick' Chandler,
rgeant 'Tug' Wilson
oncealed), Sergeant Les
llard and Sergeant R.A.
rrard at Mildenhall Oct-Nov
43.

elow) Flight Lieutenant
ooks receives his DFC from
1 King George VI at
denhall on 5th July 1944. (*L*
R) Princess Elizabeth, Air
mmodore McKee, Queen
zabeth, The aide-de-camp,
oup Captain Young, HM
g George VI and Flight
utenant Brooks.

Standing proud and erect, Flight Lieutenant Oliver V. Brooks stood motionless, his eyes level with the cap of the man who stood before him, the man in whose name he had fought, King George VI. It was one of the proudest moments of his life, as the King pinned the medal and ribbon of the Distinguished Flying Cross on his 'best blue'.

Flight Sergeant Ken Pincott also has proud memories of that occasion:

> Just like Oliver, I too received a telegram ordering me to return to Mildenhall, where I discovered that an investiture had been arranged. I remember that twenty-nine officers and one NCO were to be invested, so I stood alone in the middle of that vast hangar, the last to be presented to HM King George VI.

For a man who initially had no great ambition to fly, Oliver Brooks' record was an impressive one. After a period instructing at No 1651 Conversion Unit at Wratton Common, he finished the war with No 156 Pathfinder Squadron at Upwood. He stayed in the RAF after the war and qualified as first pilot on at least seventeen different types of aircraft, including helicopters, before transferring to less exciting but important duties in the Fighter Control Branch. He finally retired in 1972.

CHAPTER NINE

The Born Survivor

Flight Lieutenant Len 'Dusty' Miller DFC

As young Len Miller played and made camps near his home during the late 1920s, he was unaware that in less than a decade and a half circumstances would force him, as a fugitive, to make camps and survive in a foreign country, with whom he was at war.

'Dusty' Miller, as he is known to his friends, was born on 7th September 1922, in London's East End where he subsequently grew up. The depressive years of the 1920s were not the best in which to be brought up. Len and his family, like many others at that time, lived hand to mouth. Even today he still remembers the feelings of hunger.

As a child, Len was left very much to his own devices; his mother had a job, which kept the family going, and his father was out most of the time looking for work. Being left on his own, young Len learned how to look after himself. He liked the outdoor life and spent much time making camps, where he could hide away especially after scrounging food, either by fair means or foul.

His father's determination to find a job was eventually rewarded when he was offered employment in the London Docks. A regular income bought in more food, but the scrounging and survival instincts Len had developed were to stay with him.

By this time, Len Miller had procured an interest in designing and making paper aeroplanes. The interest grew, he progressed to wooden models and, like most boys, set his mind on being a flyer when he grew up. Unfortunately for Len, his father had other ideas about his son's future and secured a job for him in the docks, with the intention that Len should become a marine engineer apprentice.

By the time Len was sixteen he had grown up. His general attitude to life, at that time, was based on survival and looking after himself as much as he could. This philosophy paid off when he started work, for he remembers:

> The dockers I worked with were very nice people to be with, but if you got in their way they would give you a 'thick ear'.

Working in the docks meant that one had to be alert and aware of what was going on. Cargo in those days was lifted from the ship's holds in very large nets which, due to the irregular shape or weight of the load, could and sometimes did break. Day dreaming or a pensive mood could come to a sudden and abrupt end if crates or carcasses of meat came crashing down.

Of this period of his life, Len Miller recalls:

> I was taught all aspects of marine engineering, foundry work and machine brass finishing, with a view that I could take this knowledge to sea. However, I still hankered after aeroplanes and had other ideas. When war was declared in September 1939 I was more or less ready to go. At the appropriate time, I volunteered to join the RAF, but was returned to 'civvy' street when they realised that, as a marine engineer apprentice, I was in a reserved occupation. I was wiser when I made another attempt to join up. On that occasion I said I was a plumber's mate and was accepted. By the time the deception was realised I was in Canada.

Having joined up, Cadet Miller was instructed to report to the Aircrew Receiving Centre at St John's Wood, London, in August 1941, for kitting out. He was then moved to No 10 Initial Training Wing at Scarborough for the usual square bashing and physical jerks, etc, but returned to St John's Wood prior to going to RAF St Athan in preparation for going overseas.

With the rest of his contingent, Len Miller boarded the SS *Volendam* at Milford Haven and set sail on 2nd January 1942 with an escort of destroyers, bound for Canada.

Being winter, the weather was not very good and the ship was caught in the biggest storm that many of the men had ever seen. The *Volendam* was tossed around as reported ninety foot swells rose and fell. The ships crew were as frightened as the 500 RAF men on board. The storm reduced in velocity, but maintained its presence throughout the crossing which did not help, when first the steering went and then the engines broke down. The ship drifted on the Atlantic, at the mercy of the winds and currents, until repairs had been carried out, enabling it to reach its destination of St John, New Brunswick.

At New Brunswick, the RAF contingent was billeted at No 31 Personnel Depot, prior to boarding a train for the journey across Canada. The route took them through Winnipeg to No 2 Manning Depot at Brandon, then on to a place called Assiniboia, Saskatoon, where No 34 Elementary Flying Training School was situated.

Of his time in Canada, Len Miller remembers:

> On arrival at Assiniboia, we immediately settled into our ground studies and flying training, the latter being carried out on Tiger Moth aircraft. On completion of the EFTS course we moved further west to No 34 Service Flying Training School at Medicine Hat, in Alberta, where we converted to twin-engined Oxford aircraft.

On completion of the training in Canada, the contingent returned to No 31 PD at Moncton for return to England for further training.

Len Miller boarded the liner *Queen Mary* in New York accompanied not only by his own contingent, but also by 26,000 US troops. Compared to the outward journey, it took only about three and a half days to complete the west-east crossing. Recalling the trip, Len Miller stated: 'The ship must have been doing about 38 knots; every time it zig-zagged we were pinned against the walls by the G-force'.

It was December when the ship docked at Southampton, just a few days before Christmas. The CO of the RAF contingent, who was permanently based on the ship, called the men together and stated that as they were the host country the RAF would remain on board and clean up after the 'yanks' had departed. It was Christmas Eve when the CO issued them all with brooms and sacks, which were immediately tossed overboard and he very nearly went with them.

Early 1943 saw Len Miller moving around England to various RAF establishments in order to complete his training, until he finally arrived at No 26 Operational Training Unit at Wing in Bedfordshire, where he converted to Wellington bombers.

His crew was formulated at Wing and consisted of the wireless operator, Flight Sergeant Matthews, Peter Slater who was to prove an excellent rear gunner, twenty-year-old Sergeant Eastman, as navigator and Flight Sergeant George Mead, the bomb aimer. Alf Pybus, the flight-engineer from Newcastle, and 22-year-old Wilbert Cully, the rear gunner, were to join the crew a little later. They became a close knit team who lived, worked and played together. Sometimes, on warm summer evenings, the seven of them would ride on two bikes to a local pub. Len Miller recalls how this was achieved:

> We used to tie the bikes together with rope. One bike carried four people and the other carried three. One person sat on the handlebars, one stood and peddled the machine, one sat on the saddle whilst the forth person balanced on the rear wheel wingnuts. We used to hurtle around the countryside in this manner, much to the amazement of passers-by.

From Wing, the whole crew went to No 1651 Conversion Unit at Waterbeach, where they converted to and trained on Stirling bombers. Len insisted that the crew got to know the aircraft intimately. They therefore carried out training whilst the Stirling was on the ground. At least three times a week they practised ditching procedure and parachute dropping, by jumping from the escape hatches. So that they knew exactly how to remove the hatches in the dark, they often closed their eyes or blindfolded themselves to carry out the drill. Finally, on 19th October 1943, they were declared ready for duty and posted to No XV Squadron, based at RAF Mildenhall.

Len Miller recalls:

> Our first trip was a mining operation, or as they were more commonly known a 'Gardening' sortie, to the Frisian Islands on

(*Right*) Flight Lieutenant Len Miller DFC

(*Below*) (*L to R, back row*) Sergeant Matthews, Sergeant Culley, Sergeant Miller, Sergeant Alf Pybus.
(*Front row*) Sergeant Mead, Sergeant Eastman, Sergeant Slater.

> the night of 24th October. We took off at 17.40 hours in Stirling BF533 H and headed for the planting area. The weather deteriorated to such an extent that we could not carry out our mission, so I reluctantly turned the Stirling for home, with the mines still on board. Although I had followed orders, nobody was particularly pleased when it was discovered I had bought the mines back.

The second sortie was another mine laying operation, on this occasion to the Gironde Estuary, in the Bay of Biscay. Approximately twelve aircraft from No 3 Group were detailed for the mission, including two from XV Squadron. The weather was not very good and in addition to the thick cloud, ice began building up on the wings. By reducing altitude, Len managed to overcome the latter problem and pressed on. The rest of the journey was uneventful until they were over the Bay, when without warning strings of 'flaming onions' of flak slowly arced up into the night sky. As they flew on, the crew gave passing thought to the poor sods who were receiving the attention from the flakships below. Being a sprog pilot Len Miller flew by the book, straight and level and at exactly the right height for planting the mines. The 'onions' continued to arc upwards and again the crew commented on the poor sods being fired at. Upon their return to Mildenhall they were informed that a recall signal had been transmitted to the attacking force. For some reason they had not received the message and they were therefore the poor sods being fired at.

In Len Miller's words, 'As far as can be ascertained, our Stirling was the only Allied aircraft over the Bay of Biscay that night'.

The crew only carried out three operations on Stirlings before the squadron converted to Lancasters. The battle-weary Stirlings were flown to Winthorpe and the crews made the return journey to Mildenhall aboard a Handley Page Harrow, which had wicker passenger seats!

Len Miller was granted a commission on 14th December and flew his first operation as a pilot officer exactly one month later. The target was Brunswick and he flew Lancaster ED376, F. It was a quiet trip, the aiming point being obscured by cloud and he later reported, at debriefing, 'Little flak and no fighters'.

At 17.50 hours on 27th January 1944, he lifted ED376, F, into the night sky and headed, with the rest of the squadron, for Berlin. Owing to the failure of the rear turret, Len had to abandon the mission and return to Mildenhall.

The following night the crew headed for Berlin again, but on this occasion Len Miller was piloting Lancaster R5904, G. An Australian pilot normally flew R5904 but on each of his last three misisons the Australian had returned early, claiming each time that most of his instruments had gone u/s. When the aircraft was air tested during the day no faults could be found. Finally, Len Miller was instructed to fly the aircraft operationally. During the day, prior to the raid, the ground crew whilst preparing the Lancaster removed the armoured glazed screen which protected the flight engineer, an action that was unfortunately to prove a fatal mistake.

Len Miller recalls:

> I took off in R5904 at 00.20 hours and headed east. Shortly after crossing the coast at Cromer, the majority of the instruments failed, leaving me with the compass, altimeter and turn and bank indicator. A subsequent investigation revealed that when the temperature dropped at night, condensation froze in the tubes thus creating the problem.
>
> A quick deliberation and I decided to stay with the bomber stream and head for the 'Big City'. Berlin was obscured by very thin cloud, but we had no difficulty in seeing the target indicators, which appeared to be well concentrated.
>
> At 03.28 hours I was holding R5904 steady at 20,000 feet on the bombing run when I spotted a Ju88 nightfighter turning in to attack from low on the front port quarter, at a range of about 600 yards. As I warned the gunners, the enemy aircraft opened fire with cannon and machine guns. I swung the Lancaster into a side slipping bank and the enemy's fire overshot. Aggressively, the Ju88 broke away to starboard prior to commencing its second attack. Coming in from the starboard quarter it dived, and then climbed up towards us firing a long continuous burst.

Cannon fire struck the starboard mainplane and engines, but fortunately did not put the latter out of action. As the Ju88 turned it raked the length of the fuselage and starboad side of the tailplane.

Len Miller continues:

> Alf Pybus, the flight engineer, was struck in the head by a bullet and collapsed to the floor. The Ju88 then came down and passed underneath us. As it emerged from under the tail, Peter Slater was waiting; he fired a long burst which appeared to go straight into the cockpit canopy and engines. The enemy aircraft reared up, turned onto its back and fell away, shedding fragments as we watched it silhouetted against the fires of the burning city below. Our troubles were, however, not over, for the mid-upper gunner reported another Ju88 coming in for a head-on attack. The nightfighter and the mid-upper gunner opened fire simultaneously; the former, however, did not press home the attack and was lost from view as it dived down on the port side. As I left the target area, and set course for Mildenhall, Peter Slater warned me he had spotted a single engined fighter stealing up from below and dead astern. Having identified it as a FW190, Peter opened fire with several long bursts; the intruder turned and dived away without having fired a shot.

As the aircraft headed for home, the gunners naturally stayed at their stations while the other crew members attended to Alf Pybus, who had not moved since the initial attack.

Len Miller again:

> They put Alf on oxygen and wrapped him up to keep him warm; none of us could tell what his condition was. I was still at 20,000 feet and so decreased height in order to assist Alf's comfort. On the way down I tested the undercarriage and flaps; the former seemed to be OK but the latter did not work very well. I continued to fly on course for England and Mildenhall.
>
> As I reached base, the runway was ahead of me. I flew over the perimeter fence, crossed the threshold and lowered R5904 as gently as I could onto the runway. It was the smoothest landing I ever made, but unfortunately Alf Pybus was not to know; he was, as it transpired, dead on arrival at Mildenhall.

About 100 yards from the end of the runway, without warning, the port undercarriage leg collapsed, ripping the tyre to shreds. Sparks flew as the rotating port propellers struck the concrete runway like giant grinding wheels, buckling the propeller blades. The aircraft pivoted off the runway, its port wingtip ploughing a deep furrow in the grass. R5904 came to rest with the rear section of the Lancaster protruding across the runway, obstructing the path of the other aircraft behind it.

Len Miller takes up the story:

I thought to myself, 'What the hell, she must be a write-off anyway', and pushed the throttles forward, almost through the 'gate'. Slowly, the wounded aircraft edged forward in a curving movement, still pivoting on the broken port undercarriage. The airframe vibrated and shuddered from the strain, as I kept the throttles open. Earth and debris was thrown everywhere as slowly and painfully R5904's tailplane cleared the runway.

After the noise of the crash, the silence that descended over us was almost eerie. It seemed ages, but must have been only a few seconds, before the rescue crews were in action. Their first duty being to place Alf Pybus on to a stretcher and get him into the waiting ambulance, albeit too late.

Alf's death was a great loss to them all. As a crew they were, by this time, a closely integrated team. They slept in the same billet and went everywhere together. Even on leave the crew went home with their pilot, as he lived in London and they all came from much further afield.

They were granted a few days' leave, during which they attended Alf Pybus' funeral and then returned to Mildenhall. Upon their return they found a new aircraft awaiting them. Lancaster LL801 was coded J – Jig and was powered by four Rolls Royce Merlin 24 engines with paddle-wheel propellers. The aircraft had no H-2S, but could carry about 1,000 lb more bomb load than any other squadron aircraft, and was certainly much faster.

Being proud of their aircraft, the crew often used to assist the ground crew in servicing the aircraft. Len would take his crew out to dispersal every morning and check the aircraft over. After all, like everything else, survival was the name of the game.

Peter Slater, the rear gunner, was a great asset and comfort to

Len Miller, apart from being a close friend. After every trip Peter Slater would remove the guns from the turret and, before he went to sleep, would clean them. As he and Len shared a room, the latter would sometimes assist him, thinking that Peter might otherwise sit up all night. When they were clean, Peter would put the guns into little canvas bags under his bed and check them the following morning before putting them back into the turret.

Peter Slater, an ex-policeman, was married with a young son. He was 32 years of age, quite old for a member of aircrew, about five feet tall and was quite thick-set. Because of a popular song of the time, the rest of the crew used to call him Mr Five by Five. He had an aquiline nose, very thin, piercing blue eyes, which afforded him superb night vision, and very short hair.

When Peter wore his flying suit he would literally waddle out to the aircraft. Unfortunately, due to his natural metabolism, he would sweat a great deal often to his own discomfort.

Len Miller remembers:

> One night on a raid he had switched on his electrically heated suit. About half way out to the target, screams emanated from the rear turret. He had perspired so much he had short-circuited his suit and was giving himself electric shocks.

As a rear gunner Peter Slater ranked amongst the best; knowing he was guarding the rear of the aircraft made Len feel better. Peter could somehow sense the presence of an enemy nightfighter and invariably he was right. The crew had several brushes with fighters and he was eventually credited with five confirmed kills.

The crew returned to operations on the night of 19th February, with their pilot wearing the ribbon of the Distinguished Flying Cross below the Wings on his tunic, the decoration having been awarded a few days earlier.

They took J – Jig to Leipzig but abandoned the mission due to the failure of the rear and mid-upper turrets. The bomb load, a mixture of high explosive and incendiaries, was jettisoned from 21,000 feet over the North Sea one hour and ten minutes after take off.

Apart from being their first trip with LL801 and their first

(*Right*) Pilot Officer Peter Slater, rear gunner and close friend of Len Miller. Slater was not flying with the crew the night they were shot down. He finished the war with five confirmed 'kills'.

(*Below*) Lancaster LL801, LS-J, being prepared for battle.

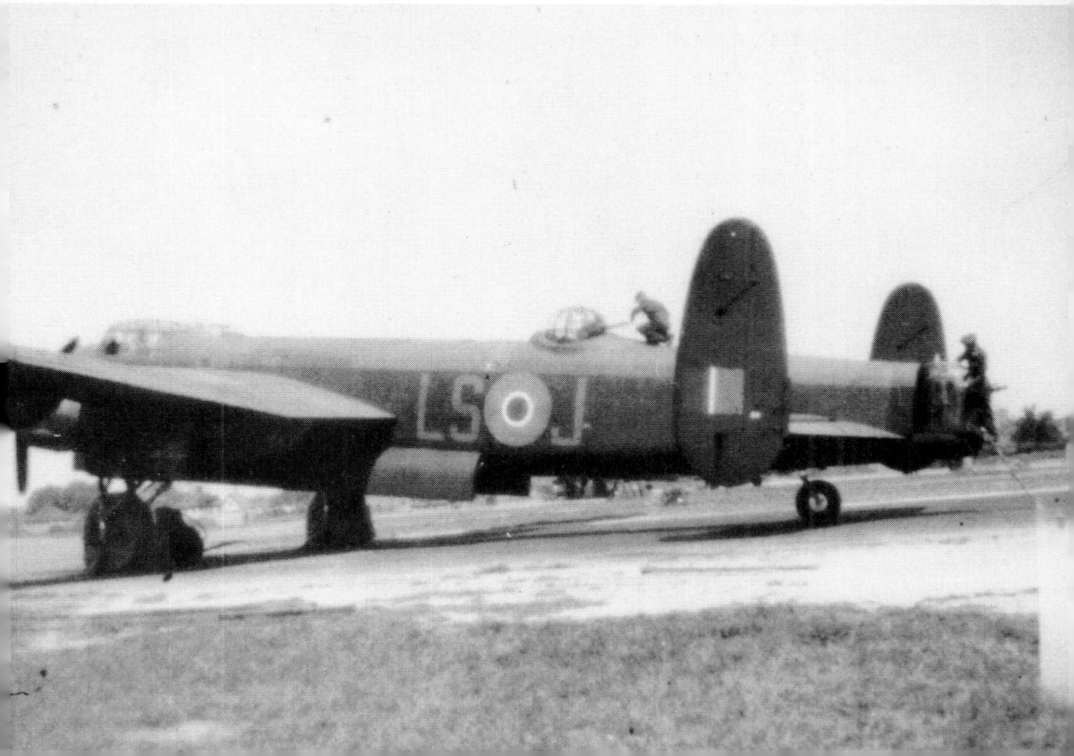

operation to Leipzig, the night of 19th/20th February was also the first time they flew with Sergeant Alf Beazley-Long, who joined the crew as Alf Pybus' replacement.

On the night of 25th February the crew were detailed for a raid on Augsburg. The target area was clear and the red and green target indicators were well concentrated. The flak defences were very weak and the participating crews were able to drop more than 2,000 tons of bombs accurately on the old city centre.

George Mead, the bomb aimer, reported seeing one of their 4,000 pound 'cookies' exploding on the railway junction, adding to the fires already burning and the smoke which was rising to 15,000 feet.

The weather started to deteriorate and the homeward journey was made in ever thickening cloud, with the cloudbase getting lower and lower. By the time LL801 reached Mildenhall the aircraft was flying in torrential rain and the cloudbase had descended to about 300 feet over the airfield.

Len Miller circled the airfield, with almost empty tanks. He called the tower for permission to land, but there were other aircraft requesting priority landings, some damaged and some with wounded aircrew on board. The tower advised Len to divert to Bourn, some eight miles away. He reset the compass and pulled back on the control column, climbing LL801 up into the cloud and through the milling hoard of aircraft from both XV and No 622 Squadrons. The cloud remained thick and the rain did not relent. Len continued to fly blind until instinct told him to decrease height. He broke cloud dead in line with, and about half a mile out from Bourn's illuminated runway.

There was a frenzy of activity on Len Miller's part, knowing the fuel had almost gone. He lowered the flaps, dropped the undercarriage and put the props into fine pitch ready for immediate landing. He called Bourn tower and landed simultaneously. The tower instructed Len to turn right once he had landed to which he instantly replied, much to their surprise, 'I am not turning right'. As he carried out the manoeuvre, all four engines died!

The first day of March started with Pilot Officer Miller being appointed to the rank of acting flight lieutenant. It ended with his taking off from Mildenhall at 23.40 hours to participate in a raid on Stuttgart.

The target was cloud covered with occasional gaps through which the brilliant red glow of fires could be seen. As LL801 crossed the target area Len Miller held the aircraft steady, in accordance with the bomb aimer's instructions. George Mead pressed the tit and the bomb rained down to join the conflagration below. As with all raids, George checked the bomb switch panel and, on this occasion, reported the hang-up of two 90 x 4 lb incendiary canisters. They didn't have time to worry about them, for as Len banked LL801 out of the target area the wireless operator, on watch in the astrodome, reported a Ju88 nightfighter effecting a diving attack from astern at a range of approximately 600 yards. Flight Sergeant Cully, the mid-upper gunner, and Peter Slater, the rear gunner, traversed their turrets, sighted the enemy aircraft and opened fire simultaneously. The tracer from the nightfighter passed over the Lancaster's starboard mainplane as the bomber dived and then banked to port. Cully and Slater continued to fire as the enemy aircraft dived way to the starboard quarter, to be lost in 10/10th cloud below. The nightfighter was later claimed as damaged.

The rest of the trip home was uneventful, although they still had to face a landing with the two incendiary canisters in the bomb bay. Len Miller eased LL801 gently onto Mildenhall's runway at 07.45 hours without any mishaps.

Fifteen days later, LL801 was detailed for another operation against Stuttgart, but the mission was abandoned when Peter Slater reported the rear turret had gone u/s. Having jettisoned the bomb load at 20.38 hours Len Miller turned LL801 for home and landed at Mildenhall less than one hour later.

By comparison, the raids at the end of March and April were very quiet trips for LL801 and the crew. However, this situation was to change on the night of 27th/28th April, when the crew was detailed to attack Friedrichshaven, as back-up to the Pathfinder Force.

Len Miller always flew wearing engineer's overalls because they were denim with epaulettes and military style pockets. Into the seams he had sewn a number of bar compasses, the theory being that if he were shot down and captured and one of the bars was found, whilst he was being searched, he would hopefully manage to retain the others. He also had hacksaw blades inserted in his flying boots. The rest of Len Miller's survival equipment included a bag of pepper, for use against dogs or anybody else who sought to interfere with his freedom, bars of chocolate, a sheath knife, razor, shaving creme, mirror and a tooth brush. His uniform cap he kept inside his battledress under the overalls. This was how Acting Flight Lieutenant Miller was dressed on the night he flew to Friedrichshaven.

Peter Slater was not on the crew list that night. He had sometime earlier jumped over a barbed wire fence and almost left his testicles decorating the wire. It was obviously a very uncomfortable situation for him, as he was unable to sit in the tight confines of the rear turret for hours on end. Therefore, the crew had a new chap as rear gunner, a young man named Robert Watson.

Out at dispersal, Len Miller spoke with the new rear gunner and learned that this was to be Watson's first trip. Len, therefore, decided that Bert Cully, the mid-upper gunner, being experienced would occupy the rear turret and Watson could fly in the mid-upper position.

They took off from Mildenhall at 21.44 hours and headed south. Their route took them over southern England, crossing the coast at Shoreham, out over the English Channel and on a direct route across northern France to Friedrichshaven.

The flight over northern France worried Len because there was no activity from either searchlights or flak, which usually meant that nightfighters were on the prowl. The pilot was getting his usual feelings, but because Peter was not in his rightful place there was no reponse from the rear turret.

J – Jig was approximately eighty miles from the target, near Strasbourg, when they spotted the first flak bursts arcing up in search of the first wave of bombers which had arrived over the aiming point. Suddenly LL801 was illuminated by the brilliance of an exploding Lancaster nearby. A marauding Ju88 nightfighter spotted LL801 and swung in to attack, opening up with cannon fire as Len took instant evasive action.

Cannon fire raked the complete length of the fuselage and also hit the port outer engine, setting it ablaze. The fuel tank also ignited, causing fire to spread. Long tongues of flame streamed out from the trailing edge of the port wing as the pilot continued to take evasive action.

Of the action, Len Miler recalls:

> Bert Cully in the rear turret was firing non-stop at the enemy aircraft. His guns were hammering away, he must have fired 1500 rounds in one burst. He was hurling abuse and obscenities with equal intensity, then I heard him yell, 'I've got the bastard'.
>
> Realising J – Jig was doomed I ordered the crew to jump. George and Alf clipped on my chute. While they went down to the forward escape hatch, I called the rest of the crew but there was no response. George yelled up to me that he could not open the hatch cover. In my frustration, I kicked out with my legs and told him, through gritted teeth, to get the bloody thing open. The aircraft was at this time going down in a dive, but as I kicked out I must have pulled back on the column, for the Lancaster started to level out. At the same instant the hatch gave way and George, who was leaning on it, went out with it.

In an effort to leave the stricken Lancaster, Len Miller put the aircraft on auto-pilot, released his intercom cable and climbed out of his seat. It was then that he realised that Alf Beazley-Long was still sitting by the open hatch, Len gave Alf a shove and the flight engineer disappeared through the black gaping hole into the night.

Len Miller continues:

> I had a feeling 'Mac' Matthews, the wireless operator, and Sergeant Eastman, the navigator, had not left the aircraft. I think they may have been killed in the first attack. I could also hear the gunners firing. I started to make my way down the aircraft when it suddenly lurched. I climbed back into my seat and tried to pull LL801 back on to a more even keel. I plugged in my intercom and screamed a warning for them all to get out of the doomed aircraft, when the port wing folded and there was a hell of an explosion.

An eerie silence prevailed as Len Miller came to and realised he was falling as one does in the darkness of a nightmare:

> I must have been catapulted out through the top of the aircraft, and rendered semi-conscious. I felt as though I was lying on a woolly cloud and, as my sight came back into focus, I could see the stars above me spinning round and round. I now began to tumble haphazardly and therefore reached for the parachute release handle to open my 'chute. Unbeknown to me, the shoulder harness straps had become undone and the parachute pack, still clipped to the harness straps, floated about two feet above my head. I managed to pull the pack down and yanked the canopy out manually.
>
> As I floated down I had time to take stock of the situation. Looking up into the bright moonlit sky I could see George and Alf above me. Returning my gaze earthwards I could see the fiercely burning wreckage of LL801 which, with the bomb load still on board, had exploded on hitting the ground.

Len Miller landed in the forest at Rhein Wald, south of Strasbourg. The 'chute canopy caught in the top of a spruce tree and he swung down into total darkness.

Recovering quickly from the shock of the situation, the downed pilot decided on his next course of action. Grasping hold of the tree trunk with both his arms and legs, and being mindful of the injuries other people had received believing they were only just above the ground, he gingerly pressed the harness release with the intention of edging his way down the tree. Unfortunately, Len's ankle had caught in one of the 'chute shrouds as he began his descent and he immediately toppled backwards. The pilot's inverted weight made it difficult for him to release his foot, but after a few minutes' struggle he achieved his aim and promptly fell head first to the ground – some two feet below!

He remembers: 'I sat there thinking "Jesus Christ" and then, even in the seriousness of the situation, I saw the funny side of it and began to laugh.'

*

The Evasion

A short while later, Len Miller heard a clock in the distance chime three o'clock, which caused him to look at his watch. He could just see it had stopped at ten minutes past two. Extricating his 'chute from the tree created a problem, insomuch as it refused to budge from the branches. Taking out his knife, Len reached up high as he could and cut the shroud lines, which he buried along with the harness.

Slowly, Len edged away from his immediate landing area and after some distance located a holly bush in which he settled down for the remainder of the night. He slept quite well and was awoken at dawn by the chiming of the clock he had heard earlier. Reasoning that the Germans would not waste any time looking for him once they realised that the whole crew had not perished, Len decided it was time to move on.

His natural survival instincts began to take over. Locating a small stream Len waded slowly along it until he felt it was safe to climb back onto the bank. The sound of people thrashing about in the undergrowth, obviously searching for him, made him change course and make a quick but silent run for it. It was then that Len decided he would only move about at dusk, which would enable him to disappear more quickly if the need arose.

It was not until he took time out to look at his silk scarf map that Len realised that he had landed near Schoenau, a village about half a kilometre from the French bank of the River Rhine. The Lancaster had actually crashed into the ground on the river bank.

With the aid of his map and a bar compass, Len Miller set off in a southerly direction, keeping to minor roads. His instincts told him not to wander across fields, leaving tell-tale trails through the crops. He came to a small stream, where having ascertained he was alone, Len had a wash and a shave. He followed this with a meal consisting of two squares of chocolate and a Horlicks tablet. Meditating on his escape, Len rose from his reclining posture and set off again, still heading south. He arrived at a town called Neuf Brisach, not far from the German border, during the evening of April 29th.

As Len walked cautiously along the road he noticed ahead of him a German soldier riding a ~~peddle~~-cycle. The soldier was not cycling

PEDAL.

very fast and Len was able to keep him in view until the former dismounted, lent the bike against a wall and disappeared into a café.

He remembers the incident well.

> As there was nobody about, I continued walking towards the bike. As I drew level with it, I placed my hands on the handle bars and kept going, pushing the bike along by the side of me. After about fifteen yards I leapt onto the saddle and peddled like bloody hell.

Len nearly came a 'cropper' when he tried freewheeling down a slope and found that the bike had a fixed wheel and back-peddle brake. However, he soon mastered the controls and continued on his way.

Continuing to cycle south by way of the back roads, Len headed for Mulhouse. When he arrived at his destination he was aware that there was nobody about and nothing moved. It was after all between midnight and two o'clock on the morning of Sunday 30th April. His natural instincts giving way, on this occasion, to his self confidence, Len happily cycled into the centre of Mulhouse. Arriving at the end of a street off of which many other streets radiated, Len was unsure of which direction he should take. In the middle of the road stood a large lamp standard with various street and place names indicated on arms pointing in all directions. As he stood perusing the name on each arm, Len became aware of the sound of uneven footsteps approaching him. Too late to run, he froze as a German officer stepped out of the shadows and stood in front of him. Len's heart missed a beat as he suddenly remembered the curfew. The officer barked in German obviously asking a question, the smell of Schnapps penetrating the airspace between them as he stood right in front of Len. The one word Len understood was one of the place names on the signpost, the direction of which Len quickly indicated. Much to Len's surprise the German snapped '*Danke*' and swayed off into the night. Len didn't waste any time; he mounted the cycle and rode off as fast as possible before the soldier remembered the curfew and came back.

Len spent the rest of the night asleep in suitable foliage away from prying eyes, and woke refreshed and recovered from the shock of meeting the German face to face. However, that Sunday he seemed fated to meet Germans; lots of them.

Looking very much like an engineer in his overalls, Len cycled towards Altkirch, which he reached that afternoon. Totally at ease he cycled through an archway not knowing he had just ridden into the courtyard of the local barracks. There before him lined up in ranks, for inspection, were the local divisions. One or two civilians stood quietly watching the parade, and Len dismounting from the bike stood near them. Expecting his legs to give way at any moment Len lent the cycle against the wall and in turn lent himself against the cycle.

Recovering his composure and hoping his shaking legs were not too obvious, he nonchalantly scrutinised the German posters and notices on the wall, a word of which he could not read except for '*achtung*' and '*verboten*'.

After a short while, having composed himself, Len wheeled the bicycle back through the archway, remounted and cycled on. As he left Altkirch he passed an assortment of German officers, some walking with young ladies and others with comrades, but fortunately they took no notice of him.

Having ridden for some distance Len decided to sit and rest awhile amongst some trees. He recalls:

> Against my better instincts I pondered on my good fortune at not having been captured. My musing was interrupted by the distant barkings of dogs. Shielding myself with the undergrowth I spotted three Dobermanns with their handlers, whom I took to be forestry guards. I liberally sprinkled pepper around, then quickly jumped onto the bike and cycled away from the area.

Proceeding onwards, still heading south, and getting closer to the Swiss border each day, Len began to give some thought as to how he should approach the frontier. He was by this time at Wittersdorf, some ten miles from the border, and it was here he decided to abandon the bicycle and continue on foot.

The escaper's journey took him through the villages of Feldbach, Bendorft, Winkle and finally Lucelle, on the French/Swiss border, where he arrived on the evening of 1st May. His footsteps seemed to echo about him as Len walked down the dark deserted cobbled street. Suddenly, he saw ahead of him a frontier crossing point complete with sentry box and guard. With some amusement he recalls:

> I kept walking thinking, 'Jesus Christ, what do I do now?' Without realising what I was doing I carried out my smartest parade drill, stamped my feet, turned and marched away parallel to the frontier fence.

The frontier consisted of two parallel wire fences approximately eight feet high and ten feet apart. Along the top of each were three rows of 'flying' barbed-wire, angled inwards. Between each fence, at regular intervals of some two feet, were posts the same height as the fence. Except for no man's land this was the obstacle between Len Miller and Switzerland.

Len gave some thought to the sentry who ignored him when he marched away, and realised there could be another guard ahead and possibly marching towards him. No sooner had Len dived into the undergrowth and concealed himself against the base of a tree, than the sentry he had wondered about came into view. As Len watched, the guard about faced and retraced his steps. It took some twenty minutes for the sentry to reappear. He remembers:

> I decided to move further along, looking at the fence and surrounding area to find a suitable place to get across. Having got this far, I had no intention of getting caught now. At one point I found the wire of the fence nailed to a young tree. Using the wire as footrests and holding onto the tree, I gingerly climbed up and over the fence. My heart was thumping against my chest, and I felt sure the guard would hear it if he came near. I managed, by supporting myself on the tree, to reach and stand on top of the first of the posts spanning between the fences. Using the tops of the other posts as stepping stones, with a fair amount of balance and a silent prayer I jumped from post to post and dived over the wire on the far side, hitting the ground in a forward roll.

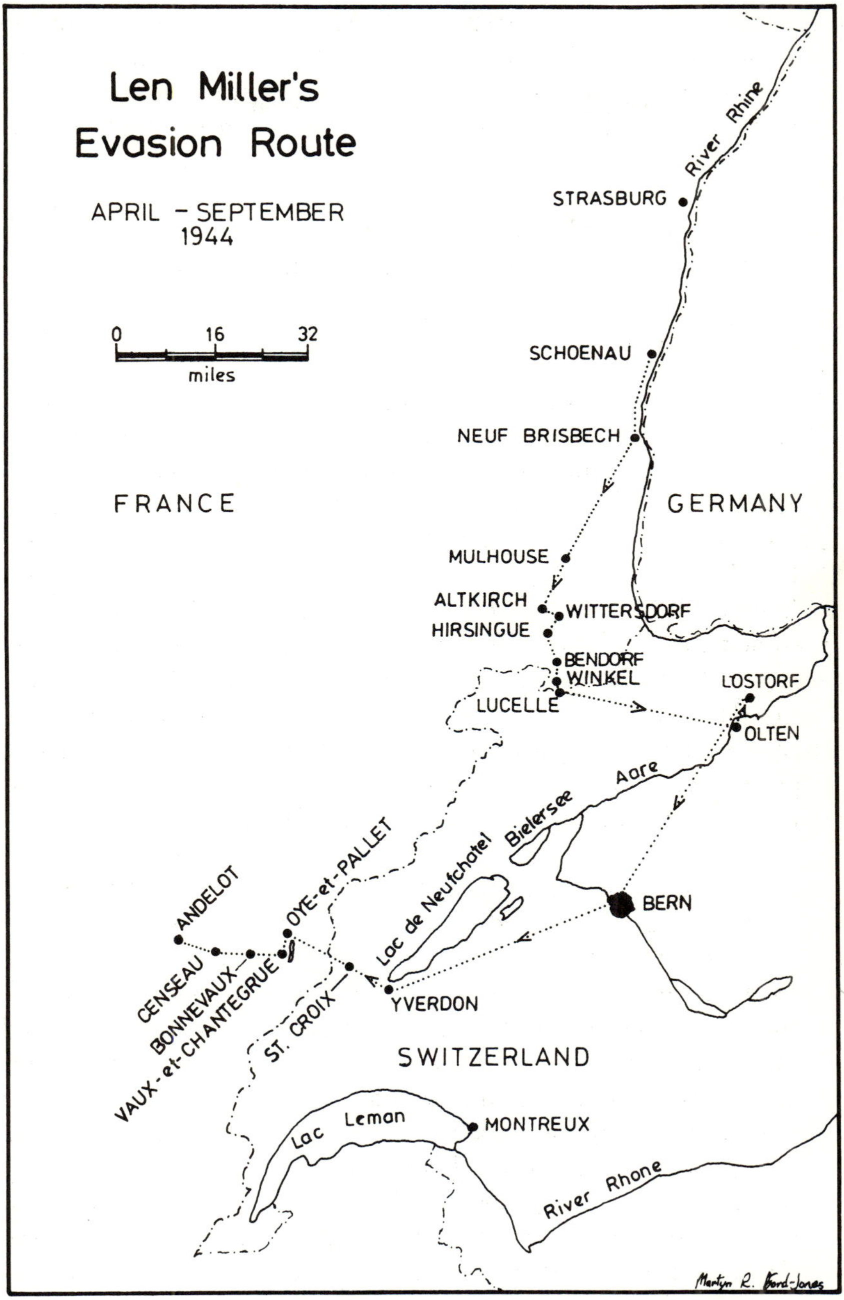
Len Miller's
Evasion Route
APRIL – SEPTEMBER
1944
0 16 32
miles
FRANCE
GERMANY
SWITZERLAND
River Rhine
STRASBURG
SCHOENAU
NEUF BRISBECH
MULHOUSE
ALTKIRCH
WITTERSDORF
HIRSINGUE
BENDORF
WINKEL
LUCELLE
LOSTORF
OLTEN
Aare
Bielersee
Lac de Neufchatel
BERN
OYE-et-PALLET
ANDELOT
CENSEAU
BONNEVAUX
VAUX-et-CHANTEGRUE
ST. CROIX
YVERDON
Lac Leman
MONTREUX
River Rhone
Martyn R. Ford-Jones

> I lay exactly where I dropped, hardly daring to breathe the only noise still being the thumping of my heart. After a short while, I got up in a crouching position, ran forward a few yards and dropped back to earth. I repeated this action two or three times until I was well away from the wire.
>
> I rested a while in the foliage to regain my breath and took stock of the situation. I had become disorientated and to some degree was not sure of my location.

Len emerged from his hiding place and pursued his course. He came to a small valley with a road just below him and a river beyond. He was slightly concerned for he could also see what looked like a blacked out power station, a fact which worried him.

Len clambered down onto the road and walked cautiously along it until he came to a large house. It was only as he drew level with the building that he realised there was a sentry box outside it. At that moment, a guard with a rifle stepped forward to challenge him, Len's instincts immediately came to the fore as he grabbed the soldier by the throat. He continues:

> The sentry was somewhat shorter than I and as I slid my arm round his neck, I stretched him up onto his toes, the rifle falling from his grasp. As I closed my arm round his windpipe, applying more pressure, he slowly began to sink to the ground. To my horror I suddenly noticed emblazoned on the side of his steel helmet the white Cross of Switzerland. I immediately released my grip and gently lowered the guard to the ground, where after a few minutes he revived.

Fortunately, there were no recriminations from the soldier or his companions who entertained and fed Len in the guard house for the rest of the night, after he had given his name, rank and number. During the course of the evening Len learned the power station he had seen earlier was in fact occupied by the Germans. It appeared that Len's instincts had guided him correctly again.

The following day, the grounded airman was escorted to a town called Pruntrut, where he was interrogated by the Military Authorities, but the only information he offered was his name, rank and number.

At an hotel where he spent the night in Pruntrut Len met several other chaps who had crossed the border into Switzerland, in the same area as himself. One of them, Flight Sergeant Colin Campbell, an air gunner, had worked his way down from Belgium with the help of the French Resistance and had crossed the frontier the night before Len.

On 3rd May, the group from the hotel was taken to Olten, where they were placed in quarantine for six days. Whilst there, their heads were completely shaved and they were sprayed all over with an anti-louse detergent.

From Olten the group was moved to Bad Lostorf, where they were placed in quarantine for a further fourteen days. Their accommodation was a castle or Schloss, complete with drawbridge and mediaeval dining hall. It housed prisoners of all the fighting nations, including Germans. There was one German in particular they called Adolph. He was a weedy little man with thick horn-rimmed glasses, who had decided that Germany was finished and he therefore made his escape to Switzerland. He was by nature a scrounger and came in useful to the group to whom he attached himself.

Colin Campbell and Len Miller had a visit from the Air Attaché to the British Embassy in Bern, on 23rd May. He took them both back to the Embassy where they met the British Consul. They were given some money and taken out to buy some civilian clothes, Len having long since discarded his overalls in favour of his RAF battle dress.

Two days later, the group was on the move again, this time to Montreux, where they were interned, until 12th August, in a large expensive hotel which overlooked the lake. There were about eighty people there, all airforce types, including a South African lieutenant and a 'penguin' (non-flying) type, who had been captured in his pyjamas.

Being an active type, Len Miller did not appreciate being interned and neither did Colin Campbell. He recalls:

> Compared to some, we lived a life of luxury and yet it became very boring. I used to get up in the morning, look across the lake and say, 'What shall we do today?' I'd see the same bloody lump

of rock and the same stretch of water that people now pay a fortune for, and I was bored to tears.

Colin Campbell and I decided we weren't going to have too much of this situation. We didn't like or get on with 'Clots', our name for the Senior British Officer in charge of us, so we devised a plan to get away, but first we needed money. We were given a small allowance but not enough to save any. We were told we could take up any pastime we wished and the authorities would pay the expenses incurred. I decided to learn to play the piano, for which I was allowed out after hours three times a week, to visit an ageing Polish woman who taught me. Each time I had a lesson she would give me a bill which I had to take back to the authorities, who then issued the money which I would hand over to the teacher at the next lesson. In the interim period between her giving me the bill and it reaching the authorities, I used to add a figure to the total. This of course was deducted, by me when the money was handed over, before settling the account for the lesson. In this manner I quickly accumulated a fair sum of money, certainly enough to purchase maps, boots, a small rucksack and two rail tickets for Ste Croix, near the border on the north-west side of Switzerland.

On 12th August, Colin Campbell and Len Miller set out on their homeward journey. They caught a train to Yverdon, where they had to change and catch another to Ste Croix. Having reached their destination, Colin and Len walked from the station down into the town where they had a good meal and stocked up with all sorts of provisions. After the money supply had been exhausted, the pair of evaders set off on foot up the mountainside. Somewhere over the top lay the French border. The climb presented no difficulties, but as they neared the frontier Len thought he heard a dog barking. He remembers:

I heard barking and thought, 'Bloody Hell, they've got dogs out' and told Colin to run. We ran and ran, but the barking stayed close to us. Out of breath, we had no choice but to stop and rest and in doing so saw that it was not a dog but a fox that was barking. We had obviously frightened each other and in our panic all taken off in the same direction.

Being somewhat experienced, Colin and Len had no difficulty in crossing into France, which they managed away from prying eyes and trigger-happy fingers, up in the high ground.

They continued heading west and arrived at Oye-et-Pallet, which is at the head of Lac de St Point. They skirted round the lake, along the west bank and on to Vaux-et-Chantegrue.

Feeling fatigued they sat down under a tree and both succumbed to the dormancy of sleep. They awoke, shivering, in the cold light of dawn. Pulling themselves together they then set off on the next stage of their journey, which was to take them through Bonnevaux, Pt Villard and Censeau.

By the time they reached Censeau, Colin Campbell was experiencing trouble with his feet and Len was having to carry Colin part of the way on his back.

Although Len Miller was a very fit man there was a limit to his endurance, and by the time they had reached Andelot-en-Montagne Len felt he could carry Colin no further.

The two men discussed their situation and decided the best course of action was to try and enlist the help of some local people. At that moment, a small boy of about seven years of age came along. He stopped and looked quizically at the two airmen, with his head on one side. Len tried his French and asked the boy where his father was. He also explained to the lad that they were RAF and asked for some food. Without a word the boy turned and ran off up the road, as fast as his young legs could carry him.

Len realised that one of two things could happen; either they would be assisted or if the boy told the wrong people both he and Colin were in trouble. Looking around him Len spotted a tree some two hundred yards away, which looked a suitable hiding place. He made his way to the tree, still carrying Colin on his back. Colin reached up and pulled himself onto the lower branches and then assisted Len by offering a helping hand.

Together they climbed up to some of the higher branches where the foliage, although thicker allowed them a view down the road in the direction of which the child had run.

Len mused to himself for a moment on the fact that he started his escape in a tree; he hoped it wasn't going to end in one.

The two men sat silently in the tree not daring to move, trying to ignore the cramp which was setting on due to the awkward positions they had adopted in sitting on the uneven branches. Eventually Len espied in the distance two men slowly ambling down the road. They appeared to be engaged in conversation, but both were casting glances towards the hedgerows as they walked. As they approached the tree they stopped walking, but continued to talk, still glancing about them. Len reasoned that he and Colin could not sit in the tree for ever; he motioned to Colin to stay where he was and slowly Len climbed down from his hiding place. Keeping his hands clear of his body, so they could see he was unarmed, Len slowly approached the two men. Having told the boy that he was an RAF airman Len saw no point in lying about his identity. The Frenchmen agreed to assist him and asked where his companion was. Len indicated towards the tree and called Colin, who climbed down and painfully made his way towards them.

They were taken to the house of a forest engineer in a village called Supt, where they were locked in a room and guarded by two men with machine guns. It was obvious the Frenchmen were dubious about their identity and so Colin and Len gave their full names, ranks and service numbers.

Len Miller comments:

> The men were obviously members of the French resistance and were playing the situation very carefully. They must have sent a message to London, for some twenty-four hours later they returned to inform us that our identities had been confirmed.

The leader of the resistance group was Captain Paul, a Frenchman by birth who spoke excellent English. He had spent some time in England and was later parachuted back into France. He asked Colin and Len to join the group in an attack on Dijon. Both refused saying that it was important for them both to get back to their respective squadrons as quickly as possible.

Both Len and Colin were provided with a bicycle each and given identity cards; Len's bore the name Louis Dupont.

Len adopted the character of a Frenchman with a terrible stutter, who had been invalided out of the services. To add to the illusion, he put a stone in his boot to make him limp. The stone also ensured that if he were stopped by the Germans, he would not limp away on the wrong leg. Colin didn't have this problem; although somewhat healed, his feet were still giving him trouble.

As it turned out, they were stopped by the Germans, but Len quickly realised that Germans didn't like people who stuttered and spat all over them. He also found that they didn't like people who picked their noses and by doing both Len and Colin managed to make a hasty departure from them.

The two evaders' next encounter was with a Communist Group who, like the previous resistance group, wanted Len and Colin to join them. Again, the pair refused giving the same reason as before. They were therefore passed on to a Free French Group.

The Free French Group was a tough and very active unit, well organised and well run by a man with the code name of 'Zabia'. Zabia was in charge of a large area in the Burgundy Region and had many successes, including capturing many German vehicles, which the group had put to better use.

The authorities in London were well aware of Len and Colin's situation, having received regular radio transmission from Zabia. Len was also aware that London knew he had become involved with the resistance group's activities. The Allies were by this time advancing, whilst some German units were attempting to get back to the Fatherland by whichever route they could find open.

Len Miller remembers:

> One day, Zabia informed me that London had transmitted a message saying that two RAF Dakotas were flying in loaded with men and equipment from a special unit, to assit in cutting off the retreating German forces in our area. Zabia, Colin and myself were then to return to England aboard one of the aircraft.
>
> At the appointed time, the two aircraft landed on the designated landing strip and disembarked soldiers and equipment. Speed being of the utmost importance we all lent a hand, and the first Dakota having discharged its duty took off into the night. We assisted the soliders with their equipment and then hurriedly clambered aboard the second aircraft, in preparation for our flight home. Just prior to take-off one of the engines coughed and spluttered and then died. No amount of

persuasion would coax it back to life. The aircraft, fortunately, was not far from the edge of the field around which were plenty of bushes and shrubbery. Whilst the wireless operator tapped out a signal to London, informing them of the situation, the rest of the group frantically cut some of the branches from the bushes and trees in an effort to camouflage the aircraft as much as possible.

The aircraft remained concealed all the following day, much to their relief. That night another aircraft flew over and dropped men from the RAF Commando Servicing Group, mechanics who were to repair the engine and return to England with the aircraft.

The various pre-arranged, dropping signals having been correctly exchanged, the men parachuted down under the cover of darkness and landed nearby. Len Miller's feelings were running high and he recalls:

> Anxious about being discovered and impatient to get away, as the shadowy figures approached I blurted out, 'Where the hell have you been?'
>
> 'Is that you, Len?' a somewhat puzzled voice asked.
>
> I replied that it was, equally puzzled, then the leader of the team stepped forward and I was amazed to see my cousin standing before me.
>
> It transpired that he was a sergeant mechanic and had been parachuting into trouble areas, doing exactly the type of work he had now come to do.

Working hard and fast the aircraft, which amazingly had not been discovered, was repaired and made ready for take-off. The branches were removed from the Dakota and the area around the field checked by Zabia's group. Without further ado the pilot pushed forward the throttles, released the brakes and lifted the aircraft into the air.

Flight Lieutenant Len Miller DFC was going home.

CHAPTER TEN

The Lucky Face

Warrant Officer Bernard Dye

Nearly every morning Bernard Dye sat on the top deck of a bus full of admiration for the young man, not much older than himself, who sat across the aisle from him wearing an RAF uniform with the coveted 'Wings' of a pilot above his left breast pocket. As the bus meandered through the streets at Ipswich, where he worked, Bernard eavesdropped on the stories related by the young man to his friends who listened eagerly to his vivid tales of combat in the 'wild blue yonder'.

Knowing he probably wouldn't make the grade as a pilot, Bernard had long since decided that when his turn came to join up he would volunteer for aircrew duty as an air-gunner. Not that he had any illusions of grandeur; he read the papers and knew what the eventual outcome might be.

When the young man suddenly ceased catching the bus Bernard thought the worse had occurred, but Bernard's admiration for his 'pilot hero' was shattered when he read in the local paper that the young man had been arrested for impersonating an RAF officer.

Bernard, nevertheless, obtained his wish when he qualified as an air-gunner at Penrhos, North Wales, during July 1943. His confidence was boosted when he read the chief instructor's remarks on his report which read, 'Has worked hard, but requires experience. Should be a good gunner'.

From Penrhos, Bernard Dye was sent to No 82 Operational Training Unit at Ossington, eight miles north-west of Newark. The course lasted a total of ten weeks, eight weeks of which covered air training and two weeks of ground studies.

On his first flight out of Ossington, his career as an air gunner very nearly came to an end before it had started. He was flying in the rear turret of Wellington HE332, which was piloted by Flight Sergeant Shaw, an Australian. The crew had been on a night cross country exercise and had been airborne for just over two hours. At 23.27 pm Flight Sergeant Shaw was making a low approach towards Ossington's runway.

He had received a wrong QFE from the ground controller and therefore had set the barometer incorrectly. As the Wellington descended even lower it flew into the tops of some trees, a short distance from the runway threshold. The aircraft was flung to the ground, killing Pilot Officer F.G. Ingham, the navigator, and Sergeant R.W.Hughes, the bomb aimer. The other four members of the crew were injured and taken to the station sick bay.

Young Sergeant Dye was not badly hurt, but sustained severe shock, which confined him to bed. Bernard progressed well and three days later was sitting up, wondering how the world in general was getting on. Suddenly, a great commotion broke loose on the airfield. Fire and ambulance bells were ringing and Bernard could hear vehicles racing past at high speed. He could also hear the excited cries of people running in the same direction as the vehicles. Bernard was curious to know what was going on, but had no way of knowing until a male nurse came in and related the story.

It transpired that Wellington BK399 was sitting at its dispersal with the engines running, in preparation for a routine training flight. Flying Officer O.L. MacFarlane, the New Zealand instructor, and Sergeant L.W.C. Wheeler, the trainee pilot, were running through the final cockpit checks, prior to taxying out for take off, when there was a sharp bang from within the fuselage. One of the crew in picking up the Very pistol, squeezed the trigger not knowing, in the best traditions of crime fiction, that the gun was loaded. Within minutes, the dope fabric-covered geodetic fuselage was ablaze, and ammunition was exploding all over the place.

Two crash tenders and a domestic fire appliance were at the scene within a few minutes, but the fire had too great a hold. Even the presence of pumps from the Newark National Fire Service could not save the blazing aircraft. Fortunately, the whole crew escaped without injury except to pride! When Bernard heard the story he said to the nurse, 'Good grief, I don't think I would want to fly with a crew like that'.

Sergeant Bernard Dye, had no illusions of grandeur about being an air gunner.

Having been declared fit, Bernard was released from the sick bay and told to report to the Chief Ground Instructor. The CGI a squadron leader, informed Bernard that a number of crews required a new mid-upper gunner. The photographs of the crews concerned were pinned to a notice board, and the CGI told Bernard he could actually choose the crew with whom he wished to fly. Bernard perused the pictures and finally picked a crew, captained by a Sergeant Wheeler. 'Why that one?' asked the CGI.

'Because I trained with Joe Hayes, the rear gunner, and would like to be on his crew,' replied Bernard.

'You do realise,' said the CGI, 'that's the crew that had the fire in their aircraft!' Bernard's heart sank but he remained silent; he had made his choice.

On 13th November 1943, Sergeant Wheeler and his crew were sent to No 1651 Conversion Unit at Waterbeach, where they converted to Stirling bombers. The routine of Waterbeach consisted of flying 'Circuits and bumps' and night cross-country exercises. It was whilst flying on one of the latter exercises that the port inner engine cut and Wheeler landed the Stirling on three engines.

In December, the crew were posted to XV Squadron at Mildenhall, but due to the fact that the squadron was re-equipping with Lancaster Bombers, they were sent off to No 3 Lancaster Finishing School at Feltwell for a conversion course.

Bernard Dye and crew returned to Mildenhall in January 1944. They spent the first week settling in to their new accommodation and finding their way around the base. Flying training out of Mildenhall started on 8th January. The various exercises continued including an escape exercise which took place during the last week of January. The crews were taken out from the base on a lorry and deposited some ten miles from the camp. The intention was for them to get back to Mildenhall, without being caught by the police who were actively looking for them.

Bernard teamed up with Joe Hayes, and together they set off. As they were walking down a narrow country road, they saw in the distance a man in uniform riding a bike. Bernard and Joe departed in opposite directions into the hedgerows either side of the road. The cyclist turned out to be a postman, who stopped his bike almost between the two concealed airmen, to relieve himself. Bernard and Joe were both carrying 'thunderflashes' in their pockets, and Bernard indicated to Joe he was going to light one. As they went off, the postman, who had not finished his business, grabbed his mailbag, picked up his bike and made off down the road, much to the enjoyment of the two pranksters concealed in the hedgerows.

On the night of 20th February, the name of Sergeant Wheeler and his crew appeared on the battle order for a raid on Stuttgart. The day was spent preparing both aircraft and kit for this, their first, mission. Apart from the butterflies in the tummy everything seemed to be in order. Bernard Dye and the crew went through the pre-operation ritual of an egg and bacon meal and the mission briefing. Everyone took careful note of what was said, jotting down the important factors. An hour before take-off, Sergeant Wheeler's crew were on board the Lancaster, each man alone with his thoughts as he tested the equipment at his respective station. Their allotted preparatory tasks completed, the crew assembled outside the aircraft for a pre-take-off smoke with the ground crew. Some joking ensued but the laughter was forced. Then the time came to climb back into the aircraft. Sergeant Wheeler started the four Merlin engines, ran through the cockpit drill with the flight engineer and when ready began to taxi round the perimeter track towards the runway to line up for take-off. Bernard, sitting high in the mid-upper turret could see Lancasters in front of and behind him, all snaking round the peri-track to the take-off point. But once again Bernard Dye faced a setback to the start of his operational career. There was a difference of opinion amongst the crew which could not be settled and take-off had to be aborted. Just over a month later the pilot, Sergeant Wheeler, was lost over Berlin.

By that time, however, Bernard Dye had been posted to No 622 Squadron and a new crew. The pilot was an older man who Bernard recognised from his days at Ossington as one who always wore white gloves when he flew and Bernard used to refer to him as 'The Duke of Purduker'. At least he has a lucky face, thought Bernard when he met Arthur Horton, the pilot. How right he was.

CHAPTER ELEVEN

The Luck Held

Flying Officer Arthur Horton

When Arthur Horton joined No 622 Squadron in February 1944, he was almost 32 years of age, an old man by comparison to the other members of aircrew, some of whom had yet to have their twentieth birthdays.

Arthur was born on 18th June 1912 at Leeds where his father had a gents' hairdressing business. He attended St Luke's Elementary School at Beeston Hill, where he became eligible to sit a scholarship. Unfortunately, Arthur's father vetoed the idea saying that further education was not necessary. One Friday during his fourteenth year, Arthur finally left school and by 4.30 pm that same day was working in his father's shop, where he served his unpaid apprenticeship until he was nineteen.

In 1936, at the age of 24, Arthur was working for himself in a business he had bought for £120, but thoughts of moving into another profession were in his mind. He therefore enrolled for maths classes at Leeds University, on his half-day.

The outbreak of war, in September 1939, altered the course of many lives and Arthur's was no exception. In May 1940, he volunteered to join the Royal Air Force. He continued his studies at University, and with the assistance of the local Air Training Corp, learned the rudimentaries of drill, morse and navigation.

In April 1941, Arthur Horton received his papers and along with many others reported to Padgate for kitting out and basic drill. Thinking his educational limitations would preclude him from becoming a pilot Arthur volunteered for training as a wireless op/air gunner. However, when a call came for volunteers to train as pilots he thought he would try his luck. Arthur's application proved successful and in October 1941 he was posted to the Aircrew Receiving Centre in London. The following month found him at Aberystwyth with No 16 Initial Training Wing. Arthur's luck held as he found he was able to absorb and keep up with the various studies, which included maths, navigation, law, administration and morse.

On 1st April 1942, having successfully passed the ITW exams Arthur Horton was posted to No 21 Elementary Flying Training School at Booker, where three days later he made his first flight in a DH82 Tiger Moth. A further seventeen days later he flew solo.

The summer of 1942 saw Arthur travelling across Canada and America. His destination was an airfield in the Mojave Desert near a small town called Lancaster. At the airfield, known as War Eagle field, further ground and flying instruction took place including Arthur's final check flight. He passed the course and on 23rd December 1942 was presented with his Wings and sergeant's stripes.

Returning to England in January 1943, Sergeant Horton filled in time with an assortment of duties until 4th May when he was posted to Lulsgate Bottom for conversion on to twin engined aircraft.

Training flights did not always go according to plan. During a check flight on an Airspeed Oxford with an instructor, the rudder control stuck. The instructor being somewhat taller than Arthur was able to free the control with a hefty kick. Having landed Arthur suggested having the control checked, but the instructor said it should be all right and sent Arthur off on his solo. The first circuit went well but as the Oxford was taking off for the second circuit the rudder jammed. As the ground school buildings loomed up a quick decision was called for, whether to hit them or raise the undercarriage and attempt to climb over them whilst kicking the rudder control for all he was worth. Arthur chose the latter and almost made it. The retracting undercarriage just touched the apex of the roof. The aircraft shot up into the air, turned over on to its back and came down nose first into the ground behind the buildings. Hanging in his harness, Arthur wondered, in his bemused state, why no one came to his aid. Then he thought he

(*Left*) Flying Officer Arthur Horton.

(*Below*) end of tour photograph with Lancaster LM241, LS-Q, on 12th August 1944.
L to R Sergeant Grant, unknown, Flying Officer Horton, Sergeant White, Sergeant Parsons, Sergeant Monether, unknown, Sergeant Gray, unknown, Sergeant Dye.

could hear water dripping – water? *Petrol*! He released the straps and tore his way through the wreckage and was half way across the airfield, running like hell, before the rescue teams arrived. Result of the accident was two black eyes, a cut head and badly cut hands received when tearing his way through the wreckage. Arthur's luck held.

Training continued with postings to No 82 Operational Training Unit at Ossington, where Arthur crewed up and flew Wellingtons, then to No 1657 Conversion Unit to fly Stirlings. A conversion course on Lancaster took place at Feltwell.

On Friday 4th February 1944, Arthur, who by now had been promoted to flight sergeant, and his crew reported for duty at RAF Mildenhall where they were to join No 622 Squadron.

Flight Sergeant Horton flew his first two operations as second pilot to Pilot Officer Sutton. Arthur has cause to remember those trips.

> During my first two Lanc' trips as 'second dicky', it became very obvious that after several hours in the air, one's bladder began to clamour for relief. This had to be done by making the lengthy trip through the aircraft to the elsan situated near the rear turret. For use by the five of us at the front of the aircraft we acquired a gallon can which was painted yellow and named '7th heaven'. This we used to pass round some 20 minutes before we reached the target. (Had we got into serious trouble and had to get out in a hurry, a full bladder was the last thing we wanted.) Having filled the can it then suited our peculiar sense of humour to tip the contents down the flare chute, a practical demonstration of 'pissing on them from a great height'. It helped morale.

The first of those two raids was on Stuttgart, the second to Schweinfurt, both raids producing heavy flak and a lot of fighter activity. The raids left Arthur, as pilot, in no doubt as to his responsibilities towards his crew. Therefore, when it became necessary to replace two of his team he did so without any qualms. The new mid-upper gunner, nineteen-year-old Bernard Dye, and the navigator, Ken Monether, were quickly accepted by the rest of the crew and under Arthur's guidance they lived, trained and flew together as a close knit crew.

The crew's first mission was a raid on the marshalling yards at Laon on the night of 10th/11th April. Approximately 86 aircraft took part in the raid which was led by Group Captain Cheshire. Although the flak was reported as moderate, nightfighters were very active, and the mid-upper gunner reported sighting a Ju88. No action occurred and the crew returned safely.

Their second mission was an operation against Essen and a complete contrast to the previous one. The searchlights were weaving across the night sky in search of the aerial intruders. The nightfighters were also airborne, engaged in the same search. A Messerschmitt 110 strayed too close to Lancaster LM477 and Bernard Dye fired a short burst from his mid-upper turret, the Me110 abruptly disappeared into the cover of darkness.

Flight Sergeant Horton set course for home with the crew keeping a watchful eye for nightfighters. What occurred next is recalled by Arthur Horton.

> Suddenly, we were attacked by what appeared to be four stubby winged rocket projectiles. I did not know what they were or what they contained and told the gunners not to fire in case they exploded. Whatever manoeuvre I put the aircraft through the projectiles followed. One of them disappeared, but for at least fifty miles, out of France and over the coast, I put the Lancaster through twists and turns that it was never designed to do. The throttles were through the 'gate' and over that fifty miles we lost some 14,000 feet of height. At one point, I called Dave Parsons, the flight engineer, 'What about the engines, Dave?' I asked, concerned for we were not supposed to run them at full bore for more than three minutes. His typical and laconic reply filtered back through my headphones, 'F … the engines'.
>
> The aircraft was vibrating and shaking due to the speed which must have reached 300 mph.
>
> Shortly after crossing the coast, the projectiles lost speed and fell away out of sight, much to our relief. Once again, the Horton luck had held and we landed at Tuddenham near Mildenhall.

May 21st saw an operation against Duisberg, during which Bernard Dye sighted two Ju88's and opened fire at one of them. Over the target area Arthur's Lancaster was caught by the blue beam of the master searchlight. To most crews this signified the luck had run out, for moments later flak would come up from every available gun. True to form, the guns opened fire and some of the flak hit the self-sealing petrol tank, but by skilful evasive action and corkscrewing Arthur escaped the tenacious beam and returned safely to Mildenhall. His luck still continued to hold.

On 27th May, Arthur was assigned charge of Lancaster LL859. The crew's hearts sank when they saw GI-Q on the fuselage, since a phenomenon peculiar to No 622 Squadron was that whenever an aircraft was coded GI-Q it failed to return from operations.

Flight Sergeant Horton had flown Q – Queenie on two previous occasions but both were training exercises; now she was to be his permanent charge for as long as the luck held. They flew their first mission in Queenie that same night when they attacked gun emplacements at Boulogne.

The following day, Q – Queenie was on the battle order for a raid against the marshalling yards at Angers. Arthur Horton lifted Q – Queenie off the runway at Mildenhall at 18.40 hours and, with the rest of the squadron, flew at low level towards the south coast. As it was late May, the evenings were still light and as the formation roared low overhead cars stopped and people ran into their gardens to wave with great enthusiasm. The squadron flew on to Land's End and crossed the Bay of Biscay staying low to avoid detection by German radar.

When Q – Queenie arrived over Angers the target was being remarked. Arthur Horton commenced his bombing run under the instruction of Brian Gray, the bomb aimer. Arthur recalls:

> We were running up to the aiming point with Aussie giving the usual instructions, 'Left, left, ri-right, steady, steady', then at the last second, his favourite epithet 'Pig's arse'! This meant he was not satisfied and had not released the bombs. I then had to close the bomb doors, ease the Lancaster out of the bomber stream, make a 180 degree turn and head back until we could make another 180 degree turn and rejoin the stream for another attempt. During this time, Aussie would be entreated by the rest of the crew in very basic Anglo-Saxon terms, not to miss the aiming point on the second run.

Brian Gray didn't miss. He released the load from 8,500 feet onto the marshalling yards below. As death and destruction rained down from the bomb bays of the Lancasters, emergency vehicles could be seen, by the crews, speeding along the roads leading to the target area.

After a spot of leave, during which Arthur had been commissioned, the crew returned to operations on 14th June when they attacked the docks at Le Havre.

The raid was carried out in a clear night sky with a full moon, which assisted Group Captain Leonard Cheshire who was leading the attack, and marking the target, in his Mustang aircraft.

Everything went well for Arthur Horton and he and the crew were very pleased with the raid. As they flew home, Bernard Dye, in the mid-upper turret, could see other Lancasters flying in formation on either side of Queenie. Suddenly, two Ju88s dived in from astern to attack a Lancaster about 600 yards off Queenie's rear port quarter. Sergeant Dye reported their presence to Arthur Horton, and continued to watch the action. Bernard could not see any tracer emanating from the rear turret, but informed Arthur that the mid-upper gunner was 'blazing away'. The first Ju88 started to emit smoke which immediately gave way to fire. Tongues of flame licked the aircraft as it peeled over and crashed into the sea. The action was duly entered in Queenie's log. Without any hesitation, the second nightfighter swung into the attack, to avenge its comrade's demise. The mid-upper gunner kept firing and much to Bernard Dye's astonishment, it too burst into flame and spun down to share the same watery grave. This action was also recorded in Queenie's log.

Back at Mildenhall, at the debriefing, the crew were relating the night's events. As Bernard Dye told his story the door burst open and a tired but happy crew entered the room exclaiming, in a state of excitement, that they had shot down two Ju88s. When the times and co-ordinates were checked, they were found to correspond.

The following day, Arthur and his crew participated in a raid on the marshalling yards at Valenciennes, which they bombed from 8,500 feet.

A raid on Montdidier was called off by the master bomber, a few minutes after midnight on 18th June. Feeling somewhat peeved at having reached the target and not being allowed to bomb, Pilot Officer Hortun turned Queenie for home and brooded on the prospect of having to land with a full bomb load. His musing was interrupted by the crew who had suddenly realised that it was in fact Arthur's 32nd birthday.

Various targets in France were bombed throughout the rest of June including Rimeulx on the 24th, when the V1 flying bomb launch sites were bombed, and Biennes on the 27th. It was during the latter raid that Queenie was attacked twice by the same Me110. On both occasions, Bernard Dye and Brian Grant, the rear gunner, were waiting, and as the nightfighter dived into the attack, both gunners opened fire. The Me110 was seen to fall away and was later claimed as damaged.

Three nights later Arthur Horton and his crew were detailed for a raid on Villers-Bocage, the target being the Panzer Divisions and troop concentrations in the area. Due to the smoke, dust, rubble and debris being thrown into the air during the attack, there was not a lot for the crews to report when they returned to Mildenhall.

Targets in France were still on the battle order during July, starting with a low-level daylight attack on the V1 rocket sites at Wizernes, on the 5th of the month. During the attack, Sergeant Jock White, the wireless operator, was on look-out in the astro dome. He spotted and quickly reported a FW190 emerging from the clouds. The enemy aircraft was flying at 7,500 feet, the same height as Queenie and in the same direction. It gave no indication of having seen the Lancaster. Bernard Dye traversed his turret, cocked the guns and opened fire. A shriek of delight emanated from the astro-dome as Jock White yelled, 'You've hit him, keep firing'. Even in daylight the flashes from the gun muzzles began to destroy Bernard Dye's vision as he continued to fire, but he was able to see the FW190 dive, apparently out of control, before it disappeared into cloud below.

The Horton luck continued to hold.

A raid against Hamburg was scheduled for the night of 20th July. The names of Pilot Officer Horton and his crew did not however appear on the battle order, but that of Queenie did.

Another crew were to fly LL859 over Germany that night. They took off with the squadron but the jinx returned and Queenie did not. Lancaster LL859 Q – Queenie was listed as missing on 21st July and officially struck off charge two days later.

Arthur Horton was promoted to the rank of flying officer on 25th July. He also took charge of a new aircraft the same day. The Lancaster carried the serial LM241 and was coded ... Q – Queenie! As he was to fly her on operations that night, an air test lasting 45 minutes was flown during the afternoon in preparation for an attack on Stuttgart.

During the raid, the aircraft was hit by flak but returned safely to Mildenhall. Repairs were carried out and Queenie was ready for the operation detailed for the night of 29th July. The target was again to be Stuttgart. Of this mission, Arthur recalls:

> It was the only time our navigator went wrong. We had flown over the target before the raid started and had overshot by about 50 miles. The bomb aimer was reporting that there was nothing to be seen, only darkness, when the gunners advised me that target indicators were going down behind us and that there was intense activity going on in the form of bomb bursts, guns firing and searchlights. I turned the aircraft onto a reciprocal course in order to rejoin the main stream, but by the time we were over the aiming point the raid was almost over. We dropped our bombs from 22,000 feet above most of the flak. I think we must have been over the target alone, this thought being verified as we crossed the coast of Normandy on the return journey, on a beautiful summer morning, with not another aircraft in sight. We could have been on a training flight, no guns fired at us and the Luftwaffe left us alone.
>
> We arrived home very late and with barely enough fuel left to fill a cigarette lighter. Bomber Command reportedly lost 52 aircraft that night, but our luck held.

Further raids on targets in France took place during the first week in August, including attacks against oil storage depots and further flying bomb sites.

On 11th August, Flying Officer Horton and his crew participated in a daylight operation on the marshalling yards at Lens. They bombed from 15,000 feet and then turned for home, arriving back at Mildenhall after having been airborne for only 3 hours and 50 minutes.

Arthur taxied Q – Queenie back to her dispersal and shut down the engines, as it turned out for the last time. As the crew disembarked from the aircraft they were congratulated on having completed their tour of operations with the squadron.

Lancaster LM241 Q – Queenie was assigned to another crew. Both the aircraft and crew were lost two weeks later during an attack against Russelsheim.

Arthur's luck held.

CHAPTER TWELVE

The First Hurdle

Flight Sergeant Harry T. Bysouth

The Lancaster emerged out of the murk for the second time as it attempted to land again on the runway at Lakenheath. Sergeant Harry Bysouth was still sitting in the mid-upper turret unable to see anything due to the poor visibility. He then made the best decision he was ever likely to make. Harry:

> At that moment, I decided to leave my turret. I climbed down and as my feet touched the fuselage floor it all happened.

The aircraft ran off the runway, the undercarriage sunk into the soft ground and ED383 cartwheeled over onto its back, in a crescendo of noise and splintering glass and wrenching metal. The last thing Harry remembered was being thrown about like a pea on a drum. Slowly, the blurred figure bending over Harry took the shape of Franklin, the navigator who, although slightly injured, was endeavouring to extricate Harry from the wreckage. At that moment, the rescue crews arrived, cut Harry free from the twisted fuselage and placed him in the waiting ambulance. Looking back through the open ambulance doors Harry could see flames flickering over the mangled remains of ED383. As Harry watched, he saw his past dance in the flames, then he receded into the oblivion of a faint.

*

Harry Bysouth was born in Tottenham, North London, on 2nd December 1919. He attended All Hallows Boys School, where he

Sergeant Harry Bysouth had an inauspicious start to his career as an air gunner, but later won the DFM.

found some of the lessons more difficult than others. However, he persevered until he was fourteen years of age and then decided to venture into the adult world.

When he was eighteen, Harry joined a searchlight unit of the Territorial Army, based at Tottenham. He stayed with the unit until July 1938, when he left to join the Royal Air Force. The RAF sent Harry to Grantham for training, on completion of which he was directed to North Weald as 615782 Aircraftman H. Bysouth, assigned to general duties.

In 1936, a suggestion for a national balloon defence organisation was approved by the Committee of Imperial Defence. This was put into operation during March the following year and was, initially, manned by members of the Auxiliary Air Force. Just before the outbreak of war, Harry was transferred to a balloon squadron based at Dulwich, South London. He was later transferred to another balloon squadron in Manchaster. It was whilst he was at Dulwich that Harry met a charming and very attractive young lady named Renee Clark. Renee made quite an impact on Harry and they became close friends.

As the war progressed into 1940, Harry thought about the situation and his future. He felt he could serve his King and Country in a better capacity than balloon operator, and therefore volunteered for aircrew. He was to wait a year before he was called to Manchaster for an interview. He was told that he would be notified of a decision in due course, but for the meantime was posted to another balloon site near the Barrett sweet factory at Wood Green, not far from his Tottenham home. Whilst based at Manchester, Harry had decided to make his relationship with Renee a permanent one; they married in November 1941.

Harry's application for aircrew was eventually vetted and approved and he was instructed to report to the Aircrew Receiving Centre at Viceroy Court, St John's Wood. Because his academic qualifications were not totally adequate for pilot training, Harry was sent to St John's College, Cambridge, for intensive tuition. The going was hard and Harry experienced difficulties in keeping up with the studies, so he decided to remuster to air gunner. Initially, he was sent to Brighton and then Bridlington before being sent to No 1 Air Gunnery School at Pembrey, where he arrived on 18th

July 1943. Eleven days later, Harry had his first experience of flying when he went up in a Blenheim, for an air to air exercise. He was airborne for 1 hour 25 minutes during which he fired 200 rounds of ammunition. A further sixteen flights were made before the course ended on 27th August.

Harry converted to Wellingtons at No 1483 (Bomber) Flight at Newmarket before reporting to No 1657 Conversion Unit, at Stradishall, where Stirlings were flown. It was at Stradishall as a sergeant that Harry Bysouth joined the crew of Flight Sergeant Richards, as mid-upper gunner. Upon being declared ready for operations the crew was posted to No 622 Squadron at Mildenhall.

In accordance with the rule that every pilot new to operations should fly his first mission with an experienced crew, Flight Sergeant Richards was detailed to fly with Flight Sergeant Morecombe and his crew on the night of 18th/19th November 1943, on a raid against Mannheim. Unhappily, Flight Sergeant Richards was killed when Stirling EF128, in which he was flying, failed to return.

The feelings within Harry on joining an operational squadron ebbed away as the reality of the loss of his pilot and what his future held sank in. Being without a captain to lead the crew, Harry was returned to a conversion unit, No 1651 based at Wratting Common.

On the 1st December, Harry made two flights in Stirling R9147. The pilot on the second flight was Tony Davis, a young man from Shrewsbury. Harry flew regularly with Davis and took a liking to him. When Davis was posted to Feltwell, at the end of December, for conversion to Lancasters, Harry had no hesitation in accepting Davis' offer of joining the crew as mid-upper gunner. The rest of the crew consisted of Sergeant J. 'Geordie' Carrott, the navigator, Sergeant Doug Haydock, the flight engineer, from Swinton near Manchester, Sergeant W. 'Bill' Geraghty, the bomb aimer, Warrant Officer G. Franklin, the wireless operator, from New Zealand and Sergeant Ernest 'Mick' Harbridge, the rear gunner. On completion of the course at Feltwell, in mid-January 1944, Harry returned to Mildenhall when Davis and the rest of the crew were posted to No XV Squadron.

The same feelings within Harry returned as he thought of his

Sergeant Tony Davis, killed on the night of 26th February 1944, when Lancaster ED383, LS-C, crashed at Lakenheath.

previous posting to Mildenhall. For the first month, various exercises were carried out which included practice bombing, fighter affiliation and 'bull's eyes'. Davis also few his first mission with an experienced crew and to Harry's relief, returned safely.

On 20th February, the battle order for a raid on Stuttgart that night was posted. The names of Davis and his crew were on it. Sergeant Harry Bysouth recalls:

> I sat alone in the mid-upper turret high on the back of the Lancaster, my stomach churning, the back of my throat dry and various thoughts racing through my mind. 'You're on your own now, mate', a voice in my head told me. I endeavoured to remain calm as I thought 'This is what I've trained for and now I'm here'.

The Merlin engines roared as Sergeant Davis pushed forward the throttles and released the brakes of Lancaster LL781. At ten minutes past midnight on 21st February, with full fuel tanks and bomb load, B781 lifted off Mildenhall's long runway.

With Harry at its controls, the top turret rotated back and forth, his keen but inexperienced eyes scanning the darkness for any potential intruder. A voice in his headphones broke Harry's concentration; somebody informed the pilot he could smell petrol. Davis called the flight engineer for his comments, Doug Haydock replied in the affirmative. Davis unsure what to do asked each member of the crew for their respective opinions. By this time, LL781 was out over the North Sea and Sergeant Davis eventually decided to return to base.

Their early return was an unwelcome one, as Harry remembers.

> The whole crew was paraded before the commanding officer who gave us a good 'rollicking' for our action. The smell of petrol was normal, due to the full tanks and would have dissipated in due time. Because of our inexperience, however, no further action was taken, the lesson having been learned.

For Harry this was an inauspicious start to his tour of operations, bearing in mind the false start due to the loss of Flight Sergeant

Richards, but unbeknown to Harry and the rest of the crew there was worse to come.

Four nights after their early return, the crew's names appeared again on the battle order for a raid on Augsburg. At 21.30 hours, Sergeant Davis lifted Lancaster ED383 off the runway. Ignoring the smell of petrol and mindful of the previous raid, everybody carried out their respective duties as the aircraft headed for Germany. The raid progressed well for the novice crew, as it did for the 593 other crews participating. The weather was clear and the Pathfinder marking was accurate, allowing the attacking force to completely destroy the centre of the weakly defended target. Davis's crew bombed without mishap and the tension of being over enemy territory for the first time subsided as the Lancaster came within sight of the English coastline, on the return journey.

It was then the problem started. Owing to poor weather conditions at Mildenhall, Davis received a signal diverting ED383 to Lakenheath. With the visibility not much better than at Mildenhall, Davis approached the airfield perimeter, keeping the aircraft straight and level. Harry suddenly heard the excited warning from the flight engineer, that the flaps would not fully extend. Davis overshot and made a second approach; the problem re-occurred. Doug Haydock warned Davis that they did not have enough fuel for another attempt and that they would have to land. It was then that Harry made the decision that was to save his life. As he climbed down from the mid-upper turret to take up his crash position, the Lancaster hit the runway hard and fast.

With the exception of Warrant Officer Franklin, who had been thrown clear and 'Mick' Harbridge, who was trapped in the rear turret, the rest of the crew had been killed instantly. Unfortunately, the badly injured rear gunner died the following day. Harry Bysouth was taken to the station sick bay where he was examined by the medical officer. In pain and fearful of what his injuries might be, Harry decided to ask for a drink. He reasoned that if it was refused it was a fair chance he had stomach injuries. His request brought forth a cup of hot sweet tea, which allayed his fears. He had suffered facial injuries, bruising and concussion and was transferred, first to Ely and then to Littleport Hospital, for treatment.

Franklin recovered from the crash fairly quickly and was preparing for his return to operational flying. Prior to going up on an air-test he visited Harry, who was still undergoing treatment and trying to regain his nerve for his own return to operational flying. Harry Bysouth remembers:

> Franklin told me he was going up with Flight Lieutenant Jarvis in Lancaster D – Dog on an air test, as the usual wireless operator of that crew was sick. As Franklin left the room he raised his hand in salutation and said, 'Don't worry, I'll be all right. See you later'.

With a feeling of apprehension, Harry watched his friend depart swinging his flying helmet in carefree mood as he went. How can he, Harry wondered with envy, take this first flight so light-heartedly. Within an hour of Franklin leaving, a loud explosion was heard and a great pall of black smoke rose into the air. Flight Lieutenant Jarvis's Lancaster had crashed; there were no survivors!

When Harry received the news he was devastated. First Richards was killed, then Davis and the others, now Franklin. Harry felt alone and empty. He had lost his 'family' and now wondered what the future would hold. His only comfort came from his young wife, Renee.

During a period of leave, Harry carefully considered his future and decided to stay on operations. That's what he had trained for, the war still had to be won and aircrew were still needed, but he was not totally sure whether he was ready to return 'ops' yet.

Harry Bysouth returned to Mildenhall during mid-April and started to fly again. His first trip was as a passenger on a cross country exercise with Flight Sergeant Thompson, aboard Lancaster LM465, U, the aircraft in which Thompson was to be shot down two months later.

On 29th April, Sergeant Bysouth flew a fighter affiliation exercise and a 'bullseye' with Pilot Officer Jones and his crew. A week later, Jones and his crew failed to return from a raid.

During the morning of 10th May, Harry was approached by Flight Lieutenant Alan Amies, the pilot of a crew who required a rear gunner for their next mission. Harry carried out an air test that morning with the crew, but was indecisive about the actual raid. He was swayed by pressure from Flight Lieutenant Amies, who agreed to accompany Harry to the MO's office for clearance to return to active duty. As they walked they talked, but Harry had doubts. Upon reaching the MO's office, Harry was about to knock on the door, he hesitated, turned to the pilot, made his apology and stated he did not feel settled inside himself and wanted a few more days. Feeling somewhat disgruntled, Flight Lieutenant Amies stalked off never to be seen again; he and his crew failed to return from the raid that night. Harry experienced a cold shiver when he heard the news. As he reflected on what might have been, he wondered if he was some form of jinx to other aircrew. In his mind he had still not really cleared the first hurdle of becoming operational.

Harry was sent on leave with the knowledge that when he returned he would be crewed-up, but it was an unfortunate incident which took him to his next crew.

On 30th June 1944, Lancaster ME695 was flying in formation with a number of other aircraft north of Ford, in Sussex, when it was struck from below by another aircraft. The other aircraft, a Lancaster from No 514 Squadron, was attempting to join the formation when it collided with ME695 of XV Squadron, killing the rear gunner Flight Sergeant A. Pawlyk. Although the crew were ordered to bale out, the pilot, Flight Sergeant Johnny French, a tall, powerfully built man, managed to regain control of the spiralling XV Squadron aircraft and made a difficult but safe landing. Harry joined this crew to replace the dead rear gunner and returned to operational flying on the night of 28th July. The rest of Johnny French's crew consisted of Flight Sergeant Geoff Stubbings, navigator, Flight Sergeant Ron 'Tug' Wilson, mid-upper gunner, Sergeant J. Hope, wireless operator, Flight Sergeant F. Smith, bomb aimer, and Flight Sergeant Ted Pavey, flight engineer.

When the battle order for that night was posted, Harry went cold; the target was Stuttgart. His first 'op' with Davis had been Stuttgart, on the night they had returned early due to the heavy smell of petrol.

Again, Harry remembers those feelings:

Pilot and plane. Flight Sergeant Johnny French (*above*) leans out of the cockpit window of his Lancaster NG364, LS-P. (*below*)

> I sat in the rear turret, my stomach churning, the back of my throat dry, I thought to myself, 'I've been here before'.

His breathing was deep but even, he was perspiring slightly, trying to push thoughts of the past out of his mind. At 21.30 hours, Johnny French lifted Lancaster LL923, O, into the air and set course for Stuttgart. The Lancaster had only been airborne for some 35 minutes when it developed a malfunction and French informed the crew he was returning to base. The problem was a leak in the starboard petrol tank. Although French struck Harry as a confident man and a competent pilot, Harry's anxiety began to increase, and he prayed 'not again'. Flight Sergeant Smith, the bomb aimer, jettisoned four 1,000 lb bombs over the Wash at 22.22 hours, from a height of 5,000 feet.

Harry recalls:

> I need not have worried, for even with two 1,000 lb and four 500 lb bombs still in the bomb bay, Johnny French made a smooth landing at Mildenhall.

It was not until 3rd August that Harry Bysouth was to complete an operation without incident. The target was a flying bomb storage deport at Bois De Cassan and although the mission was carried in daylight, with clear visibility, both the aircraft and crew returned to base safely. He had finally cleared the hurdle.

Harry flew against targets in France during the first two weeks of August, then on 15th August he participated in a raid against St Trond, the Luftwaffe night-fighter base in Belgium. The raid was successful and of the 1,004 aircraft which took part only three Lancasters were lost. This mission was in support of Operation Anvil, the invasion of southern France by US and French forces, which started in the early hours of that same day.

Harry Bysouth completed a tour of 29 operations against targets in France, Germany and Holland. In early September 1944, he was promoted to flight sergeant and was awarded the Distinguished Flying Medal on 21st May 1945.

CHAPTER THIRTEEN

Operations Manna and Exodus

Flight Sergeant D.A. (Pat) Russell

Whilst still in the sixth form at Hitchin Grammar School, 17-year-old Pat Russell travelled to London, on 29th November 1941, to volunteer, at Adastral House, for pilot training. His application was accepted and he was told to report for a medical on 4th December. Five days later, a further medical took place followed by three days of exams and an appearance before a selection board. Having been passed fit for flying training, all those accepted, including Pat, were sworn in by the attestation officer, Pat then became an aircrew cadet on deferred service, due to his age, until being called to start training.

The call came on 29th June 1942 when Pat was told to report to Lord's Cricket Ground where he was 'one among thousands'. He was billeted at No 6 Hall Road, St John's Wood, where he shared a room with another cadet named Kenneth Griffiths, who was later to become the well known character actor.

Three weeks later, the cadets were moved to No 26 Elementary Flying Training Wing, where they lived under canvas for a month. The next move was made on 18th August to No 17 Initial Training Wing at Scarborough. After six weeks at Scarborough, the cadets moved again, this time to No 9 EFTS at Anstay. Anstay was a grading school where up to twelve hours' flying on Tiger Moths was carried out to assess the potential of the cadets, and to see if it was worth sending them to either Canada or Rhodesia for further training.

The cadets spent a few days at the Aircrew Distribution Centre at Manchester before moving to No 1 RAF Regiment School at

Filey. After a month the cadets returned to Manchester, proir to boarding the *Empress of Scotland* bound for Canada.

Arriving in Moncton, New Brunswick, on 2nd March 1943, Pat stayed at No 31 Personnel Depot for thirteen days before being moved to No 31 EFTS based at De Winlon near Calgary in Alberta. Here, they flew Tiger Moths. Pat's course was the last to use these aircraft before the school converted to Cornells. The trainee pilots put the Tiger Moths through various exercises including cross-country trips, during which some fine aerial views of the Rockies were experienced.

On completion of the course, the cadets moved to No 36 Service Flying Training School at Penhold, between Calgary and Edmonton, where they converted to twin engined Airspeed Oxfords.

Taking off and flying presented no problem to Pat. His troubles began when he tried to land the Oxford. For six weeks he persevered until finally his instructors scrubbed him from the course, and he was sent to No 3 Manning Depot on 26th June 1943.

By 5th September, Pat had remustered to bomb aimer/navigator and started training at No 8 Bombing and Gunnery School at Lithbridge. For his navigational studies, which took place between 11th December 1943 and 28th January 1944, Pat attended No 2 Air Observer School at Edmonton. Having graduated on both these courses, he returned to No 31 PD at Moncton to await space on a troopship to England.

Postings to various units continued once Sergeant Russell had arrived back in Britain, until he eventually arrived at No 14 Operational Training Unit at Market Harborough. Here, Pat Russell crewed up with a pilot and crew, made up of the navigator, John Sheppard, from London, the wireless operator from Australia, Phil Smeeton, Jack Turner, the front gunner, from Cheltenham, with the rear gunner, Paddy Kirrane, from County Mayo, Eire. During OTU their pilot was 'scrubbed out' due to a number of mistakes whilst flying Wellington bombers. His place was taken by an Australian by the name of Doug Hunt, from Mount Barber, South Australia.

The new crew began to move around. They went to ACCS Balderton, then to No 1654 Conversion Unit at Wigsley, where they converted to Stirling bombers. The day they reported to Wigsley, the wireless operator went absent without leave, an action which resulted in the whole crew being sent back to Balderton. Having satisfied his superiors as to his reasons for going 'AWOL', Phil Smeeton was reinstated and together with George Pitkin from Luton, who had now joined them as flight engineer, they reported to No 1668 Conversion Unit at Bottesford on 3rd November for conversion to Lancasters.

They were declared combat ready and posted to No XV Squadron at Mildenhall, where they arrived on the penultimate day of 1944.

Because the range of the fighters escorts had increased so dramatically, since the mid-war years and the Luftwaffe was less in evidence, Bomber Command was by this time carrying out daylight operations. Pat Russell and the rest of the crew were hoping for a short daylight raid, in support of the advancing ground forces, as their first operation. Their expectations were shattered as they learned that a maximum fuel load of 2,154 gallons was being pumped into the aircraft's six fuel tanks and 8,160 lb bombs load being winched into the belly of the Lancaster. Their initiation into bomber operations was scheduled for the night of 7th/8th January 1945, when a night raid on Munich was detailed: a round trip which was to last 8 hours 34 minutes.

The squadron commander, Wing Commander Nigel MacFarlane, flew as captain, with Doug Hunt as second pilot in their Lancaster HK648 F. Pat Russell was flying in the bomb aimer's compartment where, whilst flying in the target area, he incurred the silent wrath of his crew. Pat Russell recalls:

> I was playing it by the book and as I couldn't see the target indicators over which we were briefed to bomb, I called a dummy run and instructed the pilot to go round again. As we then had to turn back against the stream of several hundred other Lancasters I got this distinct impression that this was not a popular move.

Their second operation was a daylight trip to Krefeld, but no results were obtained due to the target being obscured by cloud.

The crew's third mission was another daylight mission, this time

Two photographs of Lancaster NG357, LS-G, in which Pat Russell flew as bomb aimer. (*Above*) returning from a raid on Wanna Eickel, on 7 February 1944 and (*below*) being prepared and fuelled-up for another mission.

against Saarbrucken, which was then only just inside German lines. As the aircraft taxied out at the start of the raid, Mildenhall resembled a car park at the end of the races. There were dozens of Lancasters from both XV and 622 Squadrons swarming around the peri-tracks lining up for take off. Most of the ground staff, having finished their work, took time out to watch the Lancasters get airborne. A small group of people around the Flying Control van waved them off as each aircraft sped down the runway past the line up of 'bloodwagons' and rescue vehicles waiting in case a Lancaster incurred trouble during its heavily laden take-off.

Lancaster LL854, S – Sugar, piloted by Doug Hunt, lumbered off the runway at 12.05 hours, carrying a 4,000 lb 'cookie' and twelve 500 lb bombs in its bomb bay. The aircraft climbed slowly towards the clouds 1,000 feet above the airfield.

> We climbed through the cloud and gradually the gloom on the ground of that January morning gave way to brighter conditions until we emerged at 3,000 feet on top of a perfect layer of cloud, with blue sky and sunshine above. Over the Channel the cloud cleared and I was, once we reached the enemy coast, able to map read right up to the target, where I obtained the satisfaction of seeing our 'cookie' explode right in the centre of the railroads.
>
> Crossing over the lines at Luxemburg, we thought we had had an uneventful trip, so much so that skipper Doug put S – Sugar on to George, the automatic pilot, and came down into my compartment. George Pitkin, the flight engineer, was however keeping an eye on things up in the 'office'. I suddenly thought I heard an engine splutter, when without warning the aircraft went into a dive. We had inadvertently flown over the area between Dunkirk and Calais, which was still in German hands. The spluttering was in fact the noise of exploding flak, which was so close we could hear it above the throbbing of the four Merlin engines.

The aircraft was hit and sustained some damage, but nothing vital. To add to the problem, Phil Smeeton, the wireless operator, advised Doug that East Anglia was 'cloud bound' and that they had been instructed to divert to Predannack in Cornwall. This was interesting news to Pat Russell as his sister Sybil was serving there in the WAAFs, and he was looking forward to seeing her and her friends.

It was however not good news for John Sheppard, the navigator, who did not have charts covering that particular area, which would have enabled him to use the 'GEE' navigation system. Instead, navigation was to be by conventional means with possible fixes from the wireless operator. It was by now late afternoon, and in the gloom all eyes were on the lookout as the crew found themselves crossing a stream of Halifaxes on their way out for the 'night shift'.

> Once again, we were above cloud, but as darkness set in we descended through it and found we were flying over the sea. At one point, we saw rockets being fired up towards us but didn't get the message at the time; we just noted the position.
>
> By the time our ETA had expired, Doug Hunt was convinced we had overshot and therefore turned on to 090°, which should have got us back over the UK. We were now below the cloud layer, which was by this time less than 1,000 feet above ground level. Added to this was the fact we were rapidly running out of petrol. Thirty-five minutes later, with the fuel gauge needles almost reading zero, we saw searchlights on top of the cliffs with an aerodrome amongst them. We did not know which airfield it was until we were in the circuit, when Phil Smeeton announced he had a fix and we were in fact landing at Predannack. After we landed we were informed that the rockets we logged were in fact part of the 'Granite' emergency system. The rockets had been fired from the Scilly Isles, 25 miles past Land's End, and were to warn us that we were heading for New York and a watery grave!

The crew stayed at Predannack for three days, while repairs were carried out to S – Sugar. Unfortunately for Pat, his sister was on leave but he and the rest of the crew enjoyed the company of her friends.

The return journey to Mildenhall was an exhilarating daylight flight made at low level. Pat lay in the bomb aimer's compartment watching the rolling hills of Devon, Dorset and Wiltshire unfolding like a map as the Lancaster sped over the undulating countryside.

(*Right*) Sergeant Pat Russell adjusts the bomb sight on Lancaster NF953, LS-A (*right*).

(*Below*) Flying Officer Doug Hunt pilots Lancaster NG358, LS-H back to Mildenhall after a Manna operation to the Hague on 2 May 1945.

About half of the operations in which Pat Russell participated were carried out at night, including the controversial Dresden raid on 13th February. It was, however, another daylight raid which stood out in Pat's mind. The target was Gelsenkirchen, the date 22nd February. The crews were told at briefing that aircraft from Bomber Command, the US Army Air Force, 2nd Tactical Air Force and Fighter Command would all be operating over Germany, an estimated 6,000 sorties. The Lancasters were to fly at 12,000 feet and were routed, much to the crews' concern, through the heavily defended 'Happy Valley' – the Ruhr.

> We were miles from the target when we saw the box barrage ack-ack bursts. The sky was cloudless and the squadron was getting shot up; every aircraft sustained some damage. Planes could be seen peeling off and parachutes floating down into a large area of smoke and fires. It seemed ages as we made the long run in, watching the casualties mount. The next moment, I witnessed a great explosion just ahead of us. 'Must be one of those "scarecrows",' I thought. At earlier briefings we had been told to watch for them. 'Scarecrows' were reputed to be shells fired by the Germans, which exploded to simulate an aircraft blowing up. I had no time to ponder on the experience for we were by this time over the target and right amongst the flak. As I released the bomb load there was a terrific bang and the Lancaster shuddered. I heard Phil Smeeton cry, 'The starboard outer's on fire!' George Pitkin hit the propeller feathering switch and pushed the Graviner fire extinguisher button, while I prepared to make a hasty exit.

Fortunately for Pat, the fire was doused and the Lancaster flew home on three engines, with one of the numerous Spitfires as escort for part of the journey.

At the debriefing Pat Russell learned, to his dismay, that the 'scarecrow' he had seen was in fact the aircraft of another squadron's commander blowing up.*

*This wartime phenomenon, as in this case, proved to be just that – not a trick shell fired by the Germans, but an aircraft exploding when hit either in the fuel tanks or in the bomb bay.

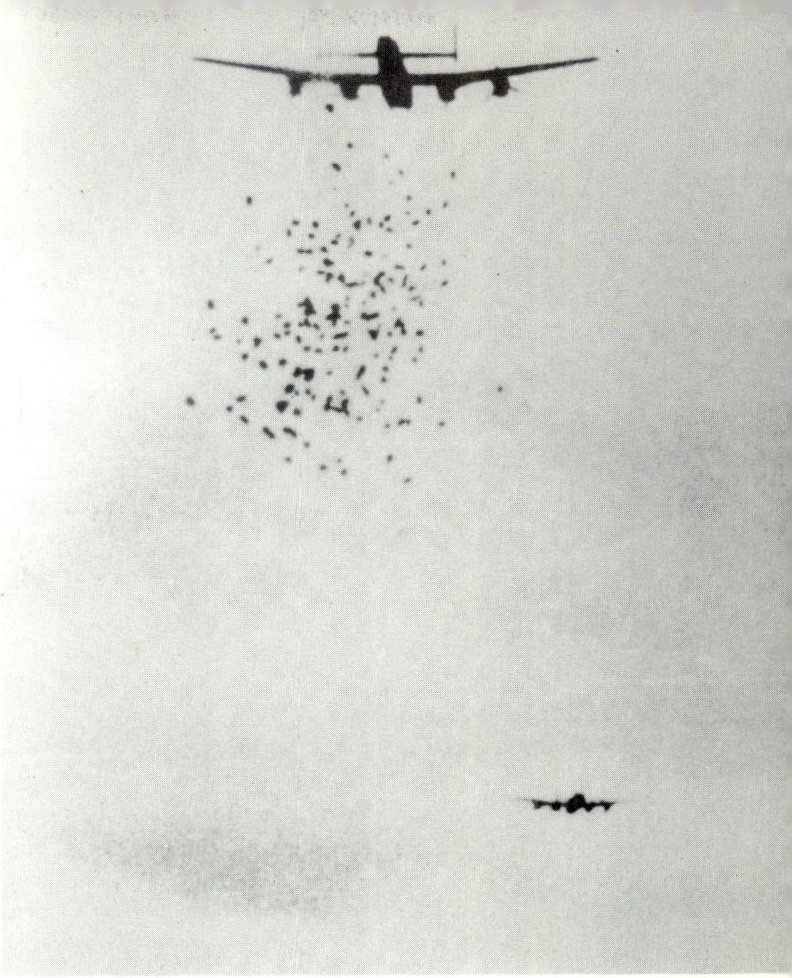

Right) Unidentified
ancasters dropped food to
ne starving Dutch people
luring a Manna operation.

Below) an unidentified
ancaster of No XV Squadron
eing loaded with food pallets
n preparation for a Manna
peration.

Just before the end of the war, XV Squadron were involved in an entirely different type of operation. It was a series of missions for which none of the crews who participated had been trained.

Back in September 1944, as the Allies were pushing into Holland, progress was such that the Dutch envisaged an early end of the occupation by the Germans. The Allied advance, however, halted and it was another seven months before Holland was finally freed in May 1945. With action by 2nd TAF aircraft and by Dutch Resistance, the railway system had ceased to work and the Germans could not get food supplies to the western areas such as Rotterdam, Amsterdam or the Hague. In early April, negotiations took place involving the Allies, the Dutch Resistance and the Germans, the outcome of which was Operation Manna. The operation called for the Lancasters to fly at 500 feet and drop some 6,500 tons of food on to designated areas. The first four areas were the Hague Racecourse, and the airfields at Ypenburg, Valkenburg and Waalhaven. The Germans had agreed not to open fire at the low-flying Lancasters, and the aircraft were supposed to be unarmed but some air gunners felt it prudent to be loaded just in case. In the event, several Lancasters were fired at. The food was protected in sacking and placed in specially designed bomb bay panniers, which were opened and released by the bomb aimer utilizing the bomb release mechanism. The foodstuff contained such items as flour, egg powder, dried milk, meat, biscuits and chocolates. One of the items which was most appreciated was the 'hard tack' biscuits. Some of the provisions proved too rich for the starving folk, but the 'hard tack' biscuits gave them nourishment without stimulating their taste buds too much.

Of the Manna Operations, Pat Russell recalls:

> On 29th April 1945, twelve crews of XV Squadron were detailed to fly individually to an airfield one mile south of Rotterdam. We were briefed to fly out of Mildenhall, at 12.39 in Lancaster HK693, B – Baker, with five panniers of food supplies in our bomb bay. On this first trip we didn't know what to expect in the form of a reception by the Germans. We flew across Holland at an altitude of about 200 feet and could see the crowds out in the streets waving anything they could lay their hands on. Here and

Food sacks scattered on the ground, having been dropped over Holland by the RAF.

Unidentified Lancasters race in low to the dropping zones during the Manna operations. The excitement of the grateful Dutch people can be seen as they hurry towards the same area.

> there, the green uniforms of the Wehrmacht stood out; needless to say they weren't waving. In fact, several aircraft came back with bullet holes in them, a Lancaster from 622 Squadron lost an engine and two aircrew were injured by trigger-happy 'Prussians'.
>
> After our previous operations when we had been dropping the 'nasties' on Germany, from 21,000 feet, the Manna flights were a joy for a number of reasons. We now had official instructions to fly low, which was normally not allowed but was highly enjoyable. We no longer expected to be shot either by fighters or flak. Finally, we were caught up in the obvious excitement of the crowds below.

The 'droppings', as they became known by the Dutch, had been expected for some days. The people around Rotterdam heard the low distant drone of approaching Lancasters, which then appeared over the rooftops like an invasion of bees. The Lancasters opened their bomb doors and the Dutch people watched as a mass of twisting, twirling sacks of food came tumbling from the sky to land on the designated areas. The recipients went wild with excitement. Pat Russell continues:

> Although the operations were known as Manna, the British newspapers called us 'Flying Grocers', while we aircrew referred to these ops as 'Spam Trips'. This gave rise to us bomb aimers being known as 'Spamardiers'.
>
> Whilst we endeavoured to drop supplies in the designated areas, some food fell in other locations due to hang-ups in the bomb bay.

It was one of these stray packs that fell towards a young Dutch girl and her friends as they watched. A young German soldier realised what was about to happen and threw the girl to the ground and protected her with his body. The soldier was killed when he was struck on the head, by the pack, but he saved the girl's life.

On 1st May, fourteen aircraft from XV Squadron took off between 13.00 and 13.34 to drop more supplies over Holland. Their designated dropping zone was a large sportsfield near the Hague.

L to R. Flight Sergeant Russell, Sergeant Kirrane, Flight Lieutenant Hunt, Sergeant Pitkin and Flying Officer Sheppard posed in front of No XV's top scoring Lancaster LL806, LS-S, at Mildenhall in May 1945. LL806 completed 134 bombing operations, 3 Manna operations and 3 Exodus operations.

Ex PoW's with Lancaster NG357, LS-G, at Juvincourt airfield, near Rheims, before leaving for Wing, Bedfordshire on 13th May 1945.

In his compartment in the nose of the Lancaster, Pat again marvelled at the obvious excitement he could see amongst the Dutch people below, who had assembled near the dropping zone, thus making identification of the target easy. Pat released the precious cargo of five panniers, which all fell to earth. Pat and the crew participated in two more Manna operations on 2nd and 7th May. A few shower storms were encountered on the route out during the latter operation, but on both occasions the panniers were dropped successfully to the accompaniment of the wildly excited and obviously cheering Dutch people. On 8th May Victory in Europe was declared and the war with Germany was over.

Two days later Pat and the rest of the crew were to participate in yet another type of operation, the codename of which was 'Exodus'. The squadron despatched fifteen aircraft to Juvincourt, France, where they landed and embarked 24 passengers to each Lancaster. The passengers were all ex-prisoners of war who were then flown back to England to a reception centre at Westcott. By mid-day, a total of 360 ex-POWs had returned home courtesy of XV Squadron. The Lancasters having faithfully discharged their duty, took off from Westcott and returned to Mildenhall. The following day, sixteen aircraft performed the same task. Again, Pat's crew participated in the operation which, on this occasion, terminated at Tangmere. On 12th May fifteen aircraft left Mildenhall at lunch time and flew again to Juvincourt for another Exodus mission. The Lancasters had to stay overnight and return early the following morning. The POWs eagerly formed themselves into groups of 24 and boarded the aircraft as instructed. Fourteen of the Lancasters got airborne safely but PP672 N piloted by Flight Lieutenant B. Bagenal crashed on take off. Although the aircraft was burnt out, both the crew and passengers escaped injury.

Pat Russell's tour of operations was now complete, but not his tour of duty. After the end of the war, he was posted to a further twelve stations before being demobbed on 10th September 1946.

Having dropped death and destruction from the bomb bay of his aircraft, Pat was pleased to have the opportunity, in the end, of reversing the role by taking part in the Manna operations. By dropping life and hope to a starving population he ended his war on a peaceful and productive note for which they had all been fighting.

Even today, Pat feels a great sense of pride in this achievement, occasionally returning to Holland, where he is warmly welcomed by the still grateful Dutch people.

CHAPTER FOURTEEN

A Collection of Memories

Other Flyers Remember

Many of those who served with No XV Squadron during the turbulent years 1939-45, when asked, comment that their tour or time with the squadron was much the same as everybody else's; nothing happened out of the ordinary!

They do, however, relate the odd incident, which at the time of occurrence could have had serious repercussions, but when brought to mind some years later are told with a chuckle.

One such story was related by Flight Sergeant Frank Watson, a wireless operator, who flew, at the time, with Pilot Officer Woodley and his crew. The incident occurred on the evening of Saturday, 2nd October 1943.

> We took off from Mildenhall, in Stirling BK818, O – Orange, at 17.35 hours, for a 'Gardening' operation in the Skaggerrak.
>
> During the flight, which was to last over seven hours, we were caught in an electical storm. St Elmo's fire danced all over the aircraft, engulfing it in blue flames six feet high. Lightning struck the trailing aerial, ran up it, earthing on the winding out handle and causing it to burn through.
>
> On landing back at Mildenhall, I informed the ground crew chief that I had lost my aerial. The chief immediately produced his note book and pencil and proceeded to fine me five shillings (25p). As so many aerials were being lost in trees and church spires, etc, due to W/Ops forgetting to wind them in before landing, it was the custom for the guilty party to be fined.
>
> I immediately put the chief in the picture and invited him to

> view the damage. A further note was made in his book and he recanted in a disgruntled voice, 'I'll have to report it anyway,' but I never heard anymore about the incident.

A more serious incident had befallen the same crew just five days previously, on the evening of Monday, 27th September.

Pilot Officer Woodley was at the controls of Stirling KB719 B having taken off from Mildenhall at 19.50 hours. His aircraft was one of a total force of 678 aircraft comprising 312 Lancasters, 231 Halifaxes, 111 Stirlings, 24 Wellingtons and five Boeing B17's which were participating in an attack against Hannover.

The Stirling was renowned for its lack of ability to gain altitude, and as BK719 crossed the target area it was bombed from above, as Frank Watson recalls:

> On the Hannover raid we were in the third wave. As we crossed the target area a string of bombs fell from a Lancaster overflying us. One of the bombs went through the wing and main petrol tank.

The Stirling immediately heaved over and fell into a spin, out of control. The compass toppled and the altimeter spun crazily round, as the rest of the instrument panel needles flickered back and forth across the dials in rapid movement.

Pilot Officer Woodley finally managed to regain control of the aircraft with the city of Hannover now only 3,000 feet below him. Climbing steadily, he regained the lost height and set a course for home, a journey which kept the flight engineer busy, as Frank Watson remembers: 'We nursed the aircraft back to Mildenhall, by changing the petrol tanks and regulating the fuel supply all the way back.'

On his return, Frank Watson recorded in his log-book, 'Hannover – Quiet Trip!'

*

Sergeant Frank Diamond, a navigator who flew with Flight Lieutenant Hugh Wilkie, will never forget the night his aircraft lost a propeller. The night in question was 11th/12th June 1943.

Flight Lieutenant Wilkie lifted off Stirling BK470, LS – G – George from the runway at Mildenhall at 23.29 hours, and headed for Düsseldorf. BF470 was one of a total force of 783 aircraft heading for that city.

The raid progressed well until a Mosquito, one of the Pathfinder aircraft, inadvertently dropped its target indicators some miles to the north-east of Düsseldorf. This led to some aircraft of the main force dropping their loads on open countryside.

Hugh Wilkie flew in over the target at 12,000 feet and dropped his bombs on the correct TI's and fires burning below, without hindrance. Although the crew had sighted enemy fighters prowling around the night sky, they had not experienced any problems, from either them or the heavy flak.

Leaving the target area, Wilkie set course for home. He had been informed that another Stirling bomber was flying close to them, but neither he nor the gunners paid any attention to it. That is, until it opened fire at them. The port outer engine was hit, putting the constant speed unit out of action. Of the incident, Frank Diamond relates:

> Being ensconced inside the fuselage, I thought we'd been hit by flak. The port outer engine started to roar and scream. I looked out of the window, on the port side, just as the aircraft went into a dive. The engine was going mad and started to vibrate.
>
> I remember John Ledgerwood, the mid-upper gunner, who had a perfect view of the port outer, saying, 'It looks as if it's about to come off.' At which point the propeller, complete with boss, sheared off and cartwheeled up and over the top of John's turret!

Flight Lieutenant Wilkie hauled BF470 out of the dive and tried to gain altitude, a difficult task with an aeroplane which had trouble climbing even on four engines.

The gyro-compass had toppled during the dive and was swinging wildly, and Wilkie needed to know a course for home. Frank Diamond takes up the story:

> The loss of the port outer engine meant no power to the GEE navigational aid; we would have to use astro-navigation.
>
> Wilkie got George above the cloud, whilst I climbed up into

(*Right*) Pilot Officer Hugh Wilkie, completed a tour of operations with XV Squadron and was awarded the DFC. He was killed in a flying accident at Stradishall.

(*Below*) Hugh Wilkie and crew.

> the astro-dome. I told Wilkie that if he kept Polaris on the starboard side we must be flying west. I took three fixes and plotted a course which, thanks to the excellent training I received in America, was spot on.

Seeing a gap in the cloud, Wilkie lost altitude and passed through it. Below and just ahead he could see Mildenhall's flashing beacon.

Another occasion when Frank Diamond, the crew and BF470 had a lucky escape occurred ten days later, on the night of 21st/22nd June when they attacked Krefeld.

Flying at an altitude of 7,000 feet over 10/10th cloud, BF470 was approximately fifteen miles south-west of and approaching the target. The crew were curious as to the lack of both searchlights and flak activity, when suddenly 'Jock' Palmer, the rear gunner, yelled a warning of, 'fighter'.

The enemy aircraft, identified as a Ju88, crossed BF470's track from port to starboard at a range of about 1,200 yards. It turned and swung down into the rear port quarter, positioning itself for an attack, closing to a range of approximately 800 yards. Sergeant Palmer instructed Wilkie to take evasive action, as he opened fire with short bursts of maching gun fire, which he later claimed hit the mainplane of the Ju88.

The twin-engined fighter gave chase to the twisting, turning Stirling, and spat out a burst of cannon fire, which was poorly aimed.

Palmer informed Wilkie that the enemy aircraft had passed somewhere underneath them. Wilkie steeply dipped first one wing and then the other in a series of steep sweeping banks to port and starboard. This manoeuvre enabled the gunners to see the fighter and fire at it when it came into view. After several minutes, the Ju88 peeled over and dived away into the cloud below.

As in the previous action, it was Frank Diamond's job to get BF470 back on course for Krefeld, which with his experience was no problem.

*

Another member of aircrew who did experience problems was John James Sparrow. Sergeant Sparrow was mid-upper gunner to Flight

Sergeant Lewis and his crew.

Posted to No XV Squadron in early July 1943, John Sparrow flew his first mining mission on the night of 25th/26th July. It past without incident, as did the second mining trip on the night of 6th August. Four nights later, on 10th August, Flight Sergeant Lewis and his crew were detailed to participate in a raid against Nuremberg.

At 22.26 hours, Flight Sergeant Lewis pushed forward the throttles, released the brakes and Stirling BF460 'F' rolled down the runway, gathering speed until it became 'unstuck' and lifted slowly into the night sky.

A total force of 653 aircraft, including thirteen from No XV Squadron, headed for Germany. The flight out was uneventful and although there was 9/10th cloud to 12,000 feet, the target was found and marked by the Pathfinders. Dummy fires were reported around the Mannheim area to the west, but all crews saw and later reported bombing on the green target indicators.

Having successfully completed their alloted task, Flight Sergeant Lewis turned BF460 towards home. It seemed to the crew as though the return journey was going to be as uneventful as the outward one. That was until they reached the area of the French/Belgian border, as John Sparrow recalls:

> Without warning, out of the darkness, a Messerschmitt Me110 nightfighter opened fired. Its first burst of cannon fire slammed into the nose and starboard wing of the Stirling, immediately setting it ablaze.

The enemy aircraft flew past its victim and turned in towards the Stirling for another attack. So fierce was the fire, the glow from the flames enabled Sergeant Sparrow and Sergeant Sheppard, the rear gunner, to see the Me110 as it turned in to inflict the coup-de-grâce on the stricken bomber. Together, they swung their respective turrets to meet the fighter's approach, and opened fire simultaneously. The Me110 took the full impact of the avenging shells. The fighter keeled over and dived earthwards, as a dark shape emerged from it; followed by a lighter colour of a parachute opening.

John Sparrow, mid-upper gunner, was shot down returning from Nuremburg on the night of 10th August 1943. He was captured and eventually interned in Stalag Luft VI at Heydekrug. During a forced-march in April 1945 Sparrow escaped from the column and was assisted by advancing British tank crews. He returned to England and was promoted to warrant officer.

There was no time for rejoicing. The fire continued to rage and the aircraft was losing height, forcing Flight Sergeant Lewis to give the order to bale out.

Hurriedly clambering down from his mid-upper turret, John Sparrow clipped on his parachute and made his way aft to the rear escape hatch. Sergeant Cave, the wireless operator, and Sergeant Bryne, the navigator, were the first two out of the aircraft, quickly followed by Sergeant Sparrow. The rest of the crew were to perish, including Sergeant Poole, the bomb aimer, who is thought to have abandoned the aircraft without his parachute.

John Sparrow landed near Heer in Belgium, but on the French side of the border. After 38 days of freedom he was captured by the Germans, having been betrayed by a local person. He spent the rest of the war as a prisoner, but that's another story.

*

Owen Sylvestre was born in Trinidad, and was one of only two coloured pilots to join No XV Squadron. He was a man who enjoyed the thrill of low flying a Lancaster, but once or twice it resulted in him having to report to his commanding officer to 'face the music'. On other occasions, it enabled him to fly out of trouble quickly as George Allom, Sylvestre's bomb aimer, relates:

> Returning from a daylight raid on the Ruhr towards the end of summer 1944, we began to trail behind the main stream until eventually we were flying alone. Gradually we lost height and flew over Brussels at a fairly low altitude. We continued our journey home flying 'on the deck', heading towards Knokke on the Belgium coast.
>
> I warned the skipper that according to that morning's *Daily Express*, the Germans were still in occupation at Knokke.

The Germans were not slow in opening fire at the low flying aircraft. As the Lancaster raced towards them, the ground defences opened-up. Tracer followed the bomber as it flashed over the German gunners, who tried to keep pace with it. Bursting shells rattled shrapnel against the aircraft's skin, but Flight Sergeant Sylvestre knew how to get away, as George Allom continues:

> As we flashed over, we heard a few 'pings', but the skipper pushed the Lancaster right down to sea level. The guns were then unable to bear down on us due to the height of the cliffs. We flew home at sea level, but had to gain height to cross our coast.

During August 1944, Flight Sergeant Sylvestre and his crew participated in a night raid against Stettin.

Approaching the target area, with his crew at their respective battle stations, Owen Sylvestre commenced his bombing run, being guided to the aiming point by George Allom.

Through the perspex nose blister, George witnessed the battle ahead and below: the kaleidoscope of changing colours of flame as fires raged in and around the port area. The battle was brought to the night sky by the searchlight beams and trails of flak, tracing patterns before bursting amongst the bomber stream.

Suddenly, as always, without warning a master beam caught PA170 N in its glare. George Allom remembers what happened:

> As we were running into the target we got caught by a radar controlled beam. The skipper immediately pushed the 'kite' into a dive and escaped before other manually controlled beams could lock onto us.

Having successfully evaded the beams, Flight Sergeant Sylvestre then returned to the job in hand, but then came another lucky escape. Both Sylvestre and Ernie Fitch, the mid-upper gunner, in his top turret, became aware that there was another Lancaster flying fairly close to them on their port side. Suddenly, Ernie's night vision was destroyed as the other Lancaster erupted into an enormous fireball of light and flames, as the bomb load blew up following a direct hit from flak.

One of those occasions when Owen Sylvestre was called before his CO was the day they flew over Ernie Fitch's home.

> We had taken the Lancaster on an air test and flew down to Welwyn Garden City, where Ernie, our mid-upper lived.
>
> Owen dropped the nose of the aircraft and made a low pass over Ernie's house. Unfortunately, the aircraft's serial number

(*Right*) Sergeant George Allom.

Below (*L to R*) Ernie Fitch, George Allom and Owen Sylvestre outside the Bird in Hand, Mildenhall during a reunion weekend.

> was recorded and obviously reported, for the minute we got back to the station the skipper was ordered to report to the CO.

During his tour of operations as a bomb aimer with XV Squadron, George Allom collected many memories but there are two missions he particularly remembers.

The first occurred on the 5th August when the squadron participated in a daylight raid against the oil storage depots at Bordeaux.

It was one of those occasions when Flight Sergeant Sylvestre was allowed to fly low, as was the rest of the force. George Allom remembers the flight, with youthful exuberance:

> We flew low level to Land's End, on the deck all the way. We flew down the runway of an airfield in that area and out over the cliffs. Dropping down to wave top height, we flew south until we were west of Bordeaux, with water splashing up onto my perspex dome. Smashing!
>
> We climbed to 3,000 feet to bomb the target and then flew north, overland, to home.

The second mission which made a lasting impression on George's mind again includes the sea. It occurred on 3rd October when the squadron detailed eleven aircraft to participate in a raid, with a total force of 252 Lancasters and seven Mosquitos, against the sea wall defences on the island of Walcheren. The aiming point was the wall around the Westkapelle area, an area heavily defended with German coastal batteries guarding the Honte of Westerschelde. The intention was to flood the area and thus submerge and render non-effective some of the German gun batteries.

The attack was successful and the wall was breached over a wide area. The result gave the impression of a mini 'Dambusters' operation. In fact, No 617, the 'Dambusters', Squadron was standing by, but their services were not required.

George Allom, again in the nose of Lancaster PA170 N, had an excellent view of the attack, as he recalls:

> We were on a daylight raid bombing the dykes to flood Walcheren island. It was spectacular watching the water pour

> through the breaches in the dykes. At Middleburg, some of the houses were standing out above the level, as were some of the German gun emplacements. Although they were surrounded by water they were still firing like hell.

Those emplacements that had not been deluged by water endeavoured to repel the attacking aircraft, but their efforts were in vain. All participating aircraft returned safely to their respective bases.

CHAPTER FIFTEEN

They Also Flew

The Ground Staff Remember

Any pilot or crew member reminiscing about his days on an operational squadron during World War II will, at some stage, undoubtedly make mention of the ground staff. A great number of both men and women were involved in keeping their aircraft in the air and many others, in the background, were involved with the operational administration side of his work. He therefore had a great affinity with many of them, particularly his own ground crew.

The aircraft they flew 'belonged' to the ground crew, the crew only borrowed it, as far as they were concerned. After having completed all pre-flight inspections, the pilot was required to sign the Form 700, as it was known, before the ground crew chief would release the aircraft into the pilot's custody.

The men (below the rank of corporal, and known as 'erks') worked all hours of the day and night in all weathers, in an effort to repair damaged or defective aircraft and keep them serviceable.

Occasionally bombers returned from an operation with damage caused by bombs from 'friendly' aircraft flying above them, but damaged incurred by bombs, flak or fighters had to be repaired. The airframe fitters, instruments fitters and armourers all carried out their duties in an efficient manner which earned them the respect and appreciation of everyone, from the station commander down.

A bomber which had been repaired, serviced or had had parts replaced was usually taken on an air-test prior to going on 'ops'. These air-tests gave some of the ground crews the opportunity to fly. It was on these trips that the lighter side of the war usually

Tony Godfrey casually leans against a 12,000lb bomb concealed on its trolley, in Mons Wood, Mildenhall, during the winter of 1944.

The groundcrew of No XV Squadron, RAF Mildenhall. Percy Pluck is seated second from right.

appeared, and the light-hearted moments of flying are recorded, as Tony Godfrey of Gil Marsh's ground crew recalls:

> I remember one occasion flying with Gil Marsh on air test, when two single-engined fighters approached us. They positioned themselves on either side of the Stirling and we identified them as American P-47 Thunderbolts. For a few minutes we flew in formation with them, but it soon became evident that they wanted to play games. One of the Thunderbolt pilots waggled his wings at us and Gil Marsh responded by doing the same with the Stirling. The fighter pilots obviously opened their throttles, because their aircraft began to pull slightly ahead of us. Not to be outdone Gil Marsh applied full throttle to the four Bristol Hercules engines, which powered our Stirling. The engines responded and the bomber accelerated away, leaving the American fighter pilots to find somebody else to play with.

On another occasion, when Tony Godfrey was flying with Gil Marsh, their youthful exuberance very nearly got them into trouble:

> We were flying along reasonably low when somebody on board spotted a hay stack with a number of figures on and around it, which we took to be Land Army Girls. Gil Marsh was urged to give them a bit of a show, and standing the Stirling almost vertically on its wingtip turned the huge bomber back towards the hay stack. He levelled out and was so low that he was almost cutting the stubble with the propeller blades. As the aircraft approached the hay stack we realised the figures were men, possibly Italian prisoners of war, who either flung themselves to the ground or took to their heels. At the last moment Gil Marsh pulled back the control column and lifted the Stirling up and over the great mound of hay. To his horror, and mine, there in front of the aircraft was a row of trees, the tops of which were lined up with the cockpit. Much to our relief the trees disappeared just under the nose of the Stirling.

Tony Godfrey did not always enjoy his work. He has never forgotten the day Stirling BK816 returned from a raid against

Berlin, battle-damaged and with the cockpit floor covered with the blood of the severely injured pilot. Tony Godfrey had the unenviable task of hosing out the cockpit floor to wash away Gil Marsh's blood. (See Chapter 7)

*

Aircraftman 2nd Class Ken Rogers joined No XV Squadron at Bourn in March 1943, just before the move to Mildenhall. He was assigned, as part of the ground crew, to Stirling EF345, M – Mother, piloted by Pilot Officer Jim Stowell.

On one of the first occasions he went near the Stirling he finished up with feelings of a guilty conscience:

> I had just climbed in the rear door of the aircraft when there was a loud explosive bang. I thought I had touched something and the electrical circuit had blown. I jumped from the aircraft and took cover behind the accumulator trolley. It was then I noticed one of the main undercart tyres had burst.

It took some time for his pangs of guilt to subside, even though he had done nothing wrong.

Ken Rogers had a good rapport with the aircrew and the rest of his ground crew. He recalls that they always saw the aircraft off on operations, and would be waiting around the dispersal area for its return. Unfortunately, as has already been recorded (See Chapter 4), one night EF345, M – Mother, did not return.

He did, however, manage to make the occasional flight:

> Members of ground crew did fly on air-tests. We usually worked with the flight engineer, notifying him of problems and what to look for during the test. Any faults found would, of course, be reported to the specific member of groundcrew on return.

*

Leading Aircraftman Percy Pluck first joined XV Squadron when they were based at Wyton. He made the move to Bourn and then to Mildenhall and stayed with the squadron until he was demobbed in 1945.

Percy, or Duke as he was known to his friends, was an aircraft electrician. His jovial personality and sense of fun make him a popular figure, which helped as sometimes the reality of war was brought onto the airfield itself.

> I remember one night the bombers were returning from a raid. As one of the Lancasters was making his final approach an 'Intruder' enemy aircraft came in behind him and opened fire with his cannons. The shells slammed into and around the rear turret in which the rear gunner was still sitting. What a mess it made of him.

Death also came without the assistance of the enemy, as an incident which occurred on Monday 30th August 1943 indicates:

> The wing commander of No XV Squadron, J.D. Stevens, together with a corporal air frame fitter took off from Mildenhall in a Defiant aircraft for a local flight. The aircraft stalled, crashed and caught fire. Both were killed. The fitter was found hanging upside down in the turret.

The aircraft, Defiant N1643, took off and instantly developed engine failure due to a coolant leak, which apparently leaked into the cockpit and affected the pilot.

Percy Pluck's sense of humour came to the fore when relating an incident which could have earned him and some colleagues a reprimand:

> Smoking on the airfield, near aircraft being serviced, was not allowed especially when the bowser was around. Occasionally, we would nip into the toilets for a cigarette. On one occasion, as a warrant officer approached the toilets, there was a mad rush of about twenty 'erks' all trying to get out one door. The warrant officer asked if we had been smoking, to which a chorus replied, 'Us, Sir; No, Sir' with clouds of blue smoke drifting above our heads.

Percy got his share of flying but the one trip which stayed in his mind was the trip over Germany after hostilities had ceased:

When the hostilities were over, the ground personnel were taken on trips over the Continent and Germany, to see for themselves the damage inflicted by Bomber Command. These trips were known as 'Baedekker' operations or 'Cooks' Tour' trips, and I made mine in the bomb aimer's compartment of a XV Squadron Lancaster. It was incredible and I took some good aerial photographs of Cologne.

*

Two other characters on the squadron who, rumour has it, managed to fly on more than one occasion were Flight Lieutenant William Prune and Flying Officer Billy Goat.

Bill Prune was a bulldog; he was also the squadron mascot. His favourite occupation when on the ground was to chase motorcycles, a ritual which was only concluded when the rider was dislodged from his machine.

It is rumoured that Bill Prune carried out more than fourteen operations over Germany and had his own log-book, although no one will lay claim to having taken him as part of their crew.

Bill was a much loved character, who appeared with the aircrew on the official squadron photographs, and occasionally on individual aircrew pictures. Pilot Bill Mason and his crew were proud to have their 'end of tour' photograph taken with Bill Prune.

Percy Pluck and some of the other 'erks' used to try and tease Prune:

> Bill Prune used to hang around the 'A' Flight dispersal area. We used to throw the aircraft engines' covers at him to try and made him annoyed.

His end came, not as one might have expected on operations, but when he tried his favourite pastime with a lorry, which duly ended his career when he ran in front of it.

Flight Lieutenant William Prune was buried with due respect in front of No 1 Hangar. His obituary was recorded in one of the national papers of the day.

Flying Officer Billy Goat was as his name implies, a goat or rather a kid. He belonged to Flight Lieutenant Len Miller DFC, who

Flying Officer Billy Goat, Len Miller's young friend who became the squadron mascot when the latter was shot down in April 1944.

acquired him after a party. Billy followed Len and his crew around the airfield and was rarely far away. Sometimes, Len would take Billy with him on air tests, much to the annoyance of the ground crews, for, like most goats, Billy would eat anything, as Percy Pluck remembers:

> After Prune died, we had a goat on the squadron. He got a liking for empire tape which was used for cables, etc. He went on a few flights but was stopped after eating the tape in flight. Sometimes he was tied up with rope, which he would eat and then wander into the NAAFI looking for something else to eat.

Once, Billy munched his way through the pilot's handling notes and the Lancaster maintenance manuals; some people commented that this made Billy the most genned-up goat, on the Avro Lancasters, in the Royal Air Force. Len Miller remembers his friend with affection.

(*Top*) (*L to R*) Flight Sergeant P. Elger, Pilot Officer Bill Mason, Flight Sergeant D. Brown, Sergeant H. Leigh and Sergeant Norman Bibbing pose for an end of tour photograph with Bill Prune, the bulldog.

(*Below*) Bill Prune, the bulldog on a squadron photograph of August 1943. Prune lies at the feet of Wing Commander N.D. Stephens who was killed in a Defiant crash on 30th August 1943. Flight Lieutenant Megginson sits on Stephens' left.

The whole crew enjoyed Billy's company and we all 'acted the goat' when we were with him. We would get down on our hands and knees and head butt Billy, a game which he thought great fun.

When Len Miller was shot down, Billy Goat was adopted as the squadron mascot.

*

The Women's Auxiliary Air Force made an enormous contribution towards the war effort, sometimes with, like other ground staff, little or no obvious credit being attributed to them.

They carried out their work with dexterity and enthusiasm, their only reward being the knowledge that they were helping the cause towards victory, peace and freedom. The WAAFs whose duties were carried out at one of the many Bomber Command operational stations, very occasionally managed to glean a different reward – a flight in one of the squadron's aircraft. These flights were against regulations and strictly unofficial, and therefore remain the private memories of the fortunate WAAFs who managed to get airborne. However, many of them got the official opportunity to fly when the 'Baedekker' operations commenced.

Section Officer Grace Archer, Intelligence Section, and her Senior NCO Flight Sergeant Kay Godfrey both put their names forward. The flight made a lasting impression, as Kay Godfrey recalls:

In July, the CO instituted what were called 'Baedekker' trips. These were flights all over the places in Europe where our bombers had been, and the ground staff could go if they wished. I was luckily able to go, with Section Officer Archer and some others, on 25th July 1945. It was wonderful. I lay on my stomach in the nose of the aircraft alongside 'Archie' Archer, for most of the trip.

The heart-rending sight was over Holland, where in some places all one could see was church steeples and tree tops, following the flood to keep the Germans out.

Upon our return, we had our photograph taken with the crew.

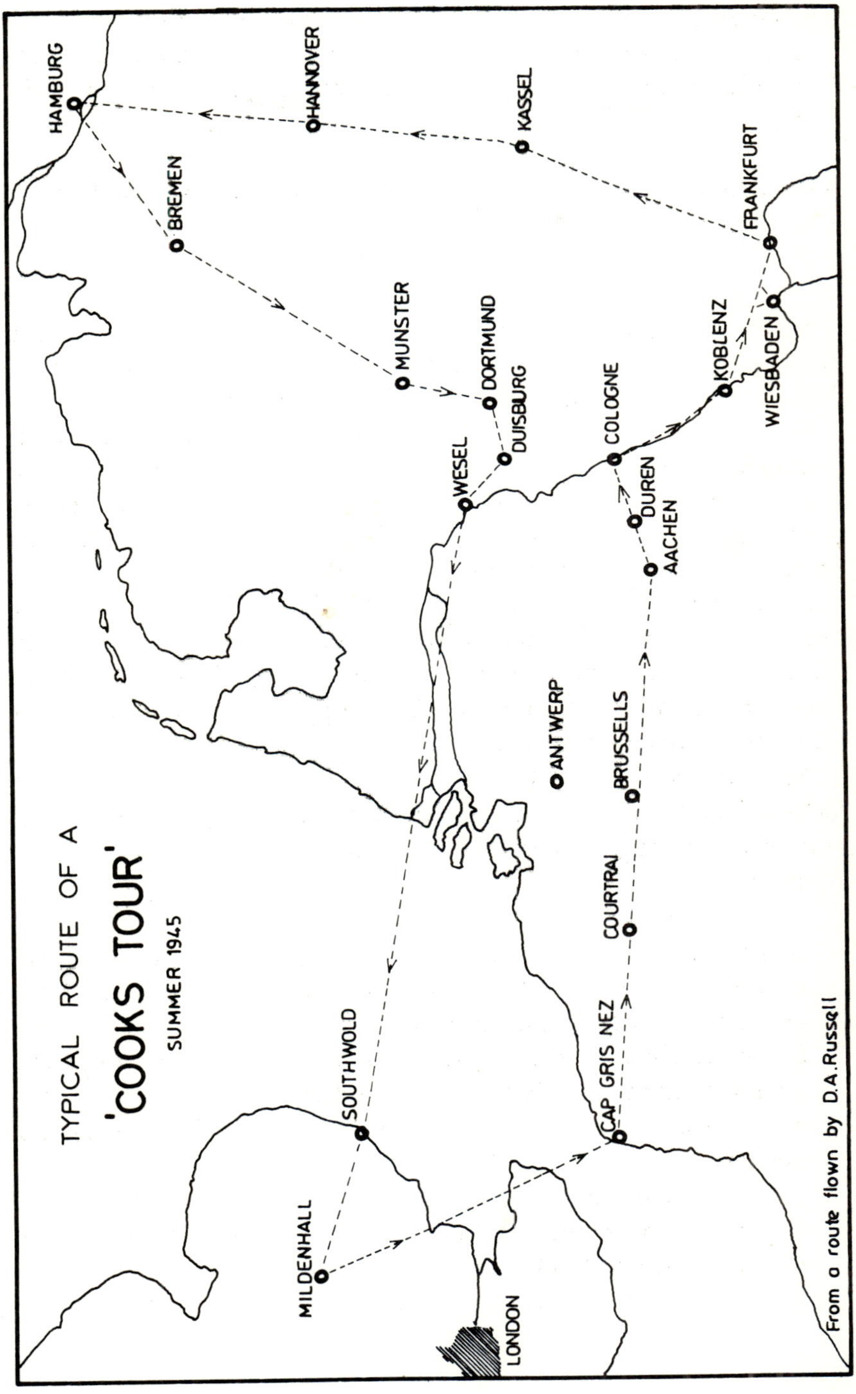
TYPICAL ROUTE OF A
'COOKS TOUR'
SUMMER 1945
HAMBURG
HANNOVER
KASSEL
BREMEN
FRANKFURT
MUNSTER
DORTMUND
DUISBURG
WESEL
COLOGNE
KOBLENZ
WIESBADEN
DUREN
AACHEN
ANTWERP
BRUSSELLS
COURTRAI
CAP GRIS NEZ
SOUTHWOLD
MILDENHALL
LONDON
From a route flown by D.A.Russell

Flight Sergeant Kay Godfrey (second from left) with Section Officer Grace 'Archie' Archer, on return from their 'Cooks Tour' trip on 25th July 1945.

An aerial view of the Krupps works taken during a 'Cooks Tour' trip from a Lancaster of XV Squadron.

To Grace Archer, the trip proved what a thoroughly devastating job Bomber Command had done.

Hostilities in Europe officially ceased on 8th May 1945. The whole country celebrated and RAF Mildenhall was no different, as Kay Godfrey recalls:

> I was there (Mildenhall) on VE night, a night to be remembered! I heard the news on the radio, and as everything was fairly quiet on the WRAF site, I thought I would take a walk over to the main camp. What pandemonium! The boys were going wild and had started a large bonfire outside the barrack block. I also saw some of our girls there, but decided not to see them.
>
> The Station Commander was trying to restore order and was brandishing a pistol to no avail. He then shouted at me to get my girls to bed. I told him that was impossible on my own, and suggested we got them singing to calm them down. We did just that and eventually things quietened down.
>
> I returned to the WRAF site and found somebody had started a fire there. I put it out with an extinguisher and gave them a good telling-off, reminding them that it was still work as usual in the morning, even if the war in Europe was ended.

APPENDIX

No XV Squadron RAF Awards

Name	*Rank*	*Award*	*Date*
R.E. Hunter	L.A.C.	DFM	9.7.40
R.A.M. Stone	SGT	DFM	9.7.40
L.H. Trent (NZ)	A/F/L	DFC	9.7.40
P.F. Webster	A/S/L	DFC	9.7.40
R.F. Davis	SGT	DFM	19.7.40
C.E.U. Thompson	P/O	DFC	19.7.40
H.R. Jones	CPL	DFM	23.7.40
A.R. Oakeshott	A/F/L	DFC	30.7.40
W.J. Stephens	SGT	DFM	30.7.40
J. Sutcliffe	SGT	DFM	30.7.40
A.F. Taylor	SGT	DFM	30.7.40
V.F.E. Trehearne	SGT	DFM	30.7.40
A.J. Box	SGT	DFM	13.9.40
S.C. Redhead	SGT	DFM	13.9.40
P.J. Camp	SGT	DFM	22.10.40
W.H. George	A/F/L	DFC	22.10.40
R.R. Higginson	SGT	DFM	22.10.40
C.A. O'Donnell	SGT	DFM	22.10.40
P. Alderson	SGT	DFM	22.11.40
W.C. Baker	SGT	DFM	22.11.40
R.S. Gilmour	P/O	DFC	22.11.40
W. Jessop	SGT	DFM	22.11.40
J.W. Mahler	A/S/L	DFC	22.11.40
R.F. Paveley	A/SGT	DFM	22.11.40
J. Cox	W/CDR	DFC	20.12.40
D.P. Boyle	SGT	BEM	17.3.41
J.R. Bushell	SGT	DFM	6.6.41
C. Raymond (NZ)	A/F/L	DFC	6.6.41
W.M. Morris	A/S/L	DFC	18.7.41
P.A. Tanton	SGT	DFM	19.8.41
A.G.A. Cochrane	A/F/L	DFC	22.8.41

Name	*Rank*	*Award*	*Date*
J.C. Galley	SGT	DFM	22.8.41
S.W.B. Menual	A/S/L	DFC	22.8.41
A.J. Putt	A/F/L	DFC	23.9.41
R.T. Jones	F/S	BEM	24.9.41
P.J. Boggis	F/O	DFC	9.1.42
R.H. Hardy	F/S	DFM	9.1.42
P.B.B. Ogilvie, DSO	W/CDR	DFC	9.1.42
C.A. Venieux	F/O	DFC	9.1.42
E.M. Brigg	SGT	DFM	10.2.41
R.J. Cook	SGT	DFM	10.2.42
M.S. Pepper	SGT	DFM	10.2.42
I.C.K. Swales, DFM	F/O	DFC	14.3.42
C.J. du Preez	SGT	DFM	14.5.42
L.R. Barr	A/F/L	DFC	26.5.42
J.F. Barron	F/S	DFM	26.5.42
R. Lambert	W/O	DFC	26.5.42
B.D. Sellick, DFC	W/CDR	Bar to DFC	26.5.42
D.A. Parkins	A/F/L	DFC	20.6.42
L.R. Barr, DFC	F/L	Bar to DFC	7.8.42
N.A. Bennitt	A/F/O	DFC	7.8.42
W.A. Shoemaker	P/O	DFC	7.8.42
W.W.O. Diggins	SGT	DFM	2.10.42
H. Meades	SGT	DFM	2.10.42
J.R. Cunningham	SGT	D.F.M.	28.10.82
C.H. Baigent	A/F/L	DFC	2.11.42
A.N. Halkett	F/S	DFM	2.11.42
E.H. McCaffery	A/F/L	DFC	2.11.42
H.T. Miles	F/O	DFC	2.11.42
D.W. Pidsley (SAAF)	Major	DFC	9.11.42
D.J.H. Lay	A/W/CDR	DSO	3.12.42
W.E. Egri	F/S	D.F.M.	12.12.42
F.F. Hamilton	F/S	DFM	12.12.42
D.D. Soderquist	F/S	DFM	12.12.42
P. Curtis	SGT	DFM	28.12.42
W.E. McAlpine	P/O	DFC	28.12.42
R.H. Phillips	F/O	DFC	28.12.42
H.H. Wright	SGT	DFM	28.12.42
H. Tilson	F/O	DFC	31.12.42
D.E.I. Clark	F/L	DFC	11.1.43
G.L. Goodall	F/S	DFM	11.1.43
F.E. Mitchell	SGT	DFM	11.1.43
T.W. Pierce	F/O	DFC	11.1.43
E.G. Powell	SGT	DFM	11.1.43

Name	*Rank*	*Award*	*Date*
W.D. Macmonagle	F/S	DFM	12.1.43
E.F. Warren	F/S	DFM	12.1.43
R. Munns	F/O	DFC	10.2.43
D.W. Newall	F/O	DFC	10.2.43
C.B. Ordish	A/F/L	DFC	10.2.43
J.A. Lithgow	F/L	DFC	14.2.43
M.M. Yudelman	F/L	DFC	14.2.43
J.C. MacDonald, DFC, AFC	A/G/C	Bar to DFC	14.3.43
F. Clark	SGT	DFM	19.4.43
J. Cope, DFM	A/F/L	DFC	19.4.43
F.C. Jackson	SGT	DFM	19.4.43
S.A. Pearce	SGT	DFM	19.4.43
W.a. Irwin	P/O	DFC	19.4.43
J.W.E. Gaylor	SGT	DFM	3.5.43
H.J. O'Conner	F/S	DFM	3.5.43
P. Devine	SGT	DFM	18.5.43
R.T. Noonan	F/S	DFM	11.6.43
A.R. Craddock	A/F/L	DFC	15.6.43
D. Craven	SGT	D.F.M.	15.6.43
R.F. Escreet	SGT	D.F.M.	15.6.43
K.W. Peters	SGT	DFM	15.6.43
I.W. Rennec	P/O	DFC	15.6.43
G.B. Tait	P/O	DFC	15.6.43
G. Wace	P/O	DFC	15.6.43
D.W. Mephan	SGT	DFM	13.7.43
G.A. Potter	SGT	DFM	13.7.43
N.J. Pawley	SGT	DFM	17.7.43
W. Towse	SGT	DFM	17.7.43
H.C. Wilkie	A/F/L	DFC	27.7.43
J. Barrass	P/O	DFC	12.8.43
J.E. Dorie	F/S	DFM	13.8.43
A.K. Sykes	A/F/L	DFC	13.8.43
W.H. Roadh	SGT	DFM	18.8.43
J.L. Smale	SGT	DFM	18.8.43
D.A. Boards	SGT	DFM	19.8.43
D.J. Watson	SGT	DFM	19.8.43
R. Waugh	F/O	DFC	19.8.43
W.J. Klufas	A/F/L	DFC	12.10.43
J. Baker	SGT	DFM	14.10.43
G.W. Gabel	P/O	DFC	14.10.43
R.R. Megginson	A/S/L	DFC	14.10.43
E.J. Phillips	F/O	DFC	14.10.43
J.V. Russell	F/S	C.G.M.	25.10.43

Name	*Rank*	*Award*	*Date*
L.G. Bentley	SGT	D.F.M.	12.11.43
R.F. Lown	A/F/L	DFC	12.11.43
N.L. Thomas	F/S	DFM	12.11.43
D. Midgley	A/F/L	DFC	29.12.43
R. Scott	A/F/L	DFC	29.12.43
K.A.H. Lawrence	F/L	DFC	17.1.44
P.K. Gerricke	F/S	DFM	12.2.44
R.P. Hayles	F/S	DFM	12.2.44
D.C. Woodruff	A/F/L	DFC	12.2.44
J. Angus	F/S	DFM	17.2.44
P.H. Cope	P/O	DFC	17.2.44
L.A. Miller	P/O	DFC	20.2.44
J.J.A. de Willimoff	A/F/L	DFC	11.4.44
L.H.J. George	F/O	DFC	18.5.44
D.H. Mansel-Pleydell	F/O	DFC	18.5.44
O.V. Brooks	P/O	DFC	19.5.44
C.K. Fabian, DFC	A/F/L	Bar to DFC	19.5.44
K.M. Pincott	F/S	DFM	19.5.44
P.J. Lamason, DFC	A/S/L	Bar to DFC	27.5.44
W.J. Boldus	P/O	DFC	30.6.44
W.J. Bell	A/F/L	DFC	14.7.44
G.M. Claydon	A/F/L	DFC	14.7.44
E.J. Moore	A/F/L	DFC	14.7.44
J.E. Cowell	A/F/O	DFC	11.10.44
G.A. Cantrell	F/O	DFC	12.10.44
L.B.A. Elias	F/O	DFC	12.10.44
S. Fisher	F/O	DFC	12.10.44
A.W. Muirhead	F/O	DFC	12.10.44
J.R. York	F/O	DFC	12.10.44
R.P. Baker	A/F/L	DFC	13.10.44
S.A. Bicknell	F/S	DFM	13.10.44
P.R.J. Child	F/S	DFM	13.10.44
F.H. Dengate	A/F/L	DFC	13.10.44
M.J. Sparks	A/F/L	DFC	13.10.44
M. Johnson	A/F/L	DFC	14.10.44
G. Allen	W/O	DFC	16.10.44
E. Grimshaw	P/O	DFC	16.10.44
W. Sneddon	F/S	DFM	16.10.44
W.J. Woodhouse	P/O	DFC	16.10.44
E.F. Glover	P/O	DFC	17.10.44
E.S. Henzel	F/O	DFC	17.10.44
R.A. Sargeant	P/O	DFC	17.10.44
E.G. Spanner	W/O	DFC	17.10.44

Name	*Rank*	*Award*	*Date*
G.W. Stokes	A/F/L	DFC	23.10.44
W.G.G. Watkins, DFC, DFM	A/W/C	DSO	5.11.44
A.W. Armstrong	F/S	DFM	12.11.44
J. Ell	F/O	DFC	12.11.44
R.A. Hearne	F/S	DFM	12.11.44
D. Rainton	F/S	DFM	12.11.44
E.C. Orchard	W/O	DFC	16.11.44
V.C. Reid	W/O	DFC	16.11.44
J. Wellings	F/S	DFM	16.11.44
P.D. Carden	A/S/L	DFC	7.12.44
G.A.M. Gallop	F/L	DFC	7.12.44
E.J. Jones	F/O	DFC	7.12.44
W.C. Parke	A/F/L	DFC	7.12.44
D.R. Bishop	SGT	DFM	8.12.44
R.J. Bell	P/O	DFC	12.12.44
G.A. Musgrove	F/O	DFC	12.12.44
W.R. Cox	A/F/L	DFC	16.1.45
P.A. Nettleton	A/F/L	DFC	16.1.45
W.M. Ferguson	A/F/O	DFC	20.1.45
W.J. Poole	P/O	DFC	20.1.45
W.H. Swent	P/O	DFC	20.1.45
A.E. Barford	F/S	DFM	15.2.45
J. Hislop	F/O	DFC	15.2.45
W.K. Perry	A/F/L	DFC	15.2.45
S.W. Stewart	A/F/L	DFC	16.2.45
W.L.S. Gapel	P/O	DFC	19.2.45
E.W. McLachlan	P/O	DFC	19.2.45
F. Wenton, DFM	W/O	DFC	19.2.45
J.R. Burnett	P/O	DFC	20.2.45
H.M. Hunt	F/O	DFC	20.2.45
O.O. Sylvestre	F/S	DFM	20.2.45
J.A.A. Gibson, DFC	A/S/L	DSO	16.3.45
W.J. Hall	A/F/L	DFC	22.3.45
A.E. Barrett	F/S	DFM	23.3.45
C.W. Ball	P/O	DFC	26.3.45
W.H. Kendall	P/O	DFC	26.3.45
W.R. McFadden	P/O	DFC	26.3.45
G. Thomas	F/S	DFM	26.3.45
W.D. Turner	F/O	DFC	26.3.45
A.A. Aleandri	F/O	DFC	12.4.45
J.S. Buchanan	A/F/L	DFC	12.4.45
R.W.P. Cameron	A/S/L	DFC	12.4.45
L.W. Marshall	F/O	DFC	12.4.45

Name	*Rank*	*Award*	*Date*
B.G.F. Payne	A/S/L	DFC	12.4.45
J.W. Sleeman	A/F/L	DFC	13.4.45
F. Wright, DFC	F/L	Bar to DFC	13.4.45
M.J. Bagan	W/O	DFC	16.4.45
R.P. Banks	W/O	DFC	16.4.45
J.H. Brown	W/O	DFC	16.4.45
K.T. Dorsett	SGT	DFM	16.4.45
D. Lowe	W/O	DFC	16.4.45
J.R. Palmer	F/O	DFC	16.4.45
G. Sim	P/O	DFC	17.4.45
R.V. Ostler	A/F/L	DFC	20.4.45
J. Williams	F/O	DFC	24.4.45
H.T. Bysouth	F/S	DFM	21.5.45
V.F. Cage	A/F/L	DFC	21.5.45
J.T. Dollisson	A/F/L	DFC	21.5.45
L.H. Marriott	A/F/L	DFC	21.5.45
J.W.L. French	A/F/L	DFC	22.5.45
J. Marpole	F/L	DFC	22.5.45
S. Anderson	W/O	DFC	24.5.45
K. Dunlop	F/O	DFC	24.5.45
R.D. Jennings	A/F/O	DFC	24.5.45
W.F. Prewer	W/O	DFC	24.5.45
A.C. Sellwood	A/F/O	DFC	24.5.45
F.J. Watson	P/O	DFC	24.5.45
B.C. Bull, DFM	P/O	D.F.C.	24.5.45
G.A.W. Stubbins	P/O	DFC	25.5.45
D.H. Haycock	A/F/L	DFC	1.6.45
J.R. Shiells	F/S	DFM	1.6.45
V.W. Brown	F/S	DFM	16.7.45
A.W. England	F/O	DFC	16.7.45
A.A. Haydon	F/L	DFC	16.7.45
C. Houlgrave	F/S	DFM	16.7.45
D.T. Bone	A/F/L	DFC	17.7.45
N. Macfarlane	A/W/C	DSO	17.7.45
L.W. Crowe	F/O	DFC	19.7.45
H.A. Jones	F/O	DFC	19.7.45
A. Schofield	P/O	DFC	19.7.45

Bibliography

The History of No 15/XV Squadron, N.J. Robertson, 1975
Sky Tiger, Norman Franks, William Kimber, 1980
The Bomber Command War Diaries, Martin Middlebrook & Chris Evertt, Viking, 1985
The Battle of Hamburg, Martin Middlebrook, Allen Lane, 1980
The Nuremberg Raid (Rev. Ed.), Martin Middlebrook, Allen Lane, 1980
The Stirling Bomber, Michael J. Bowyer, Faber & Faber, 1980
The Secret War, Brian Johnson, BBC, 1978
Form 540/541 No XV Squadron, Public Record Office

Index

A separate index of places, RAF bases and ships follows the index of personal names.

Places

RAF bases

Ships